PRESENTATIONAL
SPEAKING

THEORY & PRACTICE Fifth Edition

MELANIE MORGAN, PH.D.

Learning Solutions

Boston   Burr Ridge, IL   Dubuque, IA   New York   San Francisco   St. Louis
Bangkok   Bogotá   Caracas   Lisbon   London   Madrid
Mexico City   Milan   New Delhi   Seoul   Singapore   Sydney   Taipei   Toronto

PRESENTATIONAL SPEAKING
Theory & Practice

1 2 3 4 5 6 7 8 9 0   VNH VNH   0 9 8 7

ISBN-13: 978-0-07-338794-9
ISBN-10: 0-07-338794-0

Production Editor: Jessica Portz
Cover Photo: © Nick Dolding/Getty Images
Cover Design: Fairfax Hutter
Interior Design: Ronni Burnett
Printer/Binder: Von Hoffmann Press

Contents

Chapter *2* *Audience Analysis   30*

Chapter 3   *Selecting the Topic and Purpose   56*

Chapter 4 *Introductions and Conclusions   80*

Chapter Objectives   81

Chapter 5   *Organizing the Presentation   104*

Chapter 6   *Supporting Evidence and Research*   122

Chapter Objectives   123

Chapter 7   *Outlining the Presentation   150*

Chapter 8 *Informative Speaking 180*

Chapter 9 *The Persuasive Process 202*

Chapter 13 *Presenting as a Group* *310*

Chapter Objectives   311

Chapter 14 *Presenting Online   328*

PRESENTATIONAL
SPEAKING
THEORY & PRACTICE Fifth Edition

Chapter 1

INTRODUCTION TO PRESENTATIONAL SPEAKING

CHAPTER OBJECTIVES

After reading this chapter, you should be able to:

- Explain the differences between public speaking and presentational speaking.

- Explain the elements of effective presentations.

- Understand the different types of plagiarism.

- Describe the presentational process.

- Define communication apprehension.

- Describe methods for addressing communication apprehension.

A Northeastern University freshman sat in his uncle's office and wrote the code for a piece of software that caused a great deal of controversy. This simple piece of software changed the music industry forever, and the life of its creator. Shawn Fanning, who had been a quiet and reserved young man, was suddenly thrust into a sea of public discourse, forced to defend his creation, Napster, against huge corporate giants. Napster was a simple piece of software that allowed computer users to share MP3 music files over their computers.

Shawn was suddenly thrown into a media frenzy. He was expected to participate in interviews, make public presentations, and testify in hearings. This average American teenager was suddenly asked to be the "voice of a generation."

While this story may sound extreme, we have no way of knowing what life may hand us or when our circumstances will suddenly become newsworthy. In a blink of an eye, we can go from complete anonymity to sudden fame. There are many examples of these situations in the current news. Take for example John Walsh, host of "America's Most Wanted." He never expected to be the spokesperson for victims of crime. However, the kidnapping and murder of his young son, Adam, thrust him into this position. Similarly, the nine coal miners in West Virginia who were trapped for days in a mine shaft never imagined on that summer day in 2002 they would suddenly become heroes who were being pursued by the media for interviews and by others for speaking engagements.

All of these examples may still seem a bit removed from some of your experiences, but you never know when life will require you to stand up and engage in public discourse. Your impetus may not be as overwhelming as some of the examples, but your situation may be just as compelling for you. Imagine that you have just bought a new house, only to learn that a nearby processing plant is planning on increasing its toxic output. This would be a situation that would require you to step up and debate the issues in a public forum. You, along with other homeowners, would likely participate in city council meetings hoping to persuade local officials to ban the increase in production.

Still, many of you will not even face this kind of situation. More likely, you will be asked to be the voice of your department within your organization. Perhaps you will be asked to represent your organization in a sales presentation with a potential client. All of these situations seem far less grand than some of the other examples we have discussed, but they still have very important implications for you, your career, or the success of your organization.

This book is designed to help you prepare for common speaking situations that most of us face on a fairly regular basis. Having the ability to express one's thoughts is important to success in any career.

   Although your first job may seem a long way away at this point, you cannot underestimate the importance of strong presentational skills to your success in the workplace. This course will provide you with the basics that you will need to succeed in presentational speaking. Not only will you learn theories and skills that are vital in the workplace, but those skills will also serve you well in other courses you take while in college. Many of the courses you take at the university level will require some type of presentation. Use these presentations as practice for the presentations you will make later in your career. All of the strategies and skills you learn in this course will be valuable and applicable to the speaking you will be required to do while in college, whether that speaking occurs in the classroom or as part of a membership you have in some organization. Perhaps you will become president of your sorority or fraternity and will be required to deliver presentations to raise money, increase membership, or even remain in good standing with the university. The skills you learn in this course will help you achieve those goals.

   This course and text are designed to present communication theories and research to help you learn the fundamentals of presentational speaking. As part of this process, various guidelines will be presented on how to prepare presentations. Some of these guidelines are very specific. Elements of the presentations will be required to contain particular features. Sometimes, students report that these requirements seem constraining. However, research has shown that these guidelines work in almost all speaking contexts. You cannot go wrong if you use the fundamental guidelines this book and course advocate. Once you become an accomplished speaker, you learn which of the guidelines can be broken or adapted to specific speaking situations. Until then, these guidelines will serve you well and help ensure that your presentations are successful.

PRESENTATIONAL SPEAKING AND CAREER SUCCESS

The ability to make effective presentations is vital to obtaining employment. JobWeb, a Web site sponsored by the National Association of Colleges and Employers, reports that "year after year, the number one skill employers look for is good communication skills." The *Wall Street Journal* reports similar findings from its yearly poll of recruiters. Communication and interpersonal skills were rated as very important to 88% of the recruiters surveyed. As you can see in the spotlight on research box on page 6, communication skills received the largest percentage of responses from the recruiters.

Spotlight on Research

THE IMPORTANCE OF GOOD COMMUNICATION SKILLS

In a 2006 national survey conducted by the National Association of Colleges and Employers, it was reported that employers ranked the following qualities as the most desirable. Since 1999, communication skills have topped their list.

Job Outlook 2006

Top 10 Qualities/Skills Desirable to Employers

1. Communication skills
2. Honesty/Integrity
3. Interpersonal skills
4. Strong work ethic
5. Analytical skills
6. Flexibility/adaptability
7. Interpersonal skills
8. Motivation/initiative
9. Computer skills
10. Detail oriented

The Wall Street Journal/Harris Interactive Survey

The *Wall Street Journal* and Harris Interactive Survey asked organizational recruiters to rank the following student attributes in terms of their importance. As you can see from the table, communication skills came out on top.

Percentage of recruiters who report each of these attributes as "very important:"

88% Communication and interpersonal skills

87% Ability to work well within a team

85% Personal ethics and integrity

83% Analytical and problem-solving skills

72% Leadership potential

67% Strategic thinking

Both of these studies reiterate the fact that good communication skills are vital to success in organizations. Take advantage of the training that you will receive this semester. Use the course to build your confidence and get valuable feedback on your performance. If you put effort and determination into the presentations you make for this course, you will be on your way to building the skills required in today's job market.

National Association for Colleges and Employers. (2005, December 15). Job outlook 2006: Experience, research, preparation. Retrieved March 23, 2007, from http//www.jobwe.com/joboutlook/2006outlook/3a.htm

Alsop, R. (2005, September 21). Business schools: Recruiters' top picks. *Wall Street Journal.* Retrieved October 21, 2005, from http://online.wsj.com/public/us.

Good speaking skills may help you land that important job, but they also get you promoted once you are in the organization. In fact, organizational recruiters report that the fear of public speaking is one of the most common career-stoppers in America. Alan Greenwald, a partner at T. Bresner & Associates, a company that helps executives with presentation skills, says, "Being a poor speaker is the principle reason people don't make it into the executive ranks" (Ligos, 2001).

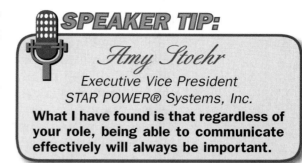

So now that you know how important good speaking is to career success, it is also important to know that potential employers have been less than impressed with the communication skills their employees are currently bringing into the workplace. An article in the Pittsburgh *Post-Gazette* reports that although communication skills are usually the most desired skills, they are often the weakest skills potential employees bring to an interview (McKay, 2005). The Web site JobWeb reports similar findings. Use the information in this course to your advantage. Take risks and try the methods and suggestions this course offers. This is a safe place to build these important skills. Take advantage of this opportunity so that you can arrive to your employment interviews with strong presentation skills.

WHAT IS PRESENTATIONAL SPEAKING?

By now you have determined that ***presentational speaking*** is something that is unavoidable and is essential to success. No matter how much you dread it, it is an inevitable part of academic and professional life. This book has been referring to presentational speaking, not public speaking. So what are the differences? Let's examine some of these differences now.

PRESENTATIONAL SPEAKING IS MORE INCLUSIVE

Public speaking can be thought of as a grand presentation. By public we usually mean it is a presentation that affects the community at large. The audience will include a "public audience." Staff meetings don't fall under this category. However, if you have ever attended a staff meeting, you know that the ability to present one's ideas in an organized and effective fashion is important. Presentational speaking includes more typi-

The ability to make effective presentations is vital to obtaining employment.

cal types of situations that people commonly find themselves facing. Therefore, the term presentational includes both the public type of presentations we often see politicians making, and those smaller types of presentations that occur within organizations.

PRESENTATIONAL SPEAKING IS LESS FORMAL

Public speaking usually occurs in a formal setting. Speakers are behind podiums and microphones. They are usually dressed in formal attire. Speakers deliver their presentations from a prepared manuscript and the presentation is rather scripted—meaning that there is little room for spontaneity.

Presentational speaking can occur around a table while everyone is seated. The speaker doesn't necessarily have to stand up to address the audience. Most likely, the presentation will be delivered from an outline rather than a manuscript; therefore, the situation is much more relaxed and allows for informality.

PRESENTATIONAL SPEAKING IS MORE INTERACTIVE

The reliance on manuscript delivery usually means that public speeches rarely adapt to the needs of the audience. Usually, the audience has little chance for interaction with the speaker. Audience members can usually stop the speaker during a presentation and ask questions if they feel they need to. The extemporaneous delivery style of presentational speaking also allows the speaker the spontaneity to talk to the audience and adapt the presentation to the needs of a particular audience.

PRESENTATIONAL SPEAKING REACHES A SMALLER NUMBER OF INDIVIDUALS

Presentations are often made to smaller audiences than public speeches. Public presentations usually reach multiple audiences through a variety of mediums. They are usually videotaped for replay, and the actual words delivered in the presentations are transcribed so that they can be reprinted in the newspaper. So, while you may not be able to see the president deliver his State of the Union address, you may be able to see it replayed on television, or read the transcript in the newspaper. This extra distribution has the ability to reach a very wide audience.

CHARACTERISTICS OF EFFECTIVE PRESENTATIONAL SPEAKING

Now that you know how important presentational speaking is and how it differs from public speaking, let's examine the factors that will make your presentations effective. These three factors are the essential elements in making a good presentation. We will refer back to these elements throughout the entire book. They will help guide you in making many of the decisions that you need to make when preparing for a presentation.

GOOD PRESENTATIONAL SPEAKING IS GOAL-DIRECTED

Good speaking is goal-directed. Each time you address an audience you should be extremely clear on what the purpose of your presentation is. What exactly are you trying to convey? What are you hoping to achieve? Are you trying to explain a procedure to a group of colleagues, or update your staff on new developments in your product line, or persuade a client to change operating systems? Whatever the purpose, the content of your presentation should be driven by your goal. Every decision you make about what to address or what to include in the presentation should be made in regard to the overarching goal of your presentation. If the material you are considering using doesn't support your goal, don't use it.

> *Presentations that aren't goal-directed seem muddled and often ramble.*

Presentations that aren't goal-directed seem muddled and often ramble. The message is unclear, and audiences often leave wondering what they should take away from the presentation.

Before beginning the preparation process, have a firm idea of what you want to achieve in the presentation. After ensuring that the goal is appropriate for the audience and the situation, use it as your guide. Every decision you make during the preparation process should be driven by your goal or purpose. If you follow this guideline, you will be on the road to delivering a presentation with a clear message that your audience can follow.

GOOD PRESENTATIONAL SPEAKING IS AUDIENCE-CENTERED

Good presenters are always aware of their audience. One of the differences between strong speakers and average speakers is the ability to relate and adapt to their audience. You have to know your audience in order to reach them. If you are delivering a sales presentation to a potential client hoping to sell them a new computer operating system and you know little about the types of features that will be most useful to them, you will probably lose the sale.

In order to be successful as a speaker, you must know the attitudes an audience holds about your message and be able to strategically plan for possible differences between your position and that of the audience.

Being audience-centered not only means that you should think of your audience during the planning phase of the presentation, but you should also respond to the audience during the presentation. It is

This speaker must tailor his message to an audience of conservative and concerned audience members.

important that you watch for audience feedback and adapt your message as their needs change. For example, if you notice that your audience seems confused by some statistical data you just presented, stop the presentation and explain it in a different way.

The bottom line is: good presentations are those that relate to your audience. It is important to make sure that, as a speaker, you are connecting with your audience. If you fail to achieve this connection, it is unlikely that you will achieve the goal or purpose of your presentation. Therefore, keep your audience in mind at every step of the presentation.

GOOD PRESENTATIONAL SPEAKING IS ETHICAL

> *Good presentations are those that relate to your audience.*

While the goal of your presentation may have great significance to you personally, you have a responsibility to your audience to pursue that goal in an ethical manner. As the expert on a given topic, you have great power over your audience. They are trusting you to provide them with good solid evidence and sound reasoning. Providing them with anything less is unethical. If you are asking your audience to change the way they eat, then it is important that you present all of the evidence so that the audience can make an informed decision about a change in their diet. This means using supporting evidence that is timely and from respected sources, and refraining from fallacious reasoning (see Chapter 10).

Additionally, make sure the goals of your speech are ethical. You don't want to ask anything of your audience that could potentially cause them harm. This becomes particularly important for classroom presentations. It is unethical to advocate any behavior that may cause potential harm to your audience. While a presentation on how to make a fake I.D. may appeal to an audience of traditional-age college students, making fake I.D.'s is illegal. If an audience member actually engaged in this behavior, they could be arrested and face serious legal ramifications. Therefore, stop and ask yourself what you are advocating. If it could potentially cause harm to your audience, pursue another topic.

Ethical speakers are always prepared. As we discuss later in the book, it is a waste of time for you and the audience both if you arrive at a speaking engagement unprepared. If an audience doesn't get what they are expecting from your presentation, they will be disappointed. More importantly, it is essential that you have prepared thoroughly and are competent to speak about the topic you are addressing. If you are not fully informed about your topic, your presentation could be misleading to members of your audience and cause them potential harm.

> *Make sure the goals of your speech are ethical.*

Ethical speakers are also honest. Be truthful in what you say. This means reporting statistics in a straightforward manner that your audience can understand, quoting experts accurately, citing sources correctly, using examples that are typical rather than unusual, and using sound reasoning.

Don't make promises your presentation can't deliver. Don't tell your audience that you hold the key to all of their dating happiness if you don't. Be realistic in what your presentation can accomplish.

Plagiarism

As an ethical speaker, it is important for you to know exactly what plagiarism is so that you can avoid it. **Plagiarism** is taking someone else's words or ideas and claiming them as your own. Plagiarism is a rising problem on college campuses (McCabe, 2005; September 9, 2003— New York Times). It is a serious offense with stiff penalties. It can result in a variety of consequences that range from failing the assignment in question to being expelled from the university.

Plagiarism isn't only an issue on college campuses, however. You have probably heard about the author of the *Da Vinci Code*, Dan Brown, and the court case brought against him alleging he stole themes and major ideas used in his award-winning book from another text. The publicity concerning this allegation has been tremendous

As this attorney demonstrates, a competent speaker cites her sources accurately throughout the presentation.

and will have an impact on his credibility regardless of the outcome of this case.

Plagiarism occurs within the organizational context as well; several important leaders in business, industry and education have been caught plagiarizing. Plagiarism is a serious offense and carries stiff penalties regardless of the context. For example, the top editor of *USA Today* was forced to retire under allegations of plagiarism. The editor, Karen Jurgensen, did not even commit plagiarism herself. It was one of her star reporters, Jack Kelley, who was actually accused of the offense, but as the editor she was held responsible (April 21, 2004—AP).

As you have seen, plagiarism carries serious consequences. In order to avoid it, it is important that you understand exactly what counts as plagiarism. Sometimes, a simple misunderstanding about what constitutes plagiarism can get someone into deep trouble. Many times students are unfamiliar with how to cite an original document and simply misunderstand when it is appropriate to give someone else credit. Familiarize yourself with the following types of plagiarism so that you can ensure that you avoid it in your own work.

Types of Plagiarism

Misrepresentation

Misrepresentation occurs when you take something someone else has written and claim it as your own. This is the most blatant type of plagiarism, and this is often what people think of when they use the term plagiarism. Buying a speech or paper on an Internet site, taking an assignment from a file, or having someone ghostwrite your assignment for you are all examples of misrepresentation.

> **RESOURCES ON PLAGIARISM**
>
> The following resources provide information on defining and avoiding plagiarism:
>
> ◉ http://www.academicintegrity.org
> ◉ http://www.academicintegrity.org/ links.asp
> ◉ http://library.law.columbia.edu/ music_plagiarism

This is a serious offense within the academic community and the larger community as a whole. Some students who engage in misrepresentation do so because they are dishonest. Other students get themselves stuck in a situation where they have waited too long to complete their assignment. At the last minute they realize they have not allowed themselves enough time and they rush to a test file and grab an old outline from a former student, put their name on it, and turn it in.

Make sure you don't get yourself into a similar situation. You would be better off turning in the assignment late than suffering the consequences of academic dishonesty.

Cut and Paste Plagiarism

Unlike misrepresentation, which pirates from one source, *cut and paste* plagiarism takes information from several sources and patches it together in one document. Cut and paste plagiarism is more common today for two reasons: first, word processors make it easy to cut and paste things into our documents and second, the Internet provides access to a wealth of information on any topic. Instead of taking the ideas of other individuals and putting them into our own words and providing proper citations, or putting the information in quotation marks and providing proper citations, the text is pasted verbatim into the new document and no credit is given to the original author.

It is important to remember that if you take exact wording from a source, the information you quote must be contained within quotation marks and cited within the document or speech where it appears. It is not sufficient to cite material you copied directly solely in the bibliography, although it is necessary. A direct quotation must be cited in the outline or speech as you use it. For example, suppose you wanted to use the following quote in a presentation you were giving. Assume that the quote was going to appear in both your outline and the spoken presentation. In order to avoid plagiarism, the following citation would be necessary in the outline.

> "ASD begins before the age of 3 and lasts throughout a person's life. It occurs in all racial, ethnic, and socioeconomic groups and is four times more likely to occur in boys than girls." (Centers for Disease Control, 2007).

The complete reference to the source of the information would also appear on your reference page or bibliography in APA style. The following spoken citation would be necessary within the speech:

> Quoting a 2007 report from the Centers for Disease Control, "ASD begins before the age of 3 and lasts throughout a person's life. It occurs in all racial, ethnic, and socioeconomic groups and is four times more likely to occur in boys than girls."

Just like your assignments in other classes, your presentations must be combined with research and your own ideas. You should conduct sufficient research and be involved enough with your topic so that you can write a presentation that not only conveys information from experts, but provides your own perspective on the topic as well.

Incremental Plagiarism

Sometimes plagiarism occurs because we just fail to give proper credit for small parts of the presentation. This is usually a result of misusing quotations or paraphrasing incorrectly.

Assume that you plan to give a speech on the consumer advocate Ralph Nader. You find the following quote from David Bollier's book, *Citizen Action and Other Big Ideas: A History of Ralph Nader and the Modern Consumer Movement*:

> While Nader did not invent the idea of consumer advocacy, he and his associates did radically transform its meaning. Before Nader's appearance, "consumerism" was often a trivialized concept that dealt with shopping for the best bargains and redeeming supermarket cents-off coupons; it did not put forth an analysis of corporate or governmental power. Nor did it constitute an independent "countervailing force" to the enormous power wielded by business in the marketplace and government policymaking.
>
> From CITIZEN ACTION AND OTHER BIG IDEAS, A History of Ralph Nader and the Modern Consumer Movement, by David Bollier

You like the quote because it captures the importance of Nader's presence in the consumer movement. If you wanted to use the quote as it is, you would need to document it with quotations in your outline and introduce it verbally in your speech in the following way:

> According to David Bollier in his book, Citizen Action and Other Big Ideas: A History of Ralph Nader and the Modern Consumer Movement, . . .

You have made it clear that these ideas belonged to someone else and have given credit to the original author. If you had decided to paraphrase the passage instead, you would simply restate or summarize the ideas in your own words. But, you must remember that these ideas were not your own. Even though you have restated Bollier's ideas, they are not original and you must still give credit to the author. Here is an example of how that passage may be paraphrased.

> Nader may not have invented consumer advocacy, but together with his colleagues, he transformed the nature of the movement from one of trivialized pursuits to an independent force with the ability to counteract the power wielded by corporations and government.

While Bollier's ideas are now presented in your own words, it would still be plagiarism if you failed to cite him for the ideas represented in the statement.

Although you would not use quotation marks in the outline, you would still cite the source. In the presentation you might present the quote in the following manner:

> David Bollier argued in his book, Citizen Action and Other Big Ideas, A History of Ralph Nader and the Modern Consumer Movement, that Nader may not have invented consumer advocacy, but together with his colleagues, he transformed . . .

Excessive Collaboration

Sometimes we ask our friends or family to read something we have written for class and make suggestions for improvement. Sometimes, however, we sit down and write the assignment with our friend or family member. While the first example is acceptable, the second is considered *excessive collaboration*, and the work can no longer be claimed as solely your own.

A couple of semesters ago, two students from this course were discussing their first presentation assignment. They decided they were both interested in the topic of baseball for the first individual informative assignment. They narrowed the topic to new innovations in baseball and went to the library to conduct research. They collected their research together and went back to their dorm and wrote the outline for their speech, together. They constructed a solid outline and turned it in to their instructors. The instructors, who were office mates, discussed the upcoming topics for their student presentations, and discovered that they had received the same outline from these two students. The students were called into a conference, where they admitted to writing the outline together. However, the assignment was not a group assignment, and the students were found guilty of academic dishonesty and punished accordingly.

THE PRESENTATION PROCESS

Select the Topic

- Pick a topic based on your interests, expertise and the audience's interest
- Adapt that topic to the specific needs of your audience

Determine the Purpose

- Write your specific purpose statement
- Write your thesis statement

Research the Presentation

- Determine what evidence you need to reach your goal or purpose
- Collect a variety of types of supporting material
- Organize the presentation
- Decide on your main points
- Choose an organizational structure
- Arrange supporting material
- Create a preparation outline

Practice the Presentation

- Construct a speaking outline
- Refine delivery
- Check the length of the presentation
- Practice in front of an audience

This example is extreme. The two students obviously cowrote the presentation in question. Be careful that when you ask for feedback or advice from friends that the work remains your own. Plagarism can be a serious infraction with undesirable consequences. Try to prevent it at all costs. If you are in doubt about how to cite a reference or how to handle a particular piece of reference material, ask your instructor. It is much better to be safe than sorry.

As we have discussed, ethics are extremely important to good presentational speaking, whether we are talking about collecting supporting material or about giving proper credit to those sources. Ethics have consequences for you as a speaker and for your audience. As an effective speaker, it is important that you take every effort to be ethical in every aspect of the presentation process. At each step in the decision making process, it is important for you to ask, is this the most ethical decision I can make? If not, reconsider.

THE PRESENTATION PROCESS

Now that you know what presentational speaking is, why it is important and what makes it effective, it is time to examine an overview of the presentation process. Just how do you write and deliver a successful presentation? There are several steps in this process. The following section presents a brief introduction to this process. It does not address everything you need to know about making good presentations, but it will get you started.

SELECTING THE TOPIC

Sometimes you are asked to deliver a presentation based on specific knowledge that you possess. In this particular situation, the topic is selected for you. The tricky part in this situation is adapting the topic to the particular audience that you will address. Imagine that you are an IBM representative making a sales presentation to the client's engineering department; it would look very different than the same presentation made to the accounting department. Or, at least, it should look very different, if you had adapted to the various needs of these diverse audiences. After all, these two audiences would have different needs, interests and motivations. It would be important that the two presentations reflect these differences.

Sometimes, however, topic choice is left up to the speaker. In this class, you will have to address the parameters of the assignment, but your topic selection will be more or less up to you to determine. When faced with this situation, you have to consider two things. First, you have to choose a topic that will be interesting and important to your audience and second, you have to adapt this topic to meet their needs. More detail on this process will be provided in Chapter 2.

DETERMINING YOUR PURPOSE

Once you have selected your topic, it is important that you determine exactly what you want to achieve with your presentation. Do you want to increase the audience's understanding of the topic or do you want to encourage them to try something new? You need to think very closely about what is realistic for you to achieve in one presentation and then focus all of your energy and preparation into achieving that goal.

RESEARCHING YOUR PRESENTATION

At this point, you need to determine what type of evidence you need in order to reach your goal. Answers to the following questions can help you determine what type of evidence you might need. Exactly what type of audience are you facing? Are they hostile, captive, motivated, knowledgeable, etc.? What types of evidence are they going to find the most compelling and useful? Will narratives be more persuasive or would statistics be more convincing?

All claims and arguments need to be supported by evidence. By performing a thorough audience analysis, you can have a much better idea of what type of supporting evidence is going to work best in your particular situation.

ORGANIZING YOUR PRESENTATION

Once you have collected your supporting evidence, you are ready to decide on an organizational structure. Using an outline, you begin developing main points and arranging your supporting material. After you have completed the body of the presentation, you craft the introduction and form the conclusion, and complete the reference list.

PRACTICING THE PRESENTATION

At this point in the presentation process, you are ready to construct a speaking outline and begin the practice sessions. One of the most important details to assess at this point is whether or not the presentation is adhering to the time constraints. Practice as much and as often as you can. Rehearsal in front of an audience is one of the best methods of practice. Speakers who practice their presentations enjoy more success.

Now that you have an overview of the process, you are almost ready to begin writing your first presentation. However, there is just one more issue that should be addressed: nervousness. Feeling some amount of stage fright is normal. After reading the following section on communication anxiety, you should be ready to jump in and get started.

DEALING WITH NERVOUSNESS

Many people report feeling anxious about speaking in front of an audience. It is an extremely common fear. In fact, Mark Twain has supposedly said that, "There are two kinds of speakers, those who are nervous and those who are liars." There is probably some truth to this statement. Everybody gets a little nervous when they have to face an audience. The *Washington Business Journal* reports that the fear of public speaking has enjoyed a top spot on Gallup polls for years. Many people report being more frightened of giving a speech than of heights, spiders, snakes, thunderstorms or even death (Washington Business Journal—September 10, 2004).

As you can see, fear of delivering a presentation is a normal anxiety. So if you feel anxious you aren't alone. The good news is that there is a large body of research devoted to this topic. From the research, many methods have been identified that you can use to alleviate this fear. The first step in reducing anxiety, however, is understanding exactly what it is. So, let's start there.

WHAT IS COMMUNICATION APPREHENSION?

Communication apprehension has been defined as "the fear or anxiety associated with real or anticipated communication with others" (McCroskey, 1977. p78). As you can see from this definition, the fear of public speaking is just one small part of communication apprehension. Individuals can feel anxious about communicating across a wide range of contexts. Some of us may feel more anxious in communication situations that involve one-on-one interactions. Still others may not feel anxious while delivering a presentation to a large group of people, but may feel more anxious about communicating with a small group of individuals. Still others may feel anxious when thinking about almost any communicative event. So, as you can see, communication apprehension

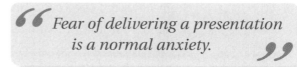
Fear of delivering a presentation is a normal anxiety.

is broad and extends across a wide array of contexts and situations. However, we are only interested in the apprehension related to the public speaking context, and so we will focus our energy on this area.

You can actually experience communication apprehension in one of two ways. First, the communication apprehension you experience may be traitlike. With this type of communication apprehension you are likely to feel anxious when delivering a presentation of any kind,

PRCA-24
(PERSONAL REPORT OF COMMUNICATION APPREHENSION)

This instrument is composed of twenty-four statements concerning feelings about communicating with others. Please indicate the degree to which each statement applies to you by marking whether you:

(1) strongly agree, (2) agree, (3) are undecided, (4) disagree, or (5) strongly disagree.

Please respond with your first impression.

1. _____ I dislike participating in group discussions.
2. _____ Generally, I am comfortable while participating in group discussions.
3. _____ I am tense and nervous while participating in group discussions.
4. _____ I like to get involved in group discussions.
5. _____ Engaging in a group discussion with new people makes me tense and nervous.
6. _____ I am calm and relaxed while participating in group discussions.
7. _____ Generally, I am nervous when I have to participate in a meeting.
8. _____ Usually I am comfortable when I have to participate in a meeting.
9. _____ I am very calm and relaxed when I am called upon to express an opinion at a meeting.
10. _____ I am afraid to express myself at meetings.
11. _____ Communicating at meetings usually makes me uncomfortable.
12. _____ I am very relaxed when answering questions at a meeting.
13. _____ While participating in a conversation with a new acquaintance, I feel very nervous.
14. _____ I have no fear of speaking up in conversations.
15. _____ Ordinarily I am very tense and nervous in conversations.
16. _____ Ordinarily I am very calm and relaxed in conversations.
17. _____ While conversing with a new acquaintance, I feel very relaxed.

to any type of audience, under any circumstance (Booth-Butterfield & Gould, 1986). In other words, public speaking in general makes you anxious.

The second type of apprehension you can face is situational. This means the current speaking situation makes you nervous, not public speaking in general. There is something unique about this particular speaking situation that makes you nervous or anxious. Maybe you are a little less prepared than usual and so you feel more anxious. The outcome of the presentation may have serious consequences and so you

18. _____ I'm afraid to speak up in conversations.

19. _____ I have no fear of giving a speech.

20. _____ Certain parts of my body feel very tense and rigid while giving a speech.

21. _____ I feel relaxed while giving a speech.

22. _____ My thoughts become confused and jumbled when I am giving a speech.

23. _____ I face the prospect of giving a speech with confidence.

24. _____ While giving a speech, I get so nervous I forget facts I really know.

Scoring: To compute your scores, add or subtract your scores for each item as indicated below.

Group discussion:

    18 + (scores for items 2, 4, & 6) − (scores for items 1, 3, & 5)   =_____

Meetings:

    18 + (scores for items 8, 9, & 12) − (scores for items 7, 10, & 11)   =_____

Interpersonal conversations:

    18 + (scores for items 14, 16, & 17) − (scores for items 13, 15, & 18) =_____

Public speaking:

    18 + (scores for items 19, 21, & 23) − (scores for items 20, 22, & 24) =_____

To obtain your total score for the PRCA, simply add your
subscores together.   **Total** =_____

Your overall PRCA score should range between 24 and 120. For scores on each of the contexts (interpersonal conversations, meetings, small group, public speaking) your scores should range from 6 to 30. Any score above 18 on any of the contexts indicates some degree of apprehension.

The PRCA is a trait measure of speaking anxiety. It is good at detecting very high or very low levels of anxiety. If your score is above 65, you feel more anxious than the normal person. If your score is under 50, you feel less anxious than the normal person. Scores above 80 indicate extremely high levels of anxiety.

Richmond, V. P. & McCroskey, J.C. (1998). *Communication: Apprehension, avoidance, and effectiveness* (5th ed.). Boston, MA: Allyn and Bacon.

feel more nervous than usual. Perhaps the audience is particularly knowledgeable about your topic and that makes you a bit anxious. You are anxious because of something unique to the situation.

  You can assess your level of communication apprehension by filling out the questionnaire in the box on pages 20 and 21. This is the Personal Report of Communication Apprehension (PRCA) developed by communication researcher James McCroskey. It can give you a very good idea of how much anxiety you feel across speaking contexts.

Regardless of the type of apprehension you experience, there are methods for addressing it. We discuss the four most popular below.

ADDRESSING COMMUNICATION APPREHENSION

Skills Training

Skills training or courses such as this one can actually end anxiety for some people. One source of anxiety results from what researchers call a skills deficit. If you perceive that you lack the appropriate skills necessary to succeed in a speaking situation, you will likely experience some anxiety (Kelley, 1984). For example, if you are worried about your ability to organize a presentation and deliver it dynamically, you will naturally be nervous when making the presentation. By taking a course such as this, you are eliminating the source of the problem, the skills deficit, by acquiring the appropriate skills. Once you have the ability to learn the theory and guidelines, practice speeches, and receive feedback, you now feel trained and competent in your ability to effectively deliver a successful presentation.

If you experience anxiety due to a skills deficit, then you are in the right place. The knowledge and experience you will acquire in this course may help alleviate your fear and allow you to feel comfortable facing speaking situations after completing this course. In order for skills training to be effective, however, there must be a high level of commitment on the participant's behalf (Richmond & McCroskey, 1998).

Systematic Desensitization

This is the most popular method used in the communication field to treat communication apprehension (Richmond & McCroskey, 1998; Hoffman & Sprague, 1982). It was designed to treat broadly defined communication apprehension. It involves two primary steps. First, a series of deep muscular relaxation techniques are taught. Second, visualization is used to simulate the participation in various communication situations while in a deep state of relaxation.

Participants engaging in ***systematic desensitization*** are instructed to tense and relax each major muscle group. This process should last about 25 minutes.

It also requires visualizing increasingly more and more threatening situations. Once you can remain in a relaxed state while envisioning a scenario, you may move on to a more threatening one. For example, imagine delivering a presentation to your best friend. If you can remain calm while picturing this scenario, you can move to the next one and the next, which increasingly become more threatening. The last situation you are asked to visualize is the most threatening and would look something like this: "You are ready to appear on a television show and give a speech, but you lost your notes" (Richmond & McCroskey, 1998, p. 104).

Systematic desensitization is extremely effective. Studies have concluded that 90% of the individuals who receive this treatment reduce their communication apprehension levels. Of those participants who are extremely apprehensive, 80% report that after completing this treatment, they are no longer categorized as highly apprehensive (Richmond & McCroskey, 1998).

Cognitive Restructuring

Another method for reducing communication anxiety is *cognitive restructuring*. This method assumes that an individual's fear of public speaking stems from irrational thoughts they have about themselves and their behaviors. These irrational thoughts or beliefs are attacked and replaced with more appropriate thoughts. Once the illogical thoughts disappear, so, too, should the communication apprehension (Richmond & McCroskey, 1998).

Cognitive restructuring is administered in five or six one-hour sessions. These sessions can extend across several days or weeks. The treatment typically involves four steps. First, the participant is introduced to the method. Second, the participant is asked to identify his or her negative self-statements or illogical beliefs. Some examples might be: "I can't ever think about anything to talk about when making my presentations." "The audience will find me boring." The leader of the session explains the illogical nature of these thoughts to the participants. Third, participants are asked to replace these thoughts with more appropriate ones: "I have something valuable to offer to my audience." "My audience will find my presentation topic interesting." Finally, the participants are required to practice these coping strategies or replacement messages (Fremouw, 1984).

Research regarding cognitive restructuring has demonstrated that it is useful in reducing self-reported levels of apprehension. Its success rates are similar to those of systematic desensitization (Richmond & McCroskey, 1998).

Current research has indicated that a combination of these three treatments, skills training, systematic desensitization, and cognitive restructuring, is the most effective treatment in reducing self-reported communication apprehension (Allen, Hunter & Donohue, 1989).

Visualization

The final method for reducing apprehension is *visualization* (Ayres & Hopf, 1992). Visualization asks the participant to imagine the day on

Spotlight on Research

VIRTUAL VISUALIZATION

Another type of visualization is currently being implemented to assist anxious speakers. This type of visualization takes advantage of virtual reality. Virtual reality actually immerses an individual in the speaking situation in order to simulate the experience. Current research seems to indicate that the fear of public speaking can be reduced if individuals are exposed to "virtual audiences" and asked to deliver presentations to avatars, or virtual audience members. Anxious speakers can reduce their apprehension after as few as four exposures to the virtual audience.

Researchers are also employing this type of technology on college campuses. At Purdue University, a virtual classroom has been created that replicates the classrooms where public speaking courses are taught. These virtual classrooms are populated with student avatars, or audience members. As you can see from the picture below, the virtual environment models an actual classroom down to small details, such as the bulletin board on the left-hand side and the clock on the back of the wall. The speaker puts on 3-D goggles and becomes completely immersed in the speaking situation. This virtual environment has provided students with the opportunity to deliver presentations to this classroom audience in an attempt to reduce their speaking apprehension and gain more speaking experience.

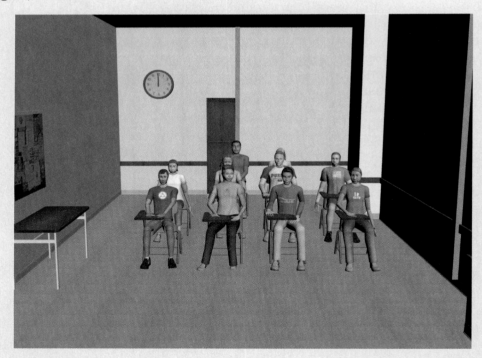

Anderson, P. L., Zimand, E., Hodges, L. F., & Rothbaum, B. O. (2005). Cognitive behavioral therapy for public-speaking anxiety using virtual reality for exposure. *Depression and Anxiety, 22,* 156-158.

Morgan, M. & Natt, J. (2003). *The virtual classroom.* Paper presented at the annual meeting of the National Communication Association, Miami, 2003.

which they are going to speak. They are told to imagine the entire day, from the moment they get up in the morning to the moment they finish their presentation. They are to imagine that everything they do that day goes extremely well. Participants are even asked to imagine themselves receiving congratulations from their classmates or business colleagues in regards to their successful presentation (Ayres & Hopf, 1992).

Visualization has also been found to be effective in reducing self-reported communication apprehension (Ayres & Hopf, 1992). Visualization techniques are also associated with enhanced speaking performance. Students who were exposed to visualization were perceived as less rigid than students who did not receive visualization treatments (Ayres & Hopf, 1992).

Communication apprehension related to public speaking is a common phenomenon experienced by almost all of us. However, it can be problematic for those individuals who experience it at high levels. By using the techniques described in this chapter, you can begin to cope with your fear.

CONCLUSION

Presentational speaking is vital to your organizational success. Remember, the guidelines outlined in this book are appropriate for both public speaking and presentational speaking situations. Regardless of your speaking situation, a presentation that is goal-directed, audience-centered, and ethical has a good chance of being successful. By understanding what counts as plagiarism, you have a much better chance of avoiding this kind of ethical dilemma. The presentational speaking process is quite manageable as long as you take the time to prepare. Even those of us who experience a little stage fright can deliver extremely effective presentations if you follow the guidelines discussed in this chapter.

KEY TERMS

Characteristics of effective speaking

Cognitive restructuring

Communication apprehension

Cut & Paste plagiarism

Excessive collaboration

Incremental plagiarism

Misrepresentation

Plagiarism

Presentational speaking

Skills training

Systematic desensitization

Visualization

EXERCISES

1. Visit this online plagiarism site (http://www.sinc.sunysb.edu/Class/sourcebk/frost3sumframe.html) and complete the exercises.

2. In order to avoid plagiarism and assure that your presentation is ethical, you must put information you uncover in sources such as newspaper and magazine articles into your own words and provide proper citations, or put the information you use verbatim in quotation marks and provide proper citations. Take the following excerpts from newspaper and magazine articles and reword them into a main point or subpoint/subpoints in your own words, with proper citation:

   From a February 2006 article by Canadian Press: It's a bit of a no-brainer that speeding down a slope on skis or zooming into the air on a snowboard puts winter sports aficionados potentially in harm's way. But a new study shows that donning a helmet can significantly reduce the risk of the most common slope-related injury—head trauma.

A study by Norwegian researchers found that alpine skiers and snowboarders who wore a proper helmet while participating in their respective sports had a 60 percent lower risk of sustaining a head injury than those who wore no helmet.

"That means that six out of 10 head injuries could be avoided if everyone wore a helmet," said principal researcher Dr. Roald Bahr of the Oslo Sports Trauma Research Centre. "If you're smart, wear a helmet—if you want to stay smart."

From a February 2006 article by *PCPro* online magazine: Apple has set a new bar for digital music sales, selling over one billion songs since the first iTunes Music Store opened in April 2003. The milestone was passed on February 22. iTunes passed the halfway mark to its first billion as late as June of last year. Doubling that figure in just eight months represents a huge increase in monthly sales to a mean of over six million, dwarfing the sales of all its main rivals.

From a February 24, 2006, article in London's *Guardian* newspaper: Britain has set up a new police task force of five senior detectives to crack down on pirated DVDs.

The 12-month 400,000-pound (696,000-U.S. dollar) pilot project will target networks illegally supplying and distributing DVDs which are being sold at pubs, markets, street corners and via the internet. The police unit has been formed by the Economic and Specialist Crime Command of the Metropolitan Police in partnership with the Federation Against Copyright Theft (Fact).

"It is a recognition that film piracy and DVD piracy is a serious crime and that the people behind it are making a lot of money. They are not just involved in film and DVD piracy but a lot of other nasty things as well," said a Fact spokesman.

He added that a survey for the British Video Association put the trade in pirated DVDs at 300 million pounds (522 million U.S. dollars) a year.

Until about a year ago, they were mainly made in the Far East and shipped to Britain. But criminals are now using DVD "burners" and PCs to make counterfeit copies on British territory.

REFERENCES

Allen, M. (1989). A comparison of self-report, observer, and physiological assessments of public speaking anxiety reduction techniques using meta-analysis. *Communication Studies, 40,* 127–139.

Allen, M., Hunter, J., & Donohue, W. (1989). Meta-analysis of self-report data on the effectiveness of public speaking anxiety treatment techniques. *Communication Education, 38,* 54–76.

Alsop, R. (2005, September 21). Business schools: Recruiters' top picks. *Wall Street Journal.* Retrieved October 21, 2005, from http://online.wsj.com/ public/us.

Anderson, P. L., Zimand, E., Hodges, L. F., & Rothbaum, B. O. (2005). Cognitive behaviora therapy for public-speaking anxiety using virtual reality for exposure. *Depression and Anxiety, 22,* 156–158.

Ayres, J., & Hopf, T. S. (1989). Visualization: Is it more than extra-attention? *Communication Education, 38,* 1–5.

Booth-Butterfield, S. & Gould, M. (1986). The communication anxiety inventory: Validation of state- and context-communication apprehension. *Communication Quarterly, 34,* 194–205.

Fremouw, W. (1984). Cognitive-behavioral therapies for modification of communication apprehension. In J. Daly & J. McCroskey (Eds.), *Avoiding communication: Shyness, reticence, and communication apprehension* (pp. 209–218). Beverly Hills, CA: Sage.

Hoffman, J., & Sprageu, J. (1982). A survey of reticence and communication apprehension treatment programs at U.S. colleges and universities. *Communication Education, 31,* 185–193.

Kelley, L. (1984). Social skills training as a mode of treatment of social communication problems. In J. Daly & J. McCroskey (Eds.), *Avoiding communication: Shyness, reticence, and communication apprehension* (pp. 189–208). Beverly Hills, CA: Sage.

Ligos, M. (2001, June 20). Getting over the fear-of-speaking hump. The *New York Times,* p. G1.

McCabe, D. (2005). Center for academic integrity assessment project. Retrieved March 24, 2006, from http://www.academicintegrity.org/cai_research.asp.

McKay, J. (2005, February 6). Employers complain about communication skills. Pittsburgh *Post-Gazette.* Retrieved November 2, 2005, from http://www.post-gazette.com.

Morgan, M. & Natt, J. (2003). *The virtual classroom.* Paper presented at the annual meeting of the National Communication Association, Miami, 2003.

National Association for Colleges and Employers. (2005, December 15). Job outlook 2005: Experience, research, preparation. Retrieved March 23, 2006 from http//www.jobwe.com/joboutlook/2005outlook/3a.htm.

Richmond, V. P., & McCroskey, J. C. (1998). *Communication apprehension, avoidance, and effectiveness* (5th ed.). Boston, MA: Allyn and Bacon.

McCroskey, J. C. (1977). Oral communication apprehension. A summary of recent theory and research. *Human Communication Research,* 4, 78–96.

Chapter 2

AUDIENCE ANALYSIS

CHAPTER OBJECTIVES

After reading this chapter, you should be able to:

- Explain why audience analysis is important.

- Explain and apply demographic audience analysis.

- Explain and apply psychological audience analysis.

- Adapt to different environmental constraints when speaking.

- Use direct and indirect methods to gather material about an audience.

- Explain how a speaker can adapt to the audience while preparing for a presentation.

- Explain how a speaker can adapt to the audience during the presentation.

$\mathcal{C}$aty, a consumer and family sciences major, decided she wanted to deliver a presentation on organizing your living space. She delivered an incredible presentation to her public speaking class. She provided strategies and tips that traditional college-age students could use to unclutter and better utilize their living spaces. Her presentation was so compelling that her instructor asked her to deliver a presentation on home organization to a civic group in the community made up of working mothers. Caty gave the same presentation she had delivered in the classroom. Unfortunately, the audience did not respond as positively as her classroom audience. Caty was very disappointed.

What Caty failed to realize is that good presentations are always audience-focused. She was addressing a different audience with different needs, and her presentation should have reflected those differences. The demographics, needs and motivations of her audience had changed. The audience members in the civic club had children and, therefore, more stuff to organize. They live in houses rather than apartments or dorm rooms, which made their organization needs extremely different. They were more concerned with organizing their children's toys than organizing their CD collections. Although Caty could have easily adapted to this audience, she failed to do so.

Caty violated one of the golden rules of good speaking: "Effective presentations are always audience-centered." Your presentation will always change based on the unique characteristics of your audience. By adapting to the distinctive needs of your audience, you have a better chance of connecting with them as individuals. This connection between you and your audience is a powerful tool.

 ## THE IMPORTANCE OF AUDIENCE ANALYSIS

As mentioned in Chapter 1, **audience analysis** is essential to a successful presentation. You have little, if any, chance of achieving your presentational goals if you don't adapt your message to the needs of your audience. As a speaker, you need to be able to answer the following questions about your audience members:

- ◇ What is the position of the audience on my topic?
- ◇ What are the interests of my audience?
- ◇ How knowledgeable is the audience about my topic?
- ◇ Why is my audience here?
- ◇ What are the demographics of my audience?

The answers to these questions help you craft a message tailored to your specific audience. If Caty had known what the primary organizational needs of her audience were, she could have delivered a message that targeted these needs. She could have provided valuable information to her audience. Instead, the material she presented had little utility for her audience.

Good audience analysis not only allows you to achieve your goals, it also helps you identify with your audience. ***Identification*** is the process of expressing ideas and beliefs that you and your audience share (Burke, 1950). It builds common ground and helps you build a relationship with your audience. Being audience-centered also helps ensure you won't alienate or offend your audience. We live in a diverse world with people from many different backgrounds. Acknowledging this diversity shows you respect your audience and that you have high ethical standards.

It is important to note that although you must adapt your message to your audience, don't simply tell them what you think they want to hear. It is not necessary for you to change the focus of your message so that your audience automatically agrees with you. Nor is it necessary to present a point of view that you don't believe. But you do want to present a message that your audience can "hear." By understanding their positions, beliefs, and attitudes, you can construct messages that will allow audiences to listen and think about what you have to say rather than shutting down and tuning you out.

There are three types of audience analysis that will aid in your planning process. These include demographic analysis, psychological analysis, and environmental analysis. Each of these three types of analyses is described in the following section.

DEMOGRAPHIC AUDIENCE ANALYSIS

One method of analyzing an audience is to examine the demographics that characterize a particular audience and then adapting the presentation to the characteristics associated with those demographics. ***Demographics*** are the traits that describe your population or audience. Demographics may include: age, gender, religion, geographical location, group membership, sexual orientation, ethnicity, occupation, and many others. At one time, demographic audience analysis was the primary tool we used in assessing our audience. However, we now know that we cannot make accurate assumptions about individuals just because they belong to a particular group. Just because an audience member is female doesn't mean that she enjoys decorating or shopping. You simply cannot make those types of assumptions.

Placing too much emphasis on demographic audience analysis can lead you to stereotype your audience. If an audience feels stereotyped, they will likely react negatively to your presentation. However, if used with caution, demographic audience analysis can inform certain aspects of your presentation. Let's examine a few of these categories in order to understand how you may utilize them to prepare your presentations. While there are many other demographic categories that this chapter does not address, the analyses of these other categories will be similar to the examples discussed below.

AGE

Age is one of the most helpful of all of the demographic categories. It is important for you to stop and think: "What are the ages of the individuals that will make up my audience?" We can predict with certainty what events a particular cohort has experienced. For example, we know that young people growing up in the late 1920's and early 1930's were greatly affected by the Great Depression. Therefore, any presentation concerning finances would have to take that event and the effects on that generation into account when putting together that presentation.

Experiences such as the Great Depression or 9/11 have a deep effect on a generation of individuals. Events such as these shape the way they view life. Individuals who experienced the Great Depression are savers and are typically frugal with money and food, for example. Given their experience with the collapse of the stock market, they are more inclined to invest conservatively in safe investments backed by the government. So, if you were planning to speak to a group of depression era individuals on estate planning, you would present conservative investment plans and strategies. By thinking about particular events an audience has experienced, you can better predict how they may react to certain policies and ideologies.

> *Placing too much emphasis on demographic audience analysis can lead you to stereotype your audience.*

By knowing the age of your audience members, you can predict basic concerns they may have as well. For example, college students planning vacations in March or April have an interest in spring break vacations. They are interested in "hot spots" and economical destinations. An audience of professionals planning vacations in March or April is probably not interested in this type of vacation planning. In fact, this age group would probably want to avoid any "hot" spring break destination. Therefore, any presentation made by a travel agent would have to take these differences into account.

Age is such an important variable in adapting to audiences that Beloit College publishes a "Mindset List" for each entering freshman class. This list is compiled to help professors relate to their students. It explains how they may view the world differently from individuals born in different age cohorts because of changes in the world. (You can visit this list at http://www.beloit.edu/~pubaff/mindset/2010.php.)

SEX AND GENDER

Sex is biologically assigned at conception. Sex is the physiological characteristic that makes someone male or female. In other words, is someone anatomically male or female? There are particular topics that would be relevant to only one sex or the other. Only men can get prostrate cancer. Only women can be physically pregnant. However, there are ways to adapt these topics so that there would be relevant information for each sex in your audience. For example, Jill gave a speech on breast cancer. Although this is a disease that normally only affects those individuals whose sex is female, Jill presented some evidence about male breast cancer as well. So, she was able to make her speech relevant to both sexes in her audience.

Gender is more complicated. Gender is more psychological and emotional than physical, and refers to an identity that is socially constructed throughout an individual's lifespan (Ivy & Backlund, 1994). Research on gender indicates that individuals today can feel masculine in some aspects of their lives, and feminine in other aspects. So although an individual's sex may be female, she may approach relationships in life with more masculine behaviors. In other words, she may be more distant and less emotional. Therefore, simply approaching an all female audience (sex) and assuming they all would approach relationships in the same way, or feel the same way about domestic responsibilities, would be a mistake. The gender differences in this all-female audience would cause them to react very differently to this topic. As a speaker, it is important that you are aware of these issues and refrain from alienating certain segments of your audience by stereotyping them based on gender differences.

GEOGRAPHICAL LOCATION

The part of the country or world an individual comes from is also part of demographic audience analysis. Individuals are often characterized by certain traits based on where they were born or raised. For example, people from the South are assumed to have a variety of attributes that individuals from other parts of the U.S. are not assumed to possess.

Southerners are often thought of as slow-talking, conservative, warm and friendly, among other characteristics. Simply adapting your speech to a group of Southerners based on your stereotyped expectations would be a big mistake. A group of people living or raised in one geographical location is extremely diverse. While it may be safe to assume that individuals who live along the Gulf Coast would be concerned with hurricane safety, it would not be safe to assume they will all vote Republican or are conservative.

GROUP AFFILIATION

Group affiliation is another demographic that may inform your presentation preparation. If it is possible to discern what groups your audience members belong to, you will have a better chance reaching them. Belonging to particular groups may indicate interests or particular positions on topics. For example, you may learn that many of your audience members belong to the American Legion. This is a veterans' organization committed to community service. Membership includes males and females who have served in the U.S. military during wartime. Learning that a large proportion of your audience belongs to the American Legion could be extremely helpful. This is a patriotic organization. It would be safe to assume that most members would not support burning the American flag. This group is also extremely supportive of the military and would be unlikely to support antiwar protests.

Sometimes you get lucky and you are asked to speak to a group that shares an affiliation. For example, you may be asked to present an informative talk on increasing study skills to a group of fraternity pledges on campus. Knowing that this group shares this affiliation will tell you a great deal about them. You can use this information to tailor your message to the needs of this particular audience and their situation. This adaptation will make the information in your presentation more relevant and beneficial for them.

More often than not, the individuals that make up your audience will belong to many diverse groups and share little in common in terms of group affiliation. In that case, you have to respect differences and approach your speech in a way that respects diverse views and opinions.

SOCIOECONOMIC FACTORS

Socioeconomic factors include occupation, income, and education. All of these factors can influence the way an audience responds to your message.

If you stop and consider an individual's occupation, it can consume a large portion of their identity. Therefore, it affects the way they think about certain topics and may even determine what types of interests they have. A group of teachers will have different concerns than a group of doctors regarding managed care. Doctors will be interested in how managed care affects their practice, while a group of teachers would be more concerned with how managed care will affect their insurance premiums and the level of care they receive from their physicians. Therefore, knowing this information in advance can facilitate the adaptation of your presentation.

The amount of income a particular individual earns can also have an impact on their attitudes, beliefs, and behaviors. Imagine giving a tax-planning seminar to a group of individuals who earn less than $35,000 a year versus a group of individuals who earn over $200,000 a year. This difference would greatly affect the material you address in your presentation. The amount of income an individual earns would suggest very different guidelines in terms of tax planning. While someone with a large income may be interested in tax shelters, this type of tax planning would not be appropriate for someone with a lower income.

> **COMMON DEMOGRAPHICS USED IN AUDIENCE ANALYSIS**
>
> ◉ Group affiliation
> ◉ Age
> ◉ Sex
> ◉ Geographical location
> ◉ Gender
> ◉ Socioeconomic factors

Amount of income is even relevant in a speech like the one Caty delivered on organization. While someone with a good deal of disposable income can purchase all kinds of organizational baskets, bins and containers, someone on a more limited budget simply cannot afford to make these purchases. Caty would need to think about less expensive alternatives for the lower income group and incorporate those into her presentation.

Knowing the amount of education a particular audience has can also be beneficial in adapting your message to fit their interests. Knowing that most of your audience did not complete college can help you adapt your message. If you were presenting material on saving for your children's college education, there would be certain aspects of the college experience that would need to be explained to this audience; for example, that the cost of textbooks is not included in the cost of tuition. Presenting the same topic to a group of individuals who possess undergraduate and master's degrees would be different. They already know the ins and outs of higher education, and this background information would not be necessary for them to understand your message.

As with any other demographic category, it is important that you beware of stereotyping your audience based on their level of education.

Just because you are speaking to a group of individuals who hold Ph.D.'s, it is not safe to assume they all enjoy classical music or National Public Radio (NPR), for example. The same can be said for a group of individuals who did not attend college; they may enjoy and be big patrons of the arts even though their educational background may not indicate as such.

One aspect of demographic audience analysis that cannot be overstated is that you should be extremely careful about stereotyping your audience. Nothing will be more patronizing and alienating to a particular audience if they feel they have been marginalized. So, while it is important that you know about demographic audience analysis, use it with caution. Some of the other types of analyses discussed in this chapter may prove more useful to you.

 PSYCHOLOGICAL AUDIENCE ANALYSIS

In the previous section of this chapter, we discussed how you might adapt your presentation based on the traits or group memberships of an audience. There is more to audience analysis than simply examining demographics, however. Understanding why your audience is there, how they think about your topic, and how motivated they are about your material are all important *psychological factors.* A good psychological audience analysis asks what attitudes does my audience hold in respect to my topic? That is, how favorable, or unfavorable, is their reaction to my position. What is their motivation for attending my presentation, and how much do they know about my topic? By answering these questions, you can better anticipate and adapt to their interests and needs. In the long run, you will be more successful as a speaker if you engage in a thorough psychological audience analysis.

AUDIENCE ATTITUDES

One of the most important aspects of audience analysis is assessing what attitudes your audience holds about the information you are planning to present. An *attitude* is an individual's evaluation of an object, event, person, policy, etc. (Fishbein & Ajzen, 1975). In other words, attitudes express how positively or negatively you feel about an object, person, policy, etc. Here are some examples of attitudes.

- ◈ Purdue's course registration system is cutting-edge and extremely efficient.
- ◈ Daily exercise is beneficial to well-being.

    ◇ College internships are excellent methods to secure permanent employment.

    ◇ Assisted suicide is harmful to our society.

Attitudes are different from values. **Values** are ideals that we hope to achieve and underlie specific attitudes (Rokeach, 1973). Examples of values include equity, wisdom, democracy or justice. These values then shape the attitudes we hold about affirmative action, assisted suicide, or gay marriage, for example. For instance, an individual's views on justice and equity might predispose them to have a positive attitude toward policies that allow for gay marriage.

At this point you may be asking yourself why should I be concerned with attitudes? You are probably thinking that you are more interested in the actual behaviors of a particular audience. After all, you want a particular audience to vote for your candidate or buy your company's software. Your concern is understandable.

> ❝ *Attitudes express how positively or negatively you feel about an object, person, policy, etc.* ❞

However, attitudes and behaviors are intertwined and actually work together. In order to affect the behaviors of your audience, you must first understand their underlying attitudes.

Let's briefly examine this relationship. Research has demonstrated that we are most comfortable when our behaviors and attitudes are consistent (Festinger, 1957). For example, if we hold the attitude that daily exercise is healthy, and we engage in a regular exercise routine, we feel good. However, if we hold this same attitude, but fail to exercise regularly, this mismatch between our attitude and behavior can be psychologically uncomfortable. When this mismatch occurs, we are motivated to change either our attitude or behavior so that they are more aligned or consistent. So, many times, if we can predict an audience's attitude on a given issue, we may also be able to predict their behaviors (Kim & Hunter, 1993).

Let's examine how this might work in terms of speaking. Let's assume that you want to increase usage of the campus co-recreational facilities. You are going to speak to a campus service organization and you hope to persuade them to take advantage of the many services the co-rec provides. You know from your audience analysis that only 15% of them are currently involved in an exercise regimen. You also know that your audience believes exercise is good for them or healthy. That's where you start, with this positive attitude toward exercise. Reinforce the attitude that they hold about health and physical activity. Next, emphasize the difference between their attitude and their current behavior. Explicitly point out that although they believe in the exercise/health benefit relationship, few of them are actually engaging in exercise.

Then call for them to attend a class or event at the co-rec. This attitude/behavior issue will be further discussed in Chapter 9, but for now it helps us understand the role of attitudes in relation to audience analysis.

Attitudes of an audience regarding your position as a speaker can be placed in three broad categories. Sometimes audiences are favorable to your position and in complete agreement with the ideas you present. Other times, their attitudes are in direct opposition to your own. Still yet, sometimes, they have failed to form any attitude at all on your topic. Whether you are delivering an informative or persuasive presentation, there are strategies for dealing with each of these types of audiences. The following section describes these strategies.

Favorable Audiences

The easiest audience to face is a favorable audience. Speakers are usually relieved to learn that they will be addressing an audience that holds attitudes similar to their own regarding the topic at hand. Audiences who share our attitudes are called *favorable* or *friendly audiences.* Sometimes, speakers wonder why they should even address a favorable audience. After all, you already share the same beliefs. However, there are many reasons to address a favorable audience. Here are a few.

Increase Commitment

With a favorable audience, your goal is to reinforce your position and, thereby, the position of the audience (see Chapter 9). They are already on your side; you just want to reinvigorate them. Basically, you act as a cheerleader explaining why they are right to feel or act the way they do. They are already excited about the issue on which you speak, so you want to reaffirm their commitment and keep them motivated. Think of campaign rallies. This is what typically occurs at these events. The audience already supports the candidate or the party, and the goal of the rally is to keep them committed or even increase commitment.

> " *Addressing a friendly audience is also an opportunity to get them more involved in the issue.* "

Inoculation

Speaking to a favorable audience is also a chance to protect them against counterpersuasion. We are bombarded with messages every day. Some of those messages may run in opposition to the attitudes we currently hold. Therefore, they have the potential to move us from our current positions. To guard against this process, remind your audience of the strengths related to their own position or attitudes and demonstrate the weaknesses in opposition arguments. This is called *inoculation* (McGuire & Papageorgis, 1961). Inoculation is extremely powerful. Sometimes people agree with you but haven't heard other positions. You have the opportunity to educate them in a way that makes them both more informed but also more confident in their current belief that they share with you. You see inoculation at work in political campaigns. At campaign rallies candidates often make statements such as "My opponent will tell you I am weak on crime. Let me show you the evidence that clearly proves this statement is false." The politician has now inoculated his supporters against his opponent's argument, should they be exposed to it at a later time.

Increase Involvement

Addressing a friendly audience is also an opportunity to get them more involved in the issue. Maybe they hold consistent attitudes with your position but don't engage in any relevant behaviors. Take this opportunity to get them to engage in consistent behaviors. For example, assume your audience is supportive of your particular candidate but doesn't currently volunteer in her campaign. Use your presentation to motivate your audience to become directly involved in your candidate's campaign. Ask them to hand out fliers, make telephone calls, or simply run errands. It can be a great opportunity to strengthen their involvement and commitment.

Hostile Audiences

Sometimes an audience is on your side, and sometimes they just don't see things the way you do because they hold different attitudes. We call audiences who are unfavorable to you or your position **hostile audiences**. None of us wants to face a hostile audience, but sometimes it is unavoidable. The good news is that research has shown that individuals perform better when they perceive the audience to be nonsupportive rather than supportive (Butler & Baumeister, 1998). So,

Spotlight on Research

INOCULATION THEORY

In an influential research article, McGuire and Papageorgis (1961) demonstrated the advantages of refuting opposing viewpoints. In their study, they gave some subjects arguments which supported common cultural truisms, such as "you should brush your teeth three times a day." Other subjects received the same argument as well as an opposing viewpoint that was then refuted. Those receiving the supporting argument, plus the refutation of the opposing viewpoint, were better able to resist later arguments challenging the truism. McGuire and Papageorgis argued that this resistance is analogous to medical inoculations where a weakened form of a virus could protect against a stronger version of the virus later on. In other words, participants in the study were "inoculated" against later persuasion attempts and more immune to counterpersuasion.

McGuire, W. J., & Papageorgis, D. (1961). The relative efficacy of various types of prior belief-defense in producing immunity against persuasion. *Journal of Abnormal and Social Psychology, 62,* 327–337.

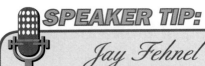

SPEAKER TIP:

Jay Fehnel
Vice President
Entertainment Products
Tribune Media Services

One strategy I use for a hostile audience is to try to disarm them. I try to mention upfront that I may not be an expert, and I may have a lot to learn from them. This establishes that I am not arrogant and that I need their input. Most audiences appreciate that honesty and the opportunity to help teach me. Also, if I feel the audience may be reluctant, I try to structure the presentation as a discussion.

even if you do have to face a hostile audience, odds are you will rise to the challenge and present more effectively.

If you have adequately prepared for the presentation, you will rarely, if ever, be surprised by a hostile audience. More than likely, you will be warned in advance so you can prepare for the challenge. There are some strategies that can make facing hostile audiences easier.

First, stress commonalities between you and your audience, or your position and the position they hold. Again, this increases identification and can be an effective tool in establishing a relationship between the speaker and audience. Here is how it works: assume you are trying to persuade the audience to build a community center, and they are opposed because of a potential raise in taxes needed to fund the center. You might express that everyone there wants what is best for the children in the community. It is safe to assume the audience will be in favor of programs that enhance the welfare of young children in their community. This is something you all agree upon and have in common. The disagreement lies in the approach to take in funding these programs. So start from a position where you both agree. Try to find an attitude that both the speaker and audience share and then move to positions where there are disagreements. The more similarities the audience perceives between their position and yours, the more likely they will respond favorably to your presentation.

Second, take small steps with a hostile audience and set modest goals. You aren't going to persuade an audience who is pro gun control to donate money to the NRA, but you might get them to listen to your position and at least understand why you believe the right to purchase arms without waiting periods is important. As we will discuss in Chapter 9, persuasion is a process. Don't get overly ambitious in one presentation. Set realistic goals and proceed incrementally. This is essential with a hostile audience.

Third, acknowledge the differences explicitly between your position and that of the audience. This demonstrates to the audience that you respect and understand their position. This may encourage them to listen fairly to your point of view, and it builds your trustworthiness.

> 66 *Take small steps with a hostile audience and set modest goals.* 99

Neutral Audiences

A *neutral audience* has yet to form an attitude about your topic. They are a blank canvas, so to speak. With a neutral audience, you have some latitude of movement; they can be persuaded (Sherif & Sherif, 1967). If you are facing a neutral audience, it is important for you to determine why they are neutral about your topic. Is the information new to them, and they are simply unfamiliar and have yet to form an attitude, or are they apathetic? Once you are able to answer these questions, you can begin preparation of your presentation.

If your audience is simply uninformed about your issues, present them with the facts and material relevant to your topic. Once you have informed them about the topic, then you can draw out the conclusion you are working toward.

If your audience is apathetic, they just don't care. You will need to focus on increasing the relevance of the topic to them. Why is it important? This idea gets elaborated on in the next section regarding audience motivation and in Chapter 4.

Although many of the examples discussed in this section regard persuasion, it is important to note that audience attitudes also play an essential role in informative presentations. Even in informative presentations, an audience's attitude may interfere with their ability to listen and process the information in your presentation.

AUDIENCE MOTIVATION

Sometimes audiences are highly interested in the material you present and actively listen to every aspect of your message or presentation. They carefully consider all of your arguments, analyze your supporting material, and critically examine your credibility. We call audiences who are engaged at this level *motivated audiences*. Other times, audiences are less interested in your material and, therefore, less likely to put forth much effort into critically examining or thinking about the messages you are presenting. We call these types of audiences *passive audiences*.

Knowing whether your audience is highly motivated or less motivated can be a big help in crafting your presentation. It can dictate specific strategies you might use in your actual presentation.

Motivation ultimately depends on how involved the audience is with your particular topic. *Involvement* is the personal relevance a topic holds for an audience member. For example, if you are delivering a speech about a proposed increase in Purdue's tuition to an audience of Purdue students, involvement would be extremely high. A change in the cafeteria menu at a local high school in West Lafayette, however, is a topic in which this same audience would have little involvement. The audience is

Good speakers use strategies to keep captive and voluntary audience members involved in the presentation.

unlikely to be affected by changes in a high school menu; however, they will be affected by an increase in tuition at Purdue. Therefore, their motivation to process the material on each of these two topics would be very different.

When topics are highly relevant for an audience, they will be motivated to engage in a good deal of thinking about the messages presented on that particular topic. This means they will actually devote a good deal of mental energy to think about the ideas you present. They will critique arguments more closely and pay attention to the minute details in the presentation. As a speaker, you must be even more attentive to the quality and strength of your arguments when dealing with motivated or involved audiences (Petty & Cacioppo, 1986).

If an audience has low involvement and motivation, and is passive, as with the example of the menu changes in a local area high school, they will be less motivated and, therefore, less likely to spend large amounts of mental energy in processing the material you present (Petty & Cacioppo, 1986). Rather than exerting the mental energy to elaborate on each of the ideas you present, they sit back and rely on cues for making decisions. For example, instead of examining the strength of each argument you present, they may only notice the number of arguments or the length of those arguments. This doesn't mean that you can be less prepared; it just means that you should refocus the type of supporting material you choose to use. Less involved audiences are going to be more interested in supporting evidence that is easier to process. So, use narratives versus statistics, for example.

A key factor in determining an audience's motivation for your topic is to examine why they are in the audience. Are they captive or voluntary? ***Captive audiences*** are forced to attend your presentation. They may include employees required to attend a training presentation or even a classroom audience. In both of these examples, the audience is there by force. In one case, they could lose their job if they don't attend, and in the other, they could receive a failing grade. Other audiences are voluntary. ***Voluntary audiences*** attend a presentation because they are interested in the material you are going to present or are interested in you as a speaker. Understanding the differences in these two types of audiences makes a big difference when planning your presentation.

A captive audience, by definition, is a tougher audience to reach. You have to work harder at gaining their attention and making the presentation relevant to them and their needs. You must be able to convince this type of audience that you have something that will benefit them. Be explicit; tell them directly how they will benefit from listening to your presentation. Once you have managed to capture their attention, you must work hard to keep it.

A voluntary audience is less daunting. They are attending your presentation because they are interested in your topic or your expertise. Therefore, it will be relatively easy to gain their attention. This audience arrives motivated and interested in your material. It is still important to use good evidence and sound reasoning. However, it will not be as difficult to engage a voluntary audience with your information.

AUDIENCE KNOWLEDGE

The amount of familiarity your audience has with your topic is another important consideration in psychological audience analysis. Are they experts or are they novices? It can be very irritating for a knowledgeable audience to attend a presentation and learn nothing new. Likewise, it can also be frustrating for novices to attend a presentation and feel like everything was above their heads.

If your audience is unfamiliar with the topic you are presenting, start with the basics. Explain technical terms, and use organizing analogies and directional transitions (see Chapter 8) to enhance their understanding. Even if you know that your audience is unfamiliar with the material you are presenting, be careful not to patronize them. Assume that they are bright and intelligent. As you move through the presentation, check for understanding; if they are following along you can adjust your material to meet their needs and increase the complexity if necessary.

Knowledge also becomes an important variable when you consider what type of evidence and reasoning to use. Audiences that are extremely knowledgeable about a given topic are able to engage in

ADAPTING TO DIFFERENT AUDIENCES

ATTITUDES

Supportive
- Reinforce their current position.
- Inoculate the audience against counterpersuasion.
- Build involvement.

Neutral
- For uninformed audiences, focus on educating them on the issue.
- For apathetic audiences, focus on establishing relevance.

Hostile
- Find common ground that you share with audience.
- Set extremely modest goals.

MOTIVATION

Motivated
- Provide very strong evidence.
- Be thorough in your treatment of the material.

Passive
- Emphasize your credibility and expertise.
- Refine delivery and involve the audience.

KNOWLEDGE

High
- Don't waste their time with rudimentary information.
- Be sophisticated in your approach to the material.

Low
- Don't patronize the audience; assume they are intelligent.
- Focus on one or two key areas they need to know to begin to understand your position.

more issue-relevant thoughts (Petty & Cacioppo, 1986). This means that if your audience is knowledgeable on your topic, they can easily engage the material you present. They can easily process your material because of their familiarity with the topic, even if it is extremely complex. Knowledgeable audiences depend more on the quality of your arguments and rely less on details like number of sources, length of argument, and how much they like you as a speaker (Wood & Kallgren, 1988) to make their judgments about your presentation.

ENVIRONMENTAL AUDIENCE ANALYSIS

In addition to analyzing the different characteristics of your audience, it is also important to examine the environment that will surround your audience. Just where will you be speaking and how will that affect your audience's ability to relate to you?

PHYSICAL SETTING

Where will you be presenting this presentation? Will your audience be seated in comfortable seating? Will the setting be formal, as in a large lecture hall, or will it be informal, as in a conference room? All of these factors will affect your audience and will require adaptation on your part. Always try and visit the actual place you will be making your presentation. If this is not possible, ask the person who is scheduling or arranging your presentation to describe the accommodations.

> **CONSIDERATIONS IN ENVIRONMENTAL AUDIENCE ANALYSIS**
> ◉ Physical setting
> ◉ Length of presentation
> ◉ Time of day
> ◉ Occasion
> ◉ Order of speakers

If you will be speaking outside, it will be unlikely that you will be able to use audio-visual equipment. PowerPoint slides will not be visible outdoors even if you had the equipment available to you. You will also be competing with the environment. If it is a beautiful spring day after a cold drab winter, it will be hard for your audience to concentrate on what you say. How might you accommodate this? Some type of novelty in your presentation may help you overcome this distraction.

If the room is large, you will need to speak louder so that those audience members in the back can hear you. You may even consider wearing a microphone. Large rooms also suggest more formality. Speakers are required to be more formal in large settings. Think about your own experiences. Classes conducted in standard classrooms are usually more informal than those conducted in large lecture halls.

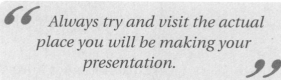

> " *Always try and visit the actual place you will be making your presentation.* "

If you notice that your audience is uncomfortable due to the room's environment, you will want to shorten your presentation. The attention of an audience sitting in uncomfortable chairs or having to stand in the back of the room will wander. Make accommodations during your presentation if you sense that your audience is uncomfortable.

OCCASION

The occasion can also affect the need for adaptation on your part as a speaker. Why are you being asked to give this presentation? Is this part of a sales presentation? Are you being asked to reveal changes as part of an organizational restructuring? The occasion will dictate how you will approach the topic as well. Take the example of organizational

The physical setting can enhance a presentation but if a speaker is not careful, the physical setting can also provide distractions.

restructuring; it makes employees very nervous. Their jobs are potentially at risk. Therefore, you would approach this occasion very differently than if you were speaking to commemorate the anniversary of the organization. In terms of the occasion, think about what the audience is expecting and feeling and how those expectations can be incorporated into the presentation.

TIME OF DAY

The time of day that you deliver your presentation can also affect your audience. You want to prepare for their reactions and adapt your message to best engage them. If you are asked to deliver a briefing at 11:30 a.m., you can anticipate that your audience will be hungry and looking forward to lunch. You would want to keep your comments brief. If you continued your presentation well after the noon hour, you would lose your audience. They would be distracted and thinking, "When will this presentation be over so I can get some lunch?"

Similarly, speaking right after an audience has returned from lunch can have profound implications on your presentation as well.

Audiences are often sleepy after eating a large meal. Therefore, you must plan very engaging and exciting material if you are making a presentation right after the lunch hour. What can you do to get your audience involved? Some type of activity might be necessary when facing this situation. For a very important presentation, it might be better to try to alter the circumstances rather than adapting to increase the likelihood of achieving the desired impact.

ORDER OF SPEAKERS

The order that you speak in can be important in terms of audience analysis as well. Do you speak first or are you sandwiched between many speakers? The first speaker in a series of presentations enjoys the advantage of facing a fresh audience. Fresh audiences are usually engaged and alert early in the program and, therefore, likely to focus on the material you present.

The opposite is true if you speak last or near the end of a series of speakers. Your audience will be fatigued and less likely to expend a great deal of effort processing your message. Use strategies for reinvigorating the audience. Involve them and use a delivery style that is animated. Use narratives and avoid long lists of statistics or other information that may be difficult to process. If there is a question and answer session, your audience may be too tired to participate. Their questions may have previously been answered by the other speakers. If there aren't a lot of questions, don't worry. It probably has more to do with fatigue than your actual presentation.

If you do find yourself speaking in the middle of a program, use that to your advantage. Relate material other speakers have presented to your own. You can use their information as context for your own material. Demonstrate how your material and ideas relate to all the others and try to synthesize the main ideas of the previous speakers to give your audience the "big picture" of the topic being addressed.

Speaking order can have an impact on your presentation. Take this into consideration when you are planning your talk. By making a few minor adjustments, you can better meet the needs of your audience. They will appreciate it, and your presentation will more likely have the impact you want to achieve.

TIME/LENGTH OF PRESENTATION

Students often complain about the time restrictions associated with their presentational assignments. What you may not know is that speakers in the real world face similar constraints that have real implications. Will Miller, Ph.D., comedian and motivational speaker, says that "the time restrictions I face from my clients are very real. If I go over my allotted time, audience members will start to leave. They have other engagements, and their schedules are very tight. If I go under my allotted time, audiences feel they haven't gotten their money's worth" (personal communication, January 15, 2005). When speakers exceed their time constraints, they send several negative messages. First, they are communicating that their message is more important than everyone else's. After all, when they go over their time limit, they are taking time away from another speaker. This implies that they think their material is more important. If they are the only speaker, they show a lack of respect for the audience by failing to recognize that audience members have other commitments and obligations. Second, it demonstrates incompetence. It implies that the speaker was unable to adapt their material to the situational constraints.

As Will Miller suggested earlier, falling way short of your time limit is problematic as well. If an audience member pays to listen to an hour-long presentation on gardening and the speaker only talks for twenty minutes, the audience will feel cheated. Even if the material you presented was valuable, they may not appreciate it because the entire presentation failed to meet their expectations.

It is the responsibility of the speaker to adhere to the given time constraints. Whenever accepting a speaking engagement, always make sure you understand the time constraints. It is important to determine if the constraint includes the question and answer session or not. During your presentation, keep an eye on the clock. Ultimately, it is the speakers' responsibility to ensure they stay within their time limit.

TECHNOLOGY

It is important as a speaker that you understand what technology you will have available to you and plan accordingly. No matter how well you plan, there can always be technical difficulties. "The show must go on" so to speak. So, have a backup plan. If the bulb of the LCD projector burns out, you need to be able to give your presentation without the use of visual aids. You can always print transparencies for use with an overhead projector as a backup (see Chapter 12 for more discussion). However, projectors are harder and harder to find and the venue you are speaking at may not have one available. Be flexible and plan for every contingency.

Speak with the event coordinator about what technologies will be available. Some questions that you will want to ask include:

- ◈ Will I have a podium?
- ◈ Will I have a LCD projector?
- ◈ Will I have access to a computer, or should I bring my own?

    ◇ Will the room have Internet access?
    ◇ Will I have a microphone? Is it cordless?

Knowing what technologies are available to you will help you plan your presentation more effectively. Remember, utilize the technology to better meet the needs of your audience. If it doesn't enhance your message, you really don't need it.

AUDIENCE ADAPTATION BEFORE THE PRESENTATION

Now that you know many of the important things you need to consider when adapting to your audience, you may be thinking, "How will I get this information? How will I know the demographics of my audience, and how motivated they will be to process my presentation?" There are direct and indirect ways of gathering this information.

DIRECT METHODS

One of the best ways to gather information about your audience is through *direct methods*. These include directly asking your audience who they are and what characteristics they possess. Interviews, focus groups, and surveys are some of the traditional tools used in gathering information directly from your audience.

    Interviews are conducted one-on-one with audience members. You should prepare a list of questions in advance that includes both closed- and open-ended questions. *Closed-ended questions* limit responses to a specific range of answers. An example would be, "Do you exercise regularly?" The respondent only has two choices: yes or no. *Open-ended questions* allow the respondent the freedom to answer any way they choose. An example would be, "Describe your exercise routine." By including open-ended and closed-ended questions in your interview, you will be able to get better and more varied information about your audience.

> **DIRECT METHODS OF AUDIENCE ANALYSIS**
> ◎ Interview
> ◎ Focus groups
> ◎ Surveys

    The *focus group* differs from the interview in one substantial way: the number of people involved at one time is much larger. A focus group is a group interview facilitated by one leader. Focus groups usually range in size from three to twelve individuals. Focus groups are advantageous because the group can often think of ideas or issues that the individual may not think of alone. However, some individuals may be hesitant to speak up in a group setting. In comparison to the interview, you are able to collect more information in less time. So from a preparation standpoint, they may be more efficient.

Surveys or *questionnaires* are another direct method of collecting information about your audience. Surveys allow you the opportunity to collect a large amount of information in a relatively short amount of time. Polls that political candidates distribute are examples of surveys. You can use the e-mail tool in VISTA to distribute questionnaires to your classmates. This is a quick and easy way for you to collect information on your classroom audience.

Many times direct methods such as the preceding are not feasible. This kind of research takes time and money. Usually, investment in this type of research would only be conducted if the stakes were high, such as corporate takeovers, political presentations, and new product launches, just to name a few.

While the direct method is the most effective method for gathering information about your audience, it isn't always available to you as a speaker. If you are unable to gather information directly from your audience, here are some indirect tools to use when analyzing your audience.

INDIRECT METHODS

Indirect methods involve collecting information from any source but your audience. You might ask the person who invited you to speak for some information about the group. This is one of the best methods of collecting information about your audience. They know a great deal about the group and have a good idea of what the group is expecting from you as a speaker. You can also ask individuals who have spoken to the group before to help you understand the characteristics of the group. They can give you a very good preview of how the audience will likely respond.

> **INDIRECT METHODS OF AUDIENCE ANALYSIS**
> - Interview the individual arranging the presentation
> - Interview other speakers who have addressed the group
> - Examine organizational Web sites
> - Examine organizational pamphlets and other materials

I recently delivered a presentation to a large group of students here at Purdue. After speaking with the individual who arranged the presentation, I asked several people who had previously addressed this group to give me some advice about how to approach this audience. All of them gave me some great information, but the most helpful was that they were a rowdy crowd. This enabled me to plan for this possibility. I knew that the style of the presentation would have to be more relaxed and involve the audience from the very beginning. If I had arrived at the speaking engagement and found the audience a bit wild, I would have been unprepared for this outcome. Knowing this information beforehand was extremely helpful.

You can also examine promotional materials associated with the group you will be addressing. If you have been asked to make a presentation for your company to a potential client, you will want to read every newspaper article about that client, visit their corporate Web site, and read their pamphlets and other materials. Anything you can learn about them will help you adapt to their needs.

AUDIENCE ADAPTATION DURING THE PRESENTATION

It is also important that you continue to adapt to your audience as you make your presentation. Stay tuned to audience feedback. Don't get so engrossed in your presentation that you fail to recognize the subtle messages your audience is sending you. Audiences send a variety of messages to a speaker during a presentation. They can indicate confusion, boredom, or they may even be nodding in agreement.

There are adaptations that you can make during your presentation to help facilitate the effectiveness of your presentation. If your audience seems confused, stop. Go back and explain that part of the presentation again. Try using a different explanatory strategy this time. If they still seem perplexed, ask them what seems to be causing difficulty. You may not be able to deliver the presentation as you had expected, but it is much better to ensure that your audience is following you.

If your audience seems bored, try picking up the pace of the presentation. This may mean that you simply speed up the delivery. However, other situations may call for you to cut portions of the presentations. A second strategy is to use more narratives and capitalize on good delivery skills. Stay away from using statistics and facts that are not completely necessary. Make sure you are making good eye contact and using a varied delivery style. You can also try to involve your audience: ask for a show of hands or call on someone directly. This will help you regain your audience's attention.

CONCLUSION

Audience analysis is fundamental to a successful presentation. As we have discussed in this chapter, there are a variety of methods a speaker can use to adapt a presentation to an audience. A demographic analysis provides a general understanding of an audience and includes items such as age, gender, sex, socioeconomic status, culture, religious background, and sexual orientation. However, demographic audience analyses are limited in nature. Be careful not to marginalize your audience by stereotyping them. More sophisticated approaches to analyzing your audience include psychological approaches. Understanding what attitudes the audience holds about your message, why they are in your audience, and what they know about your topic are all important. Environmental audience analysis helps you adapt to the situation that surrounds your audience. There are many methods to collecting the information you will use for your audience analysis. Indirect and direct methods for collecting information can be insightful, so take advantage of both. It is also important to remember that audience analysis isn't only conducted before the presentation. You must also continue to analyze and adapt to their needs during the presentation as well.

KEY TERMS

Attitude

Audience analysis

Captive audiences

Closed-ended questions

Demographics

Direct methods

Favorable audiences

Focus groups

Friendly audiences

Hostile audiences

Identification

Indirect methods

Inoculation

Interviews

Involvement

Motivated audiences

Neutral audiences

Open-ended questions

Passive audiences

Psychological factors

Questionnaires

Surveys

Values

Voluntary audiences

EXERCISES

1. Visit an organization's Web site and/or obtain printed materials (pamphlets, mission statements, ethics codes, brochures, etc.) for the organization. Using the materials as a basis for demographic and psychological audience analysis, try to decide what kind of audience you would be giving a presentation to and how this would affect your choice of presentation materials and your goals for the speech. Possible organizations include the

American Association of Retired Persons (http://www.aarp.org/) , the Red Hat Society (http://www. redhatsociety.com/), New Chauncey Neighborhood Association (http://www. newchauncey.org/) Young Democrats of America (http:// www.yda.org/), College Republicans (http://www.crnc .org/), Future Farmers of America (http://www.ffa.org/), the Sierra Club (http://www.sierraclub.org/), the Audubon Society (http://www. audubon.org/), or the Cary Club (http://www.caryclub.org/).

2. Advertising is a profession that makes extensive use of audience analysis. Choose an issue of a popular magazine like *Newsweek, Sports Illustrated, Good Housekeeping, People,* etc. From that issue, select three advertisements to analyze. Try to determine who the target audience was; what attributes of the target audience did the advertiser appeal to; and what type of analysis (demographic, psychological, environmental) did the advertiser rely most heavily on.

REFERENCES

Burke, K. (1950) *Rhetoric of motives.* Los Angeles: CA, University of California Press.

Butler, J. L., & Baumeister, R. F. (1998). The trouble with friendly faces: Skilled performance with a supportive audience. *Journal of Personality and Social Psychology. 75*(5), 1213–1230.

Festinger, L. (1957). *A theory of cognitive dissonance.* Stanford, CA: Stanford University Press.

Fishbein M., & Ajzen, I. (1975). *Belief, attitude, intention and behavior.* Reading, MA: Addison-Wesley.

Ivy, D. K., & Backlund, P. (1994). *Exploring gender speak: Personal effectiveness in gender communication.* New York: McGraw-Hill.

Kim, M-S., & Hunter, J. E. (1993). Attitude-behavior relations: A meta-analysis of attitudinal relevance and topic. *Journal of Communication, 43,* 101–142.

McGuire, W. J., & Papageorgis, D. (1961). The relative efficacy of various types of prior belief-defense in producing immunity against persuasion. *Journal of Abnormal and Social Psychology, 62,* 327–337.

O'Keefe, D. J. (2002). *Persuasion theory & research.* Thousand Oaks: Sage.

Petty, R. E., & Cacioppo, J. T. (1986). The elaboration likelihood model of persuasion. In L. Berkowitz (Ed.), *Advances in experimental social psychology.* (Vol. 19, pp. 123–205). New York: Academic Press.

Rokeach, M. (1973). *The nature of human values.* New York: Free Press.

Sherif, M., & Sherif, C. W. (1967). Attitude as the individual's own categories: The social judgment-involvement approach to attitude and attitude change. In C. W. Sherif & M. Sherif (Eds.), *Attitude, Ego-involvement and Change* (pp. 105–139). New York: Wiley.

Wood, W., & Kallgren, C. A. (1988). Communicator attributes and persuasion: Recipients' access to attitude-relevant information in memory. *Personality and Social Psychology Bulletin, 14,* 172–182.

Chapter 3

SELECTING THE TOPIC AND PURPOSE

CHAPTER OBJECTIVES

After reading this chapter, you should be able to:

- Explain the qualities of a good topic.

- Identify methods for choosing a topic.

- Identify differences between the general and specific purpose statements.

- Identify differences between the specific purpose statement and the thesis statement.

- Construct effective general purpose, specific purpose and thesis statements following the criteria outlined in the chapter.

*G*ino is taking this course and has begun the initial steps of preparing his first presentation. His assignment requires him to pick a topic with which he is familiar and share this material with his audience in an informative presentation. After hours of thinking about the assignment, he still has no topic. When his roommate, Erik, comes home and asks what he is doing, Gino tells him about the assignment and tells him that he cannot find a topic that his audience will find interesting. Erik laughs and says, "You can't find anything exciting and interesting to speak about? You have two part-time jobs, one at the coffeehouse and the other refereeing intramural athletics on the weekend. There are plenty of interesting topics related to your two jobs alone." After further discussing the specifics of his part-time jobs with Erik, Gino decides to speak on shade-grown coffee. This is a special type of coffee he sells in the coffeehouse.

Gino's situation is not unique. Often the most difficult part of preparing your presentation is choosing your topic. Students often say things like, "I have no experiences an audience will find interesting" or "I don't do anything exciting or interesting." Every semester students repeat these phrases. All of them eventually find an exciting topic to deliver to the class and so will you. That being said, choosing the right topic is an important process that takes time and effort. This chapter provides steps to assist you in selecting a topic. If you follow these guidelines, it will be easier for you to select a topic you are excited about. Following topic selection, we will discuss how to narrow your topic and transform that topic into effective purpose and thesis statements for your presentation.

Let's begin by discussing the elements of a good topic. After that, we will examine the specifics of choosing a topic that will be appropriate to you and your speaking situation.

QUALITIES OF A GOOD TOPIC

INTERESTING TO THE SPEAKER

The topics that you choose for your presentations in this course should be interesting and important to you. Because you will spend a good deal of time working on each presentation, the topic you choose needs to be in an area that you find compelling and interesting so that it continues to motivate you throughout the entire speech-planning process. Planning the presentation will be a difficult task to manage if you do not find this topic interesting. In addition to keeping you motivated while you plan the presentation, you must also be able to motivate the audience while you deliver the presentation. If you have little interest in the topic, it will be obvious to your audience. If you have little interest in the topic, your audience will as well. How can you expect to motivate an audience to listen and be excited about a topic that you do not find interesting?

INTERESTING TO THE AUDIENCE

Your topic must be one that the audience also finds interesting, compelling and useful. As we have discussed in earlier chapters, the audience's motivation to process the information in your presentation is extremely important (Petty & Cacioppo, 1984). Although you find the topic engaging and interesting, you must find a way to connect that topic with your audience so that they will be motivated to think about your message. Audiences are interested in new information that

SPEAKER TIP:

Amy Stoehr
Executive Vice President
Star Power Systems

The most important aspect of public speaking is to give something of value to those in attendance. Public speaking is NOT about YOU—deliver a win for the audience and you'll be successful as a speaker.

they can use. For example, in this course, most of your audience is made up of students who are roughly the same age and in the same situation as you are. Many are hoping to find great jobs after graduation and are preparing for that goal. Therefore, an informative speech on obtaining a summer internship or how to use the job counseling service on your campus would be very useful to your particular audience.

SIGNIFICANT

Your topic should be significant and worthy of being addressed in public. Is it a topic that audiences feel is worthwhile? While you may make the best lasagna in the world, sharing this information with your

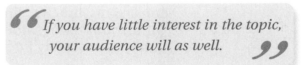

If you have little interest in the topic, your audience will as well.

audience in this particular environment is not extremely significant. You should share information that will actually have an impact on your audience.

Even in an organizational setting, you want to make sure the topic that you select is significant enough to warrant your audience's time. When employees take time out of their schedules to listen to a presentation, they are taking time away from other tasks. Therefore, make sure that when you ask for your colleagues' time and attention, you have something valuable and insightful to offer them.

FITS THE TIME LIMITS

The topic you choose for your presentation must also fit the time constraints of the situation. In today's frantic pace, we all have limited amounts of time we can devote to messages. The same is true for our audiences. Consequently, we are often constrained in speaking situations by time. More often than not, you will be given a time frame in which your presentation must fit. This time frame may be as small as four minutes or as long as several days. You must think about the topic you would like to address and determine whether you can adequately do that topic justice under the time frame you have available. For example, Jodie, a previous student in this course, wanted to explain how to write a job resume to her audience. She had a five-minute time frame to present this information. As you know, writing resumes is a difficult and timely process with many intricacies. She simply did not have time to adequately address this issue in a meaningful way. After doing initial research, she quickly realized that this was not a topic well suited to the time constraint. In the end, Jodie chose to provide information to the class on the career center on campus and the services it provided to assist students with job placement. This topic could easily be managed within her assigned time frame and still provided valuable and insightful information to her audience.

As was discussed in Chapter 2, time limits should be strictly adhered to. Speaking over your allotted time can be perceived as rude and inconsiderate by an audience. It shows lack of respect for audience members, and it has ethical implications. The same is true for speaking under your allocated time constraint. If you are hired to deliver an hour long presentation on investing in today's markets and you only speak for twenty minutes, you will be percieved negatively and damage your credibility for future presentations (see Chapter 10). Your audience will feel short changed and cheated. Respect your time constraints by choosing a topic that can be adequately addressed within your time restrictions and practice to ensure that your presentation comfortably fits the parameters of the time frame.

EASILY RESEARCHED

The topic you select for this class should also be easily researched. It should be a topic with a wide availability of resources, including traditional print media, such as books, magazines and newspaper articles; personal interviews; etc. If you are having a difficult time generating material for the topic you have chosen, move on to another topic. If the research materials you are finding for your topic are old and do not fit the criteria for the assignment, then the topic may not be novel and informative enough to meet the criteria of the assignment.

TIMELY

A good topic is also timely. This means it is relatively new or presents new information on an old topic. If you do not have new information to share with an audience, your topic will not be perceived as pertinent or useful. During the research phase of the planning process, make sure that you find new information and development within the field you are researching. If you are having difficulty finding material that is new and novel for you, perhaps this topic isn't well-suited for the presentation. For example, you might find the topic of Alzheimer's disease interesting and even know a friend or family member who has suffered from the disease. While most audience members are aware of what the disease is and the symptoms that accompany it, new breakthroughs regarding Alzheimer's are being discovered daily. A presentation that focused on the new developments would be timely for your audience. A presentation that simply described the disease would not.

Now that you know the criteria that a topic should meet in order to be considered a good topic, let's examine strategies to help you select a topic.

HOW TO SELECT A TOPIC

Although selecting a topic is a large part of the presentation-making process in this course, you will rarely have to pull a topic out of thin air for presentations outside of the classroom. When you are invited to give a presentation or are required to present material as part of a job, for example, your topic will be predetermined for you. That is, you will most likely be invited to speak because of your expertise, and your only decision will be how to address the topic in a given situation with a particular audience. In this class, however, you will be required to choose topics to develop into presentations. If you follow the tips presented in this chapter, the process will be a snap.

PERSONAL EXPERIENCE

One of the best suggestions for choosing a topic is to select something from your own personal experience. Think about something that you know a lot about. We feel more comfortable in front of an audience when we know a lot about the topic on which we are presenting. Do you have hobbies or special interests that you could share with the audience that would make a good presentational topic? For example, Shae, a student in this course, was an avid NASCAR fan. He capitalized on his passion and knowledge of racing by tracing the development of

Spotlight on Research

ANXIETY OVER TOPIC SELECTION

If you feel anxious about choosing your topic, you are not alone. Research has indicated that students feel a great deal of stress and anxiety about choosing topics for any assignment. However, this same research has indicated that social interaction can actually help reduce the stress and anxiety many students feel about this process. Discussing your ideas with a roommate, family member, or friend can actually help you narrow the topic and feel good about your choice. The people in our social networks are sometimes better equipped to recommend good directions for a topic. So when choosing a topic for this course or any presentation, talk to your friends and family about your ideas. They can be a valuable support during this phase of the preparation process.

Shaw, D. E. (1996). Information search process model: How freshmen begin research. *Proceedings of the 1996 Annual Conference of the American Society for Information Science*, 19–24, October 1996, Baltimore, MD. Retrieved February 14, 2006, from http://www.asis.org/annual-96/ElectronicProceedings/swain.html.

the organization for a classroom presentation. Use your areas of expertise to help choose a topic. Perhaps you took an excellent course on campus that led to some personal benefit for you. Tell your audience about the course or even persuade them to take it. Do you have a job that could provide interesting material? What about trips you have taken? What are your passions?

PERSONAL INTERESTS

Another good way to choose a topic for this course is to investigate something you have always been interested in. Consider topics that fascinate you that you have never had a chance to pursue. See your assignment as a way to investigate a topic that has always sparked your interest but you have never had the time to explore. You might think about other courses you are currently taking. Are there issues mentioned in those classes that you would like to know more about? If so, it may make an excellent topic for a presentation in this course.

CURRENT EVENTS

Other good places to look for topics are newspapers, talk radio programs, news magazines, National Public Radio (NPR) and news pro-

Your audience will be able to detect your enthusiasm for a topic.

grams such as *60 Minutes* and *20/20*. Topics presented in the media are usually topics being discussed in society; therefore, these topics are usually relevant for audiences and are significant and timely. Topics currently being covered in the news are also easy to find, so it may simplify your research process.

In addition to being relevant and timely, current events may also lend themselves to being **"localized"** for a presentation. Localizing is a term used in mass communication when events that are taking place elsewhere are examined for their status or effect at the local level. For instance, news reports from Kansas discussed how that state's Board of Education passed a mandate that "intelligent design"—the theory that a higher power created the universe—become a part of the public school system's science curriculum. While this story might serve as the source of an interesting informative or persuasive speech on its own, a quick check for a local angle might reveal implications for your own geographical area. A quick search revealed that your representatives also planned to

SOURCES FOR CURRENT EVENTS

◉ Google news: http://news.google.com
◉ Newslink: http://www.newslink.com
◉ Yahoo news: http://news.yahoo.com
◉ U.S. Newspaper List: http://www.usnpl.com
◉ Yahoo's newspaper list: http://dir.yahoo.com/ News_and_Media/Newspapers/
◉ CNN: http://www.cnn.com
◉ National Public Radio: http://www.npr.org

discuss your state's own intelligent design legislation in the upcoming session. Now this interesting news story becomes even more relevant for your audience.

NEWS RELEASES, NEWS SERVICES AND NEWSLETTERS

News releases are communications from for-profit and nonprofit companies as well as private and governmental entities directed at members of the news media. Most news releases claim to have some "news value" and are an attempt to garner media attention for a new product, event, new discovery, etc. Just as news releases can be a good source of story ideas for journalists, news releases can also be the source for a good topic for either informative or persuasive presentations.

> **SOURCES OF NEWS RELEASES**
>
> ◉ PRWeb: http://www.prwebdirect.com/
> ◉ PR Newswire: http://www.prnewswire.com
> ◉ U.S. Newswire: http://prnewswire.com/usnewswire/

News releases can be easily located. In 2003, both Google and Yahoo redefined the term "news" to allow news releases to be displayed in search results along with news stories. Other sites are designed solely for the purpose of making releases readily available to both the media and the public. PR Newswire (http://www.prnewswire.com/) is one of the more popular sources and reports an average of more than 1.2 million hits per month.

Most governmental, political, business and organization Web sites will make their news releases available online at their respective sites. Many of the sites have entire pages dedicated to releases. Most of these pages will be headlined "newsroom" or "media." For example, the Census Bureau's Web page (http://www.census.gov/Press-Release/www/releases/) is a popular site for journalists because of the large number of releases put out by the bureau. The Census Bureau's newsroom is accessible to everyone, as most are, and not just the news media. In addition, the Census Bureau also breaks down its news releases by date and by categories to further aid topic selection. For example, a news release published on Jan. 22, 2007, by the Census Bureau was all about the Super Bowl. It profiled information on the Indianapolis Colts and the Chicago Bears as well as the Miami site of the 2007 Super Bowl. The information provided in this news release may provide an interesting idea for a speech delivered to a classroom audience.

INTERNET SEARCHES

Using an Internet subject directory, such as Yahoo (http://search.yahoo.com/dir) or Google's Web directory (http://www.google

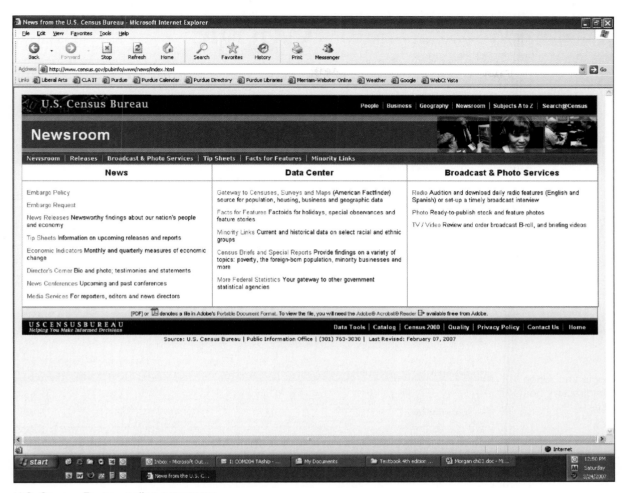

U.S. Census Bureau online newsroom

.com/dirhp), is an easy way to narrow your various interests into more specific topic ideas.

On subject directory sites, Web pages are organized by broad subject areas, and then further broken down into more specific sub-subjects. For instance, at Yahoo or Google, your initial screen will feature a standard 14 categories, such as Business and Economy, Entertainment, and Health.

Let's say you have an interest in technology but aren't sure what to give a speech on. Using Yahoo's Web directory, you can first click on the category of Computers and Internet. Your next screen will have broken this subject into an additional 49 sub-subjects.

As you peruse these, you notice the category "Personal Digital Assistants." You know a lot of your friends have recently purchased or

Web   Images   Groups   News   Froogle   Local   Desktop   more »

Search Directory   Preferences
                     Directory Help

The web organized by topic into categories.

Arts Movies, Music, Television,...	**Home** Consumers, Homeowners, Family,...	**Regional** Asia, Europe, North America,...
Business Industries, Finance, Jobs,...	**Kids and Teens** Computers, Entertainment, School,...	**Science** Biology, Psychology, Physics,...
Computers Hardware, Internet, Software,...	**News** Media, Newspapers, Current Events,...	**Shopping** Autos, Clothing, Gifts,...
Games Board, Roleplaying, Video,...	**Recreation** Food, Outdoors, Travel,...	**Society** Issues, People, Religion,...
Health Alternative, Fitness, Medicine,...	**Reference** Education, Libraries, Maps,...	**Sports** Basketball, Football, Soccer,...
World Deutsch, Español, Français, Italiano, Japanese, Korean, Nederlands, Polska, Svenska, ...		

Advertising Programs - Business Solutions - About Google

©2006 Google

Help build the largest human-edited directory on the web.
Submit a Site - **Open Directory Project** - Become an Editor

Google and Yahoo Web directory home pages

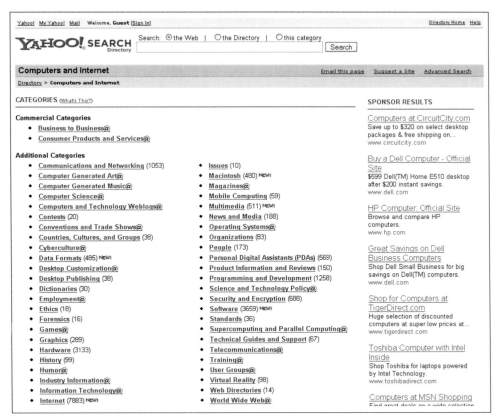

Yahoo's listing of Computers and Internet's additional categories

are thinking about purchasing PDAs, and this might make an interesting speech for a college-age audience. But you still don't know what might be new for your audience.

Clicking on "Personal Digital Assistants" brings you to yet a third screen, which further breaks down the listings for PDAs into 6 more narrow categories. The page also lists the most popular sites for PDA searches, including PDA Buzz, which features news and discussion boards for PDA users and developers. On this site, you notice a news release about the latest uses of PDAs in educational settings. Now you have a topic for your first speech.

Another option for brainstorming topic ideas is the news pages of various Web portals, including Yahoo, Google, and members-only sites such as America Online. Most of these portals break the news into various categories for readers. For instance, at **http://news .yahoo.com/**, in addition to the top national and international news stories, the day's news and news releases are organized by categories

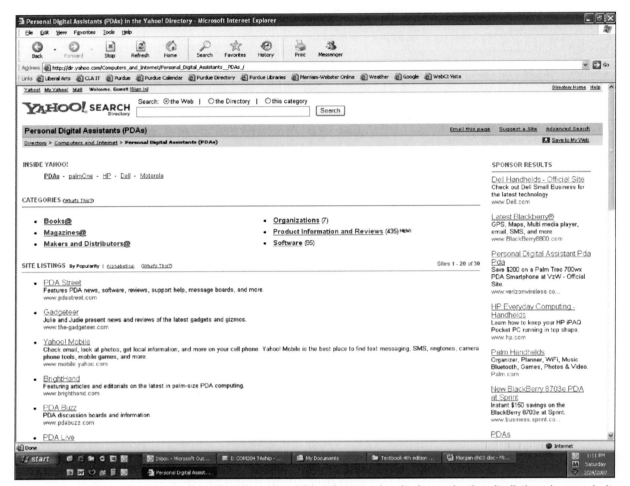

This page shows PDAs being broken down into six additional categories. It also ranks the site listings by popularity.

such as Sports, Technology, and Science. When you click on a category, such as Technology, not only do the day's top technology stories appear, but you are also provided with nine narrower topics, such as Personal Technology, where you would find information on PDAs and other similar devices.

WEBLOGS

Weblogs, or blogs as they are more commonly called, are regularly updated, self-published, online journals. Posts are in reverse chronological order and can contain original reporting, commentary, hyperlinks to news items and other sites, personal narratives, and even photos and video.

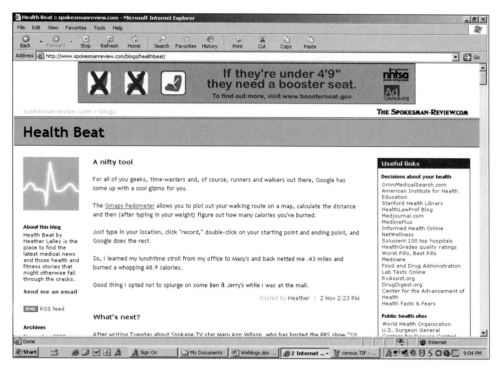

Spokesman-Review's Health Beat Weblog

Weblogs began as a form of online personal diaries, but today, many newspapers, organizations and corporations operate Weblogs as alternative sources of news delivery. In July 2006, Pew Internet put the number of bloggers at "12 million adults."

Because the format of blogs allows for quick updates on breaking stories and links to additional sources on topics, they can be an excellent source of ideas for presentations on current national news events and trends.

Also, many journalists use blogs as a way to present information to the public when space confines in newspapers and on-air television broadcasts limit the number of stories that can be presented. Health reporter Heather Lalley of the Spokane *Spokesman-Review* said she uses her blog (**http://www.spokesmanreview.com/blogs/ healthbeat/**) to inform readers of what she thinks is the most important and/or unusual health news of the day, something she would not

> ## WEBLOG SOURCES
>
> ◉ Google's blog search engine: http://blogsearch.google.com/
> ◉ Cyberjournalist's link to journalists' Weblogs: http://www.cyberjournalist. net/cyberjournalists.php
> ◉ Gallup Polling's Weblog: http://poll. gallup.com/BLOG/
> ◉ Feedster: http://www.feedster.com

have the opportunity to do daily in the newspaper because of space considerations. For example, in a recent post, she informed readers about Google's new Gmaps Pedometer, which allows you to plot your walking route on a map, figure out the distance, and then, after typing in your weight, calculate how many calories you burned. This post could have triggered a presentation about new technology weight loss aids.

And unlike traditional news stories, blogs often contain commentary and opinions of the authors and those who post responses to comments. These opinions can help gauge public sentiment on current topics and trends and guide persuasive arguments. It is an excellent additional tool to use for audience analysis.

OTHER SOURCES

Sometimes all we need is a little inspiration to get going. One technique is to brainstorm on ideas related to a topic you have a general interest in. For instance, your general interest in sports might lead you to think about exercising, which leads you to think about common stress injuries, which leads you to wonder how the casual exerciser can protect him- or herself. At this point, a possible topic for an informative speech is beginning to form. You might also use such tactics as going to the library and looking through the book stacks in areas related to your interest. You will often find interesting books that could form the basis of a presentation.

 NARROWING THE TOPIC

Once you have selected your topic, you must narrow that topic to fit the situation. A common mistake is attempting to make a presentation on a topic that is too broad. This mistake usually results in a superficial treatment of the topic. There is simply not enough time to address the topic in detail. As a result, the speaker usually presents information with which the audience is already familiar. Try to avoid this pitfall by focusing in on a particular aspect of the topic that you can develop in detail. Consider the following example. Sarah, a former student, really had her heart set on pursuing health-care reform as the topic of her speech. After determining that she could not adequately address the important issues related to this topic in seven minutes, she found an interesting alternative: student insurance coverage at her own university. She was still able to pursue her original interest in health care, but with a new spin that would both easily fit her time constraint and be highly relevant for her audience.

THE GENERAL PURPOSE

After you have selected and narrowed your topic, it is now time to begin thinking about the *general purpose* or overarching goal of your presentation. As noted in Chapter 1, effective presentations have a strong sense of purpose. Planning your purpose is one of the most important steps in your presentation. Traditionally, the general purpose of a presentation falls into three categories: to inform, to persuade, or to entertain. Because presentations with the goal of entertaining are not generally a focus of introductory speaking classes, they will not be addressed here. If your general purpose statement is "to inform," you will be providing the audience with new information to create understanding. *Informative presentations* describe, explain or demonstrate something. Your role in this type of presentation is that of a teacher. If you do not present new material or fail to enhance your audience's understanding of a topic, you have failed to meet the general purpose of the presentation.

As this attorney demonstrates, persuasion asks the speaker to advocate a particular position or course of action.

Informative presentations are discussed in greater detail in Chapter 8 of this book.

If your general purpose is "to *persuade*," you will basically act as an advocate or leader in your presentation. Your goal will be to influence the attitudes, beliefs or behaviors of your audience (Miller, 1972). You will go beyond presenting information and will actually advocate a particular position or course of action regarding that information. For example, take Gino's topic. Instead of just describing what shade-grown coffee is, he might advocate that the audience only consume coffee that was produced in this fashion. (Persuasive presentations are discussed further in Chapter 9 of this book.)

Although the preceding framework provided above is useful in getting you started, it is a bit oversimplified. The purpose of a presentation is usually never strictly informative or persuasive. For example, a successful persuasive presentation often has to be entertaining in order to win the audience over. A speech that is persuasive will also contain some informative elements.

Although the general purpose will be assigned in this course, it is important to remember that in presentations outside of this course, it is your responsibility to determine the purpose of your speech, whether to inform or to persuade. Sometimes the same topic will be persuasive for one audience and informative for another. It is your role as an effective speaker to determine what the situation calls for and to make the appropriate decisions in those circumstances.

THE SPECIFIC PURPOSE

In order to further refine and focus the scope or goal of your presentation, you need to develop your specific purpose statement. The specific purpose statement simply refines your general purpose to make it more specific. The **specific purpose statement** is a statement that conveys what you want your audience to walk away from the presentation knowing or feeling. It expresses exactly what you hope to accomplish in the speech.

> " *The specific purpose statement is a statement that conveys what you want your audience to walk away from the presentation knowing or feeling.* "

- ◇ To inform my audience. . . .
- ◇ To persuade my audience. . . .

In order to be effective, a specific purpose statement must meet the following guidelines: it must include the audience in the statement, it must be written as a full infinitive phrase, it must be written as a full declarative statement, it must contain one distinct idea, and it must be clear and precise. Each of these guidelines is discussed below along with some examples.

Qualities of a Well-Written Specific Purpose Statement

Written as a Full Infinitive Phrase

An *infinitive phrase* consists of the word *to* plus a verb. In this case, the verb will be either inform or persuade.

Ineffective:	Noise pollution and risks.
Better:	To inform my audience about the health risks associated with noise pollution.

Ineffective:	Photomicrography.
Better:	To inform my audience about the origins, techniques, and importance of photomicrography.

The ineffective examples do not adequately address what the presentation hopes to accomplish. While they announce the topic, they do not provide enough detail to indicate the direction of the presentation. Remember, the specific purpose statement guides the direction of your presentation. It is a tool used to refine and focus your material. If you cannot identify the exact content of the presentation, the specific purpose is not adequate. The effective examples provide a clear description of where the presentation is headed.

Expressed as a Full Declarative Statement

Ineffective:	What is nanotechnology?
Better:	To inform my audience about the past, present and future of nanotechnology.

Ineffective:	Is a good night's sleep necessary?
Better:	To persuade my audience that a good night's sleep provides many important health benefits.

As you can see, specific purpose statements written in the form of a question do not clearly indicate the goals of the presentation. While they introduce the topic, they do not provide enough information to reveal what the presentation expects to achieve. Similarly, specific purpose statements that are expressed as fragments also present problems. They do not give enough information about the direction of the presentation.

Limited to One Distinct Idea

Ineffective:	To inform my audience about shade-grown coffee and the plight of endangered bird species.
Better:	To inform my audience about shade-grown coffee.
	Or
Better:	To inform my audience about the plight of endangered bird species.

Ineffective:	To persuade my audience to become active in campus organizations and to reside in on-campus housing.
Better:	To persuade my audience to become active in campus organizations.
	Or
Better:	To persuade my audience to reside in on-campus housing.

Ineffective:	To persuade my audience about the benefits of productivity software and the benefits of voice activation software.
Better:	To persuade my audience about the benefits of productivity software.

	Or
Better:	To persuade my audience about the benefits of voice activation software.

While the ineffective examples are written as declarative statements and infinitive phrases, they contain more than one distinct and unrelated idea. In each of these examples, it would be better to break them into two separate specific purpose statements, one of which could then be chosen as the focus of the presentation.

Is Clear and Precise

Ineffective:	To persuade my audience that something should be done about cheating on college campuses.
Better:	To persuade my audience that an honor code should be adopted at Smith University in order to curtail cheating.
Ineffective:	To inform my audience about diabetes.
Better:	To inform my audience about the latest treatments for diabetes.
Ineffective:	To inform my audience about handheld computers.
Better:	To inform my audience about the uses of handheld computers in the college classroom.

The ineffective examples above are too general. The specific purpose statement is a tool that assists you in determining what should and should not be included in your presentation. These examples do not provide guidance in this area. They are too vague and nonspecific. What should be done about cheating? What should we know about diabetes? What it is, who it affects, or its latest treatments. What about handheld computers? The history, current uses, new developments, novel uses, or perhaps popularity? The ineffective examples are too broad and do not provide guidance in focusing the presentation. The better examples, however, are appropriate in focus and provide enough detail to assist in the preparation of the presentation.

QUALITIES OF AN EFFECTIVE SPECIFIC PURPOSE STATEMENT

- ◉ Written as an infinitive phrase
- ◉ Expressed as a full declarative statement
- ◉ Limited to one distinct idea
- ◉ Is clear and precise

THESIS STATEMENT

Once you have written a good specific purpose statement that meets all of the criteria outlined previously, you are ready to construct your thesis statement. The thesis further refines your purpose for the presentation. The ***thesis statement*** is a summary of the main idea of your presentation. It announces your topic and previews the main points of the presentation. While the thesis sentence is usually only one sentence, there are situations when it may be necessary to break the thesis into two sentences.

> *The thesis statement is a summary of the main idea of your presentation.*

The primary difference between the specific purpose statement and the thesis statement is that the specific purpose statement is what you expect to accomplish in your speech, while the thesis statement is what you will actually say to introduce your topic and main points in the introduction of your speech. There are several guidelines that you should use as you prepare your thesis statement.

Guidelines for Thesis Statement

Expressed as a Full Declarative Sentence

It is important that the thesis statement be expressed in a complete declarative sentence and not as a question. As with the specific purpose statements, full declarative sentences are better suited to detail the path of the presentation.

Ineffective:	How does the FDA approve a drug?
Ineffective:	Approving a drug.
Better:	The process that the Federal Drug Administration uses to approve drugs in this country is lengthy, complicated and consists of four major stages: pre-clinical, phase I clinical, phase II clinical, and phase III clinical.

Limited to One Idea

Similar to the specific purpose statement, if your thesis contains more than one distinct idea, the focus of your presentation will be unclear. Remember, you have a very limited amount of time to address your audience. Within your allotted time frame, you simply cannot address more than one main idea sufficiently.

Ineffective:	Our oceans are being destroyed by over fishing, pollution, and the importation of alien species.
Better:	Destructive alien species are being transplanted in our oceans through two primary means: ballast water and ocean litter.

The first thesis is too broad. Too many causes of destruction are being covered in this presentation. The presentation will be more effective if the focus centered on only one of these types of destruction.

> **QUALITIES OF AN EFFECTIVE THESIS STATEMENT**
> ◉ Expressed as a full declarative sentence
> ◉ Limited to one idea
> ◉ Uses clear and concise language and structure

Uses Clear and Concise Language and Structure

As will be addressed in Chapter 4, it is more difficult for an audience to follow a verbal message than a written one. It therefore becomes important that your thesis be stated as clearly as possible so that you can enhance your audience's ability to understand the message. This means using simple grammatical structure and avoiding overly complex sentences. It also means using language that is concise and not figurative.

Ineffective:	We live in an exciting time characterized by many new advances in dentistry that are paving the way for revolutionary treatments for both the treatment and prevention of the terrible menace, tooth decay.
Better:	New advances in dentistry are leading to changes in both prevention and treatment for tooth decay.
Ineffective:	Backpacks can damage young adults' spines. By placing too much weight in their backpacks, students create stress on their back; this may lead to spinal injuries. Young adults can avoid injury by properly using their backpacks.
Better:	In order to avoid back injury, practice safe backpack use by following these four easy steps: choose right, pack right, lift right, and wear right.

Here are several examples that trace the development of a presentation from topic selection to the thesis statement.

Topic:	Backpacks
General Purpose:	To persuade
Specific Purpose:	To persuade my audience to practice back pack safety.
Thesis Statement:	In order to a avoid back injury, practice safe backpack use by following these four easy steps: choose right, pack right, lift right, and wear right.

Topic:	Drug Approval
General Purpose:	To inform
Specific Purpose:	To inform my audience about how the FDA approves a drug for usage.
Thesis Statement:	The process that the Federal Drug Administration uses to approve drugs in this country consists of four major stages: pre-clinical, phase I clinical, phase II clinical, and phase III clinical.
Topic:	Cheating on college campuses
General Purpose:	To persuade
Specific Purpose:	To persuade my audience that an honor code should be adopted at Hometown University in order to curtail cheating.
Thesis Statement:	An honor code should be adopted at Hometown University to curtail the amount of cheating on our campus.

CONCLUSION

This chapter covered the major factors associated with selecting a topic and defining the purpose of the presentation. Many of you are likely struggling with this very issue as you prepare for your class presentations. As indicated earlier, topic selection is not as difficult in professional life as it is in a somewhat artificial classroom environment. However, topics need to be relevant and appropriate regardless of the circum- stances. This chapter overviewed quali- ties of a good topic. It then outlined how to identify and construct the general purpose, specific purpose, and thesis statements that will guide the rest of the presentation's development. By creating these statements, you will be in a better position to identify important re- sources, conduct research, and organize information you will use throughout the presentation.

KEY TERMS

General purpose	Localized	Thesis statement
Infinitive phrase	Persuade	Weblogs
Informative presentations	Specific purpose statement	

EXERCISES

1. To help with brainstorming use the following software: Open Mind. It is mind-mapping software that will help you visually as you brainstorm ideas for your speech. You can locate this software using software remote at the ITAP Web page. Contact your instructor for instructions in gaining access to this resource.

2. Critique the following thesis sentences based on the criteria in this chapter.

   a. In order to give our youth the best education possible, the education they receive must be founded on sound principles that acknowledge opposing viewpoints such as the viewpoint of evolution versus the viewpoint of creationism.

   b. In order to fully understand DNA profiling, you must first have a deeper insight as to what DNA itself is, how the DNA profile is done, and what techniques are used to create the profile.

   c. Personality is made up of four different temperaments:

sanguine, melancholy, choleric, and phlegmatic.

d. Time-reversed acoustics creates the best reversed echo in environments that have dense medias allowing for the pinpointing of hard to detect signals.

e. As we all realize that hypertension is a major killer, it will be beneficial for us to know something about this subject matter.

References

Miller, G. R. (1972). Persuasion. In C. R. Berger & S. H. Chaffee (Eds.), *Handbook of Communication Sciences* (pp. 446–483). Newbury Park, CA: Sage.

Petty, R. E., & Cacioppo, T. J. (1984). The effects of involvement on responses to argument quantity and quality: Central and peripheral routes to persuasion. *Journal of Personality and Social Psychology, 46,* 69–81.

Shaw, D. E. (1996). Information search process model: How freshmen begin research. *Proceedings of the 1996 Annual Conference of the American Society for Information Science,* 19–24, October 1996, Baltimore, MD. Retrieved February 14, 2006, from http://www.asis.org/annual-96/ElectronicProceedings/swain.html.

Chapter 4

INTRODUCTIONS AND CONCLUSIONS

CHAPTER OBJECTIVES

After reading this chapter, you should be able to:

- ☑ Identify the five components of an effective introduction.

- ☑ Identify the three components of an effective conclusion.

- ☑ Compose an effective introduction.

- ☑ Compose an effective conclusion.

*J*avier began his presentation with an interesting and humorous anecdote about his brother pulling some teenage pranks. The audience found the story entertaining and was laughing and enjoying the presentation. Javier had done an excellent job capturing the attention of his audience. After telling the story, Javier explained his thesis statement. His presentation was about recidivism rates of state parolees. The audience got very quiet and looked confused. Everyone was trying to figure out what the story of his brother and recidivism rates of parolees had to do with one another. As Javier continued with his introduction, the audience's attention remained focused on how this story was related to the content of the presentation. Rather than concentrating on the material in the introduction, the audience lost focus and missed the important details Javier was trying to explain that set up the rest of his presentation.

Javier made a crucial mistake. He opened his speech with an attention-gaining device (a story or anecdote) that was only tangentially related to his material. This mistake confused his audience and he was never able to regain their attention as he moved through his introduction. This type of mistake is common. Speakers at all levels have difficulty determining how to begin and end their presentations. Like Javier, when faced with making a presentation, many individuals immediately start thinking about how they will start their presentation. How will they begin? We often get so overcome by how we will start that we neglect some of the important planning aspects of the presentation. We want to come out of the gate running, so to speak, and so we make fundamental errors by focusing on the wrong elements of the presentation.

We have often heard that the beginning and ending of our presentations are the most important elements. We often focus so intently on how to begin the presentation, that we do not devote enough attention to the body or the major content of the presentation. This is not to say that the introduction is not important. It is extremely important. Yet, you cannot craft an effective introduction unless you have clearly formulated or articulated the body or main ideas of the presentation. After you have a firm grasp on the main ideas you want to share with your audience, you can then begin to design the introduction. If Javier had followed the guidelines presented in this chapter for preparing and delivering his presentation, he would have been far less likely to make the mistake he made with his audience.

A similar mistake is often made with the conclusion. Much like the introduction, many novice speakers jump right to the conclusion after they have worked through the introduction. Again, you simply cannot write an effective conclusion until you know what you are going to say in the body of the presentation. The conclusion simply sums up your main ideas. If the main ideas are yet to be formalized, then the conclusion cannot be written. This chapter will also help you formulate effective conclusions.

Introductions

As you recall from earlier chapters, for people to expend significant energy processing your message, two things must be in place: they must be motivated to process the message, and they must be able to process the message (Petty & Cacioppo, 1986). It is in your introduction, the first few moments of your presentation, where listeners make critical assessments about how important and understandable your message will be. If they do not perceive that your presentation will be relevant to them and that they will be able to understand or follow your presentation, then they may tune out.

The introduction in any speech sets the tone for the rest of the presentation. The ***introduction*** gains the attention of your audience, introduces the speaker and topic to the audience, and prepares the audience for the rest of the presentation by announcing and previewing the topic. All of these elements are vital in an effective presentation. You simply cannot overestimate the impact the introduction will make on your audience. First impressions are extremely powerful. Don't underestimate them.

Objectives of an Effective Introduction

An effective introduction in any presentation should:

- ◇ Capture the attention of your audience
- ◇ Establish your credibility as a speaker
- ◇ Relate the material to your audience
- ◇ Announce the topic of the speech
- ◇ Preview the main points of the speech

All of these components must be addressed in the introduction of the presentation in order to achieve maximum effect. The speaker must also be able to accomplish all of these components or goals within the allotted time frame. A guideline for the length of an introduction is about ten percent of the total speaking time. For example, if you have been asked to deliver a seven-minute presentation, your introduction should last about 45 seconds. Let's examine each of the five goals of an effective introduction so that you can get a better idea of how these components fit together.

CAPTURING THE ATTENTION OF YOUR AUDIENCE

One of the most important aspects of any presentation is the first few phrases that a speaker utters. The opening remarks in a presentation set the tone for everything that will follow. Therefore, the attention getter or opening is extremely important. The ***attention-gaining device (attention getter)*** is the tool a speaker uses to gain immediate attention from an audience. It can be a story, quotation, fact, statistic or any one of the other suggestions made in this chapter. If you are unable to gain the attention of your audience early in the presentation, it is very difficult to regain their focus. Therefore, your choice of attention-gaining devices is crucial.

> ❝ *You will always want to begin with an attention getter.* ❞

Regardless of the type of presentation or the situation, whether it is a sales presentation or a classroom presentation, you will always want to begin with an attention getter. There are many devices or strategies that you can use to capture attention. We will review several of the most popular.

Questions

Many presenters open with posing a question for their audience. Sometimes this question is purely a ***rhetorical question***, which means that you do not expect a verbal response to the question you have posed. Rather, you only want to get them to think about the question you have raised. Imagine that you are delivering a presentation about the condition of rental properties around campus. You might begin the presentation with questions such as, "Are you tired of paying sky high rents?" "Are you tired of calling your landlord about the leak in the bathroom and the broken toilet week after week with no response?" In this example, the speaker does not expect the audience to answer the questions. The goal with this attention getter is to get the audience to think about the condition of their off-campus housing.

Sometimes we want an answer from the audience. If this is the case, we ask a ***direct question*** because we desire a response. The response the audience provides may guide the way we adapt our presentation to that audience. Or, perhaps you simply ask the question in order to get the audience actively involved. For example, David, a former student in this course, gave a speech on controlling the wild deer population. He began his speech by asking his audience a direct question: "What animal, reptile, or insect kills more Americans each year?" The audience guessed many responses from spiders to snakes to dogs.

However, the correct answer, as David informed the audience, was wild deer. According to CNN, deer kill more Americans than any other animal or insect each year. He went on to support this claim by citing a 2005 published document by State Farm insurance, which reports "1.5 million vehicles collide with deer every year, resulting in 150 motorists' deaths." This attention getter was effective because it got the audience involved, and it also revealed their need for this information. He was able to easily demonstrate how uninformed they were, and this functioned to pique their interest in the topic.

Story/Narrative

One way to build rapport immediately with your audience is to begin with a story or narrative. This is often a great way to personalize your topic and intrigue your audience simultaneously. Audiences are drawn to personal stories or narratives. Additionally, narratives have been shown to help audiences comprehend material and evaluate it more easily (Pennington & Hastie, 1992).

Here is an example taken from Natalie's informative speech on LASIK eye surgery and the importance of choosing a good surgeon.

> On December 14, 2001, Sandy Keller went in for what she thought would be a "20-Minute Miracle." After her LASIK eye surgery, she would be able to throw away her unwanted glasses and contacts forever. However, things went terribly wrong for Sandy that day. The microkeratome blade used for making the incision in LASIK surgery jammed in her eye, leaving a permanent ridge in her eye and a severe infection. Days after the surgery Sandy saw through a foggy, whitish-haze and became so sensitive to light, it was difficult for her to go outside during the day. She was no longer able to judge distance and had absolutely no depth perception. Sandy's 20-minute miracle turned into two surgeries and a two and a half year nightmare. Although Sandy is now on the road to recovery, she will never regain her pre-surgery vision.

Natalie uses this story to immediately involve the audience in the topic. Audiences become interested in the plight of Sandy Keller and her traumatic experience and immediately become engaged.

There are a few things to consider when using a story or narrative as an attention getting device. First, the story must relate to the topic of the presentation. Secondly, it must also be brief. We often ramble as we tell stories. In a presentation, we do not have that luxury. Thirdly, the story must have a clear beginning, middle, and end. Audiences process information more effectively when stories build toward a conclusion (van den Brock & Lorch, 1993). So, it is important that the story has a clear structure and closure.

Quotation

Another common way to begin a presentation is by introducing a quotation. If you find a famous quotation or a quotation from a well-known figure that relates to your topic, it can be a clever way to engage your audience. Audiences appreciate comments from individuals they respect. Again, as with a story or narrative, your quotation must relate directly to your material. It should be very clear to your audience why you are using the quotation. If you have to explain the relevance of the quotation to the topic of your presentation, it is probably not the best choice.

You also need to avoid quotes that have become obvious clichés. For example, consider the following quote: "Early to bed and early to rise makes a man healthy, wealthy and wise" by Ben Franklin. This quotation is overused and has become cliché. In a presentation you want to grab the audience with a powerful quote; this one probably wouldn't do the trick. After all, we've heard it before. The following example demonstrates a more effective way to utilize a quotation.

A physician addressing a civic organization was asked to speak about health information on the Internet. He started his speech by saying, "Mark Twain once said, 'Be careful about reading health books. You may die of a misprint.' The same might be said of health sites on the Internet." He then went on to give a presentation on how to evaluate online health information sources. The quote worked well because it was relevant, humorous, from a well-known source, and appropriate to the audience.

Interesting Fact or Statistic

Sometimes the best way to introduce a topic to an audience is to surprise them in some meaningful way. This is often accomplished by sharing some interesting fact or statistic that startles or shocks the audience. A speech on healthy lifestyles started this way:

> According to the University of Colorado's Wellness Center, two out of five women and one out of five men would trade three to five years of their life to achieve their weight-loss goals.

This was an example from Jane's informative presentation on healthy lifestyle choices. She took an interesting fact and used it to engage and pique the interest of her audience. Shocking facts and statistics, like this one, are easily found while you are conducting your research. Sometimes we overlook these pieces of information. Be alert, they can really add impact to the introduction.

Humor

One method commonly used to begin a presentation is humor. Humor is a tricky device to use well. There are many pitfalls that can occur when trying to use humor. Some audiences react favorably to humor. Yet others might be offended. So think about your situation, your goals, and your audience before using humor as an attention getter.

As mentioned in other chapters in this text, the global environment in which we now find ourselves operating is extremely complex. Cultural differences in global audiences add another degree of difficulty to using humor well. Unless you are extremely familiar with another culture, you simply cannot predict what will be humorous, appropriate or offensive.

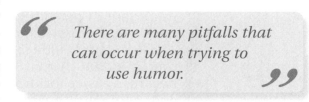

There are many pitfalls that can occur when trying to use humor.

If after doing a thorough analysis of the speaking situation you find that humor would be an effective way to engage your audience, you can begin by telling a funny narrative or example. You should not begin your speech by telling a joke. This is usually a sign that the speaker is a novice. Jokes also have the potential of alienating individuals in the audience. What is funny to you may be offensive to someone else. There are more sophisticated and appropriate ways to incorporate humor into the opening of your presentation.

Compliment the Audience

When you are asked to address an audience outside of the classroom, it is nice if you can draw on some of their previous successes and incorporate those into your opening. It demonstrates that you have done your research about this particular group, thereby enhancing your credibility but also relating their experiences with the topic of your presentation. Consider the following scenario in which this type of opening is appropriate.

Imagine that you are a fifth-grade teacher addressing a parent's group about an upcoming field trip. One thing you know about the group is they have just completed a very successful fund-raising campaign. It would be nice to compliment the organization on their successful campaign and thank them for all of their hard work. Then you can address your primary goal of presenting information about the field trip by highlighting how the successful fund-raising campaign has provided plenty of funds to cover not only normal classroom expenses, but additional frills as well, such as the upcoming field trip.

Refer to Recent Events

When making a presentation, it is important to remember that speeches never occur in a vacuum. There are many outside events that are affecting our daily lives. Many times events that are very important to a particular audience have recently occurred. Perhaps their organization has just gone through a big organizational restructuring or has had a change in leadership. If you can relate these events to the presentation topic, it might be important to address them.

Identify with the Audience

Showing similarity with audience members becomes especially important in persuasive presentations. It is important that the audience see themselves similar to the speaker in important respects. Those might include factors such as age, political views, or socioeconomic status. If you can highlight some of these similarities, it becomes easier for the audience to identify with you as the speaker and, perhaps ultimately, the goal of your presentation (Burke, 1950).

Bryan, a former student, utilized this device very effectively. He began his presentation by telling the audience that he used to be just like them, college students strapped for cash and working at low paying, dead-end jobs, but that today he is a 21-year-old college student and a successful entrepreneur. He had begun his own necktie business and was currently earning $35,000 a year. He went on to give a persuasive presentation that encouraged the audience to become entrepreneurs.

Use Technology (Audio-Visual Aids)

Sometimes the old cliché "a picture is worth a thousand words" is true, and it is possible to grab an audience's interest by demonstrating an important part of your presentation visually. Jeremy, a student at the University of Louisville, was very involved in cheerleading. He delivered a presentation persuading his audience that cheerleading should be considered a sport by the university. He began his presentation by showing a videotape of the national championship routine of the University of Louisville coed cheerleading squad from the previous year. His audience was dumbfounded. No one in the audience had any idea the level of athleticism these routines required. The video was one of the most compelling pieces of supporting evidence used in his presentation, and it had an even greater impact as an attention getter.

There are a few guidelines to consider when using a videotape, audio tape, or other multimedia device as an attention getter. First, rather than simply pushing PLAY, you must introduce your visual aid. The audience needs some indication to prepare themselves for whatever it is you want to show them. A frequent mistake made by presenters is to start the media device without orienting the audience to it. The audience can then end up missing half of the audio-visual. Secondly, cue the video or media to its exact position. It is considered unprofessional to begin the media at the wrong spot.

Finally, you must have good working knowledge of the equipment in the room. Orient yourself to the equipment beforehand, or arrange

Visual aids will enhance a presentation if the speaker uses them effectively by introducing them and using technology professionally.

to have a knowledgeable person there with whom you have discussed and practiced your presentation. If you have any doubts about how to run the equipment, choose another attention getter. Your ability to use the equipment must be seamlessly incorporated into your presentation. Anything less is unprofessional. Remember, this is the first thing an audience sees of your presentation. If you have problems right from the start, your credibility will suffer.

Solicit Participation

Another way to get the audience excited about the presentation from the very beginning is to get them involved. Asking for a volunteer to participate in some aspect of a demonstration is a way to get the audience directly involved. Another strategy is to ask specific audience members questions directly. The following is a more elaborate way to involve the audience. A presenter was delivering a speech about long-term care facilities. She asked the audience to take out a sheet of paper and list the five most important things in their lives. Then she asked them to cross off three of those items. It was a difficult task for the audience to undertake. She then explained that giving up those things most important to them (i.e., their homes, their pets) is exactly what individuals face when entering a long-term care facility such as a nursing home. This attention-getting device fulfilled two goals for the speaker. First, by getting the audience involved in the presentation, she got the audience members' attention. Second, she aroused empathy for older adults who were facing these life-changing choices, which significantly affected the way the audience reacted to the entire presentation. The audience was then able to take the perspective of the older adult, which was exactly what the speaker hoped.

CONSIDERATIONS IN CHOOSING AN ATTENTION-GAINING DEVICE

At this point you may be overwhelmed by the choices for beginning your presentation. You may be wondering where you should start and what you should choose. Below are some guidelines that should help you in this phase of the presentation process. These guidelines consider criteria such as mood, time, audience, and your individual strengths.

Consider the Tone Your Presentation Is Trying to Establish

If the presentation has a somber tone, humor would not be an appropriate way to begin. You want the attention getter to match the overall tone of your presentation. A consistent tone can be an important tool. Keeping the tone consistent in the presentation will help achieve optimal impact.

Consider Your Time Restrictions

Sometimes we can think of incredible attention getters. However, they take up a large portion of time relative to our entire speaking time. Maybe you have a wonderful narrative that relates well to your subject matter; however, the narrative takes four minutes and you can see no way to shorten the story and still achieve the desired effect. It may not be feasible to use the narrative in this case. Remember, your introduction must contain an attention getter, credibility statement, relevance statement, thesis and preview in order to be effective. This is a good deal of material to cover considering the time constraints and the 10 percent rule. You do not want your attention getter to take up too much of your speaking time.

Building identification and focusing on the relationship between the speaker and audience as this speaker is doing is critical to your effectiveness as a presenter.

Consider Your Strengths as a Speaker

It is also important that you capitalize on your strengths as a speaker in the attention-gaining phase of your presentation. If you have a terrible time using humor, do not use it. If you are a gifted storyteller, use a narrative to engage your audience. Think about what you do best and capitalize on your strengths. Choose an attention-gaining device that is not only right for the topic and presentation, but also for you and your speaking strengths.

Consider the Audience

Always choose an attention getter with your audience in mind. Audience analysis is important at every step in planning your presentation, even when planning the attention gaining phase. Ask yourself, "How will my audience likely respond to this attention getter?" In order to answer this question, you must also consider your relationship to the audience. Your role in relation to that of the audience is important. Consider this example of a student who did not recognize her relationship to her audience. Mary was in her late sixties while the rest of the class members were "traditional" college students, aged 18–23. She was delivering an informative presentation about sex education programs in public schools. In opening the presentation, she told a funny story about sex and condoms. Instead of laughing, the audience looked horrified. After the presentation, the students in her audience commented that it was almost as if their grandmother had told a dirty joke to their friends. It made them very uncomfortable. Mary had not considered how her relationship with the other students in the class might impact the effect of her attention getter. Although they may have found the same story funny from another student in the class, and even though they enjoyed and respected Mary as a classmate, her age in relation to theirs changed the impact of the humor.

Consider Your Topic

The attention getter must also contribute to the development of the topic. Many times students find an excellent example or startling statistic that they would like to use as their attention getter, but it is only tangentially related to their topic. If this is the case, do not use it. The attention getter should be the initial step in introducing the topic you will present in your speech. The link between your attention getter and your thesis statement should be extremely clear to your audience. If it is not, you need to consider another opening for your presentation.

ESTABLISHING CREDIBILITY

Once you have gained the attention of your audience, it is important that you establish your credibility as a speaker on the topic you are addressing. *Credibility* refers to an audience's perception of how believable a speaker is on a given topic. Sometimes the person who invited you to speak will establish your credibility for you in their introduction, and you will not have to devote time in your introduction to this step. More often than not, however, you will have to establish your credibility for yourself through a credibility statement. A *credibility statement* simply states what experiences or educational preparation you have had that make you an expert on this topic area.

In order to construct your credibility statement, ask yourself what specific experiences, qualifications, or educational background provides you with authority on this particular topic? Whatever those qualifications may be, you need to describe those to your audience. This is the point in the presentation when you really want to sell yourself or the company you represent. You must accomplish this task in a modest manner since being boastful could offend or insult your audience. However, you do want them to understand why you should be viewed as an expert. Research indicates that education levels, occupation and experience all work together to increase a speaker's expertise and trustworthiness (Hewgill & Miller, 1965; Hurwitz, Miron, & Johnson, 1992).

In the classroom, the speaking situation is a little different than presentations made to other groups. Although many of you will choose topics in which you have direct experience and educational credibility, some of you will not. You may choose a topic simply because you are interested in it. Perhaps you will have had no direct experience with your topic other than the research you did for the presentation. That is perfectly acceptable in this context. Simply tell your audience why you became interested in the topic and what you did in terms of research to prepare for the presentation.

Julie, who gave an informative speech on sleep, relayed her credibility in the following way: "Being a college student myself, and finding myself dozing in my own classes for the first time in my life, I wanted to learn more about sleep deprivation and remedies for this common malady. I began researching the topic through journal articles and books and finally interviewed Dr. Sharon Ward, a leading sleep expert here in our city. I would like to share some of my findings with you today." While Julie has no work or educational experience related to sleep deprivation, she, like many other college students, does experience it on a regular basis. She used her interest in the topic to lead to her credibility.

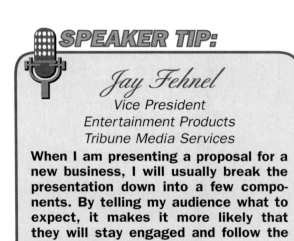

SPEAKER TIP:

Jay Fehnel
Vice President
Entertainment Products
Tribune Media Services

When I am presenting a proposal for a new business, I will usually break the presentation down into a few components. By telling my audience what to expect, it makes it more likely that they will stay engaged and follow the basic logic of the proposal.

Instructors have a variety of methods for including the credibility statement in your classroom presentations. Be sure to identify and utilize the guidelines and criteria they have established.

RELATING THE MATERIAL TO THE AUDIENCE

One important factor in motivating your audience to listen to your presentation is demonstrating how the subject relates to them and how they will benefit directly from the information you will impart (Frymier & Shulman, 1995). A speaker can easily achieve this through a relevance statement. The ***relevance statement*** makes the relationship between your topic and your audience explicit for your audience. It answers the question, "What's in this for me?" It is important that you, as the speaker, answer this question for your audience. Do not leave this important step up to them. Give them a reason to listen.

While a relevance statement is important for all types of audiences, it becomes particularly important for the captive audience. Recall from Chapter 2 that captive audiences attend a presentation because they are required to do so. They have no choice. Instead, their attendance is required, perhaps because of a job they hold or due to a course requirement they must fulfill. With a captive audience, you have to work extra hard to motivate them to listen and process your presentation.

Making your material relevant to your audience also has other benefits (Daly & Vangelisti, 2003). By increasing the relevance for an audience you can also increase the likelihood that your audience will comprehend and learn from the material that you present (Cordova & Lepper, 1996).

ANNOUNCING THE TOPIC AND PREVIEWING THE MAIN POINTS

As discussed in Chapter 3, the ***thesis statement*** encapsulates the general message and previews the main points of the presentation. In effect, it announces the topic and main ideas of your presentation. You will deliver your thesis statement during the introduction of the speech so that you can prepare your audience for the rest of the presentation.

Although it may be a bit uncomfortable to preview your main points, it is vital in helping audiences understand your message. We discussed how organizational structure in an oral presentation is not as apparent as it is in a written presentation. In contrast to a reader of "the printed word," an audience of "the spoken word" does not have the luxury of turning back a few pages in order to follow a point you have made. By previewing the main points of the speech, you will be helping the audience to organize the presentation in advance so that they will be prepared to listen when you get there. This repetition helps ensure that your message will be clear and that your audience can follow you (Cruickshank, 1985). Organizational cues, such as ***preview statements***, help audiences retain and learn information (Dixon & Glover, 1990; Kardash & Noel, 2000), so don't neglect this step. Here is an example of an introduction for a speech including its specific purpose statement.

> **KEYS FOR AN EFFECTIVE INTRODUCTION**
>
> ◉ Always start with an attention-gaining device
> ◉ Display enthusiasm for your presentation
> ◉ Display a sense of control
> ◉ Do not make apologies
> ◉ Do not make promises your presentation cannot keep

Specific Purpose:	To inform my audience about the cause and effects of childhood obesity in the U.S.
Attention Getter:	You are the parent of a six-year-old child attending the first grade at your local elementary school. One day your child brings home a note from the school. You

open up the letter, only to discover that the school has determined that your child is obese and has provided some guidelines to help curtail this situation. This is not a plot line out of a bad TV movie of the week. According to a 2001 story reported by The Associated Press, the East Penn School System in Pennsylvania and the Citrus County School District in Florida are doing just this. Childhood obesity has become a problem, and reporting to parents in this manner is one way schools are attempting to deal with it.

Credibility Statement: As a Health Promotion and Education major, I am concerned about this issue. Several of my courses and internships have dealt with this concern.

Relevance Statement: Childhood obesity is costing society monetarily as well as physically. Insurance rates are rising due to the increase in obesity related diseases. These rising costs will affect you directly as premiums for health-care plans continue to rise because of obesity related diseases.

Thesis & Preview Statement: Childhood obesity in the U.S. is a severe and rapidly expanding problem with a variety of sociological causes and consequences for our society.

Now that you understand the necessary components for constructing an effective introduction, let's examine how to prepare the final element in a presentation, the conclusion.

THE CONCLUSION

The **conclusion** is where you review the information you just presented and leave the audience with your final thoughts. There are three objectives an effective conclusion should achieve. First, you want to reiterate your thesis statement. Secondly, you want to review your main points for your audience. And finally, you want to leave your audience with a memorable thought or lasting impression; this is accomplished through a clincher and is discussed later in this

> *The conclusion is the shortest major element in your presentation. It should last approximately five percent of your total speaking time.*

chapter. No matter how tempting, it is important that you refrain from introducing any new material at this point.

The conclusion is the shortest major element in your presentation. It should last approximately five percent of your total speaking time. Therefore, if your presentation is scheduled to last seven minutes, your conclusion will take 20 to 25 seconds. If there were a motto for the conclusion, it would be, "be clear, brief, and memorable."

The conclusion will be the last impression you make on your audience. There is research to suggest that what audiences hear last, they remember best. This is called the ***recency effect*** (Insko, 1967). Take full advantage of this opportunity to leave your audience with a lasting impression. Many speakers depend on a solid introduction and body to get them through the presentation and pay little attention to the conclusion. These speeches tend to fizzle out. Don't let this happen to you. End your presentation with a bang.

OBJECTIVES OF AN EFFECTIVE CONCLUSION

An effective conclusion in any presentation should:

- Restate the thesis
- Restate the main points
- End with a clincher or memorable thought

RESTATING THE THESIS AND MAIN POINTS

The conclusion in a presentation "tells the audience what you've told them." That is exactly what you want to do. You want to take advantage of repetition. What you have a chance to repeat during your presentation, your audience will remember (Daly & Vangelisti, 2003). The more the audience can remember about your presentation, the greater your chances for achieving the primary goals of your presentation.

You will want to restate the thesis and the preview statement. This can occur in one step or two steps; you can combine the thesis and main points into one statement or separate them into two. You want the audience to leave your presentation with a clear sense of what you covered. This is where you provide them with that information.

Sometimes, as we deliver a presentation, we are unable to cover all of the material we had hoped to present because of time or other situational constraints. It is important that the conclusion review only material you presented in the body of your presentation. Even those items that may have been previewed in the introduction, but skipped due to situational constraints, should be omitted from the conclusion.

Ending with a Clincher or Memorable Thought

Just as you should fully engage your audience in the beginning of the speech, you should also seek to hold their attention at the end of your speech. The ***clincher*** is the final remark that you will make to your audience. It should be as compelling as your attention getter. Give your audience something to think about. Don't let a great presentation fizzle with a weak ending such as "Well, that's about it." There are many ways to end a speech, just as many as there are to begin a speech. Let's review some of the most common approaches.

Referring Back to the Attention Getter

One of the most effective ways to end your speech and provide a sense of closure for your audience is to tie the speech back to your attention getter. For example, if you have opened your presentation with a story, refer back to that story and end with an extension of that narrative. You can see an example of this strategy at the end of the chapter.

Quotation

It also is common to end a speech with a famous quote or a quote from a famous individual. If well chosen, this type of clincher can tie the ideas up nicely. As with using quotes in other parts of the presentation, speakers can benefit from a last additional boost to their credibility through their identification with the source of the quotation.

Call to Action

Many times at the end of a persuasive speech on a question of policy, a speaker will call the audience to action. In other words, the speaker will ask the audience to do something at the end of the presentation. Perhaps that call involves signing a petition, starting an exercise program, or voting for a proposal. Calls to actions are described in greater detail in Chapter 9.

Although you have many options when ending your presentation, think carefully about the option that would add the most impact to your presentation. All of the

> **KEYS FOR AN EFFECTIVE CONCLUSION**
>
> - Continue to make eye contact with your audience for a few seconds after the conclusion
> - Keep the conclusion brief
> - Refrain from adding new information in the conclusion
> - Stay composed as you return to your seat

guidelines that apply to attention getters also apply to clinchers. When choosing a clincher make sure to:

⬧ Consider the tone of the presentation
⬧ Consider your time restrictions
⬧ Consider your strengths as a speaker
⬧ Consider your audience
⬧ Consider your topic

An effective conclusion can help maintain the impact of an effective presentation. In order to be successful, the conclusion must restate the thesis and main ideas of the presentation and provide a sense of closure for your audience. To help clarify how all of these elements come together, let's examine the actual introduction and conclusion of Dayna's informative presentation on a new technological development.

EXAMPLE INTRODUCTION AND CONCLUSION

Specific Purpose: To inform my audience about a new instrument that allows us to detect whether drivers are over the legal blood alcohol limit.

Dayna tells a very moving and tragic narrative about her friend Lucas. It is an emotional story that engages the audience from the beginning. The detail of her story makes this narrative come to life and the audience is able to empathize with Dayna.

Introduction

Attention Getter: This is a picture of my friend Lucas Dixon when he was 12 years old. In the sixth grade, he was a percussionist in the school band, was a member of his church's bell choir, on the cross-country team, and was that class clown the teacher couldn't get mad at. He was my neighbor and my friend. We had all of the same classes and because of our last names, I sat behind him in every class. On Friday, February 9, 1996, at around 7:00 p.m., his mom, Emma Dixon, was driving him to a rehearsal for a band competition the following morning. His mom had been drinking that night, but she had to drive her son to his practice. Halfway to school, Emma swerved into the opposite lane and hit a station wagon head on. The other driver died, and so did my friend Lucas. He never got older than this picture, and I never saw him again besides in his casket. His mom had an alcohol level of about .10, which was Indiana's legal limit at the time.

Dayna continues to keep our attention by sharing statistics that show how prevalent drinking and driving are to our society. These statistics make this topic relevant for the audience. It emphasizes that they themselves, or someone they know and care about, will likely be affected by a drinking and driving accident.

Dayna explains to her audience why they should listen to her about this topic. She explains that she developed an interest because of her tragic experiences and has stayed informed of new developments in the area.

Dayna announces the topic of the presentation. The audience now understands where she is headed and what they can expect.

At this point Dayna begins her conclusion by simply reviewing her thesis sentence. This step helps encapsulate the entire presentation for her audience.

Dayna explicitly reminds her audience of her main points.

Dayna provides a nice sense of closure by tying the attention-gaining device used in her introduction to the ending of her speech. Not only does this choice add closure, but reminds her audience of the emotional costs of drinking and driving.

Relevance Statement: According to Mothers Against Drunk Drivers, an average of 59 people per hour, or approximately one person every minute, is injured in alcohol-related crashes. And about two people die every hour in alcohol-related crashes. About three out of every ten Americans will be involved in an alcohol-related car accident sometime in their lives, according to MADD.

Credibility Statement: I have a strong interest in this topic because I have had two people very close to me die from accidents related to drinking and driving. Because of my personal experiences, I stay informed about new developments in this area.

Thesis Statement: A new instrument that can test the legal blood alcohol limit is now on the market. Today, I would like to explain what this sensor is, how it works, and some of the potential benefits of the sensor.

Conclusion

Review of Thesis: As I have shared with you today, a new instrument has entered the market that can test the legal blood alcohol limit of individuals and may help save lives.

Review Statement: I hope you have a better understanding of what this sensor is, how it operates, and some of the benefits.

Clincher: Just think, if this sensor was on the market seven years ago, it may have saved the life of my friend Lucas. He might even be sitting here in this classroom in the desk just ahead of me.

CONCLUSION

Introductions are the first impression a speaker makes on his or her audience. The introduction must capture the attention of your audience, establish your credibility, provide relevance for your audience, announce your topic, and preview your main points.

The conclusion of your presentation is as important as the introduction. According to the recency effect, we remember best what we hear last. Therefore, the conclusion can be a powerful tool in reaching and persuading your audience. In order to be effective, your conclusion must review your thesis and main points, and provide closure for your audience with a clincher or memorable thought. Do not underestimate the power of the clincher. Too many presentations fizzle at this point rather than ending with a bang.

Introductions and conclusions, though brief, are very powerful tools within the overall presentation. They play very valuable roles, and you need to take them seriously. First impressions and last impressions are important. Though introductions and conclusions are relatively short compared to the overall presentation, they can have a big impact on the overall success of the presentation.

KEY TERMS

Attention-gaining device (attention getter)
Clincher
Conclusion
Credibility

Credibility statement
Direct question
Introduction
Preview statement
Recency effect

Relevance statement
Rhetorical question
Thesis statement

EXERCISES

1. Using the guidelines in this chapter, critique the following introductions. What suggestions might you make for improvement?

    ### Example A

    I.   **Attention Getter:** What would you say if I had a way to prevent adolescent smoking, drinking and drug addiction? According to a recent study, something so simple as eating family dinners nightly could do just that.

    II. **Credibility Statement:** I am very interested in the influence of family in child development and I have conducted research over this topic.

    III. **Relating to the Audience:** Maybe you have been thankful for the time you have had to eat meals together with your family. Or perhaps you feel as though you missed out by not having this opportunity. Whichever experience you had could have played a monumental role in the person you are today.

IV. **Thesis Statement:** Frequent family dining has been found to profit children physically, mentally, and socially.

Example B

I. **Attention Getter:** Gianni Vargas was born at Stony Brook University Hospital in February of 2002. He was an American citizen who had an entire life ahead of him. However, following birth he was taken to intensive care for a needed surgery. The operation went well, and Gianni would have been held in his mother's arms for the first time, except that he suddenly died 6 days after birth. Gianni's death was caused by medical error. A *Newsday* article by Barbara Durkin describes how Gianni was accidentally given 10 times the dose of potassium chloride that should have received.

II. **Credibility Statement:** Over two years ago I was misdiagnosed as being free of pneumonia when I really was still ill. For lack of medical treatment, I soon after contracted viral encephalitis, and nearly died. I know the importance of good health care firsthand.

III. **Relevance Statement:** Certainly you or someone you care for has received health care from an American hospital.

IV. **Thesis Statement:** A new computer system under development will bring significant improvement to health care in the United States by lowering medical costs and increasing patient safety.

Example C

I. **Attention Getter:** Imagine this: You take off from an airport in Chicago. Your destination is London, but on this flight, there will be no soda pop or pretzels served. Instead of this flight taking 9 hours, it will now take less than 45 minutes.

II. **Relevance Statement:** The ability to fly in space economically could change the way you live.

III. **Credibility Statement:** I have traveled all over the world.

IV. **Thesis Statement:** The Ansari X prize has begun a competition that will jump-start the space tourism industry and provide countless benefits.

Example D

I. **Attention Getter:** According to NGA, there are a lot more overweight children now than in the 1970s.

II. **Relevance Statement:** CNN reports that students spend 2,000 hours a year in school; therefore, the schools have a huge influence with vending machines, menus, soda, and candy sales.

III. **Credibility Statement:** I have eaten from those vending machines.

IV. **Thesis Statement:** Obesity is an increasing problem and schools contribute to the problem and are trying to help reduce the problem.

2. Using the guidelines in this chapter, critique the following introductions and conclusions. Remember to critique them as a unit rather than individually. What suggestions might you make for improvement?

Example A
INTRODUCTION

I. **Attention Getter:** Imagine swarms of tiny sensors sitting in your office, seeing, listening and maybe even smelling everything that goes on around you; office cubicles that change temperature depending on who's sitting in them; traffic lights that know which roads are the most crowded and bestow green lights accordingly; marshmallows that tell you when they are stale and shouldn't be eaten; and possessions that tell you exactly where you left them. And how is this brave new world coming about? Through specks of something nearly as tiny, cheap and ubiquitous as dust; I give you the revolutionary "smart dust."

II. **Credibility Statement:** As a computer engineering major, I have learned about the theory of electronics. I have especially been fascinated by electronic gizmos, and when I came across a piece of information on these smart, tiny sensors, I decided to do some more research on them.

III. **Relating to the Audience:** With uses ranging from as small as switching lights on and off in buildings to building wireless virtual keyboards, this remarkable technology will be incorporated in each and every aspect of our lives.

IV. **Thesis Statement:** In order to understand the technology of Smart Dust, it is important to know how it works, its applications and the shortcomings/limitations of the technology.

Transition: First let us see what Smart Dust is and exactly how it works.

CONCLUSION

I. **Restate Thesis:** I have discussed with you the various aspects of the "Smart Dust" technology, its functioning, applications and drawbacks.

II. **Closing Statement:** I personally think that the potential benefits of this technology, by far, outweigh the risks to personal privacy. With the global network already connecting millions of computers worldwide, Smart Dust technology is fast paving the way for more and more objects from the physical world like traffic lights or even patches of sidewalks and roadways being merged with the information network.

As John Anderson, a noted field biologist marvels, "You can literally be anywhere in the world, and know what's going on in burrow No. 43."

Example B
INTRODUCTION

I. **Attention Getter:** I'm sure everyone has heard this quote before: "Enjoy yourselves, these are the best times of your life."

II. **Credibility Statement:** As a student, I have experienced firsthand the fun of college, and the stress of college.

III. Relating to the Audience: As we all know, college can be a great experience, and it can be stressful.

IV. Thesis Statement: As college students' stress levels rise each year, we have to see that stress is bad and not be stressed.

Transition: First I will discuss how stress develops in students' lives.

CONCLUSION

I. Restate Thesis: I have discussed what causes stress in college students' lives and how to alleviate that stress.

II. Closing Statement: Hopefully you have learned to avoid stress.

REFERENCES

Burke, K. (1950). *Rhetoric of motives*. Los Angeles: CA, University of California Press.

Cordova, D. I., & Lepper, M. R. (1996). Intrinsic motivation and the process of learning: Beneficial effects of contextualization, personalization, and choice. *Journal of Educational Psychology, 88,* 714–730.

Cruickshank, D. R. (1985). Applying research on teacher clarity. *Journal of Teacher Education, 26,* 44–48.

Daly, J., & Vangelisti, A. (2003). Skillfully instructing learners: How communicators effectively convey messages. In J. O. Greene & B. R. Burleson, (Eds.), *Handbook of Communication and Social Interaction Skills* (pp. 871–908). Mahwah, NJ: Lawrence Erlbaum Associates.

Dixon, F. A., & Glover, J. A. (1990). Another look at number signals and preview sentences. *Bulletin of the Psychonomic Society, 28,* 287–288.

Frymier, A. B., & Shulman, G. M. (1995). "What's in it for me?": Increasing content relevance to enhance students' motivation. *Communication Education, 44,* 40–50.

Hewgill, M. A., & Miller, G. R. (1965). Source credibility and response to fear arousing communication. *Speech Monographs, 32,* 95–101.

Hurwitz, S. D., Miron, M. S., & Johnson, B. T. (1992). Source credibility and the language of expert testimony. *Journal of Applied Social Psychology, 24,* 1909–1939.

Insko, C. A., (1967). *Theories of Attitude Change.* New York: Appleton-Century-Crofts.

Kardash, C. M., & Noel, L. K. (2000). How organizational signals, need for cognition, and verbal ability affect text recall and recognition. *Contemporary Educational Psychology, 25,* 317–331.

Pennington, N., & Hastie, R. (1992). Explaining the evidence: Test of the story model of juror decision making. *Journal of Personality and Social Psychology, 62,* 189–206.

Petty, R. E., & Cacioppo, J. T. (1986).The elaboration likelihood model of persuasion. In Berkowitz (Ed.), *Advances in experimental social psychology* (Vol. 19, pp. 123–205). New York: Academic Press.

Swensen, R. A., Nash, D. L., & Roos, D. C. (1984). Source credibility and perceived expertness of testimony in a simulated child-custody case. *Professional Psychology, 15,* 891–898.

van den Brock, P., & Lorch, R. F. (1993). Network representations of causal relations in memory of narrative texts: Evidence from prime recognition. *Discourse Processes, 16,* 75–98.

Chapter 5

ORGANIZING THE PRESENTATION

CHAPTER OBJECTIVES

After reading this chapter, you should be able to:

- ▣ Explain the guidelines for arranging main points.

- ▣ Identify the five different types of organizational patterns.

- ▣ Explain the four kinds of transitions.

- ▣ Discuss the importance of organization.

$\mathcal{K}$elly, an agricultural communication student, wanted to give her persuasive speech on how "hydroponic" fruits and vegetables were more beneficial than those grown by traditional methods. She divided her speech into two main points: that "hydroponically grown" fruits and vegetables are healthier for consumers and that "hydroponically grown" fruits and vegetables are better for the environment, and she provided ample evidence for each point. Still, after the speech, most of her audience looked confused. It became even more evident to Kelly during the question and answer session that indeed her audience had not followed her. Kelly was certain of her goal and had planned for it consistently throughout her presentation. Why didn't the audience follow her? It was simple; Kelly did not use transitions. Transitions are one of the most important aspects of organization. They help keep your listeners on track. Many times speakers think transitions are redundant and don't use them. However, transitions, along with the other ideas presented in this chapter, will help you, and the audience, keep the ideas presented in your speech organized.

WHY ORGANIZATION IS IMPORTANT

Research has indicated that a clear organizational structure has benefits for the audience and the speaker. Some of these benefits include improved recall of the material presented, enhanced understanding of complex material, and increased speaker credibility.

Audiences are more easily able to retain the information presented when there is a clear organizational structure (Meyer & Poon, 2001; Rickards, Fajen, Sullivan, & Gillespie, 1997; Towler & Dipboye, 2001). One of the essential elements in being clear is the use of transitions, which we will discuss later in this chapter. The use of transitions has a strong impact on an audience's ability to recall content, so you want to make sure you take advantage of this organizing tool.

Complex material is also easier to understand when it is laid out in a clear fashion (Mayer, Bove, Bryman, Mars, & Tapangco, 1996). Research indicates that a clear organizational pattern marked with signposts and internal summaries (see discussion later in this chapter) actually decreases the cognitive load an individual faces when processing your material. In other words, you free up some of the working memory so that the audience can focus on the content. You have done some of the work for them, and this allows them to concentrate more closely on your message.

Finally, speakers who employ clear organization enhance their credibility as well (Sharp & McClung, 1966; Thompson, 1960). Organized presentations appear more prepared and the speakers more knowledgeable.

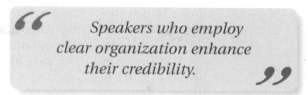

> *Speakers who employ clear organization enhance their credibility.*

ORGANIZING THE BODY OF YOUR PRESENTATION

The quality of the organization of a speech often makes the difference between an effective presentation and an ineffective one. One reason organization becomes so critical in oral presentations is that the audience can't go back and revisit your ideas. Giving a presentation is very different from reading prose on a page. Your audience does not have the luxury of examining the material at their own pace or referring back to material that was already presented. Therefore, clear organization with good use of transitions is vital to a solid presentation. Attention to organization helps ensure that your audience understands your ideas and has been able to process them in the way that you intended. In this chapter, we discuss how to organize the body of your presentation.

MAIN POINTS

As mentioned throughout this textbook, there are three main components in a presentation: the introduction, the body, and the conclusion. The body is where you present the "meat" of your presentation. This is where you place the information you are trying to convey to your audience. In order to do this effectively, you divide your material into ***main points***. Here is an example of how one student divided his material into main points.

Specific Purpose: To inform my audience about the types of mosquito repellents.

Thesis Statement: There are three types of mosquito repellents: insect-repellent sprays and creams, mosquito sticks and carbon dioxide traps.

Main Points:

I.   Insect-repellent sprays or creams containing 35% DEET repel mosquitoes from humans.

II. Mosquito sticks repel mosquitoes from small areas such as patios.

III. Carbon dioxide traps repel mosquitoes from large areas such as backyard areas.

These main points form the skeleton of the speech. At this point, we don't know much about the points this student is going to make. After deciding what your main points should be, you go back and provide supporting evidence for each of these main points.

Number of Main Points

So how many main points should you have? In a classroom speech, you will need no more than three main points. Two to three points is a good rule for the amount of time you have to speak in the classroom. Even if you have an unlimited amount of time to address your audience, you will still want to limit your main points. Good presentations will rarely have over four or five main points.

Organization of Main Points

In what order should you present your main points? An organizational pattern can help you make that decision. An **organizational pattern** is a structure that delineates the nature of the relationship between your main points. There are numerous organizational patterns. In this text we will discuss the most basic. As you become a more experienced speaker, you will add others to your repositories or adapt the ones discussed here. Let's begin by discussing each of these patterns, along with suggestions for using them, followed by some examples from student presentations.

Spatial

The **spatial pattern** is used when you want to demonstrate the relationship between your material geographically or directionally (e.g., top to bottom, inside to outside, left to right, etc.). This pattern can also be used when demonstrating how parts are related to the whole (e.g., parts of the skeleton, parts of the space shuttle).

Specific Purpose:	To inform my audience about new fashion trends around the U.S.
Thesis Statement:	There are numerous new fashion trends springing up on the West Coast, the East Coast, and in the Midwest.

Main Points:

I.   The most popular trends along the West Coast this winter will be fake fur, purple, and boots.

II. The most popular trends along the East Coast this winter will be tweed and short skirts.

III. The most popular trends in the Midwest this winter will include anything leather and vintage t-shirts.

Chronological

The ***chronological organizational pattern*** arranges material in an ordered sequence. In other words, it follows a timeline. This pattern is especially well-suited for historical topics and instructional presentations (e.g., "how to" presentations).

Specific Purpose: To inform my audience about the history of the conflict in Kashmir.

Thesis Statement: The history of the conflict in Kashmir resulted from three major events.

Main Points:

I.   On August 15th, 1947, India and Pakistan were liberated from Britain.

II.   On October 27th, 1947, Kashmir became part of India.

III.   In January 1948, the Line of Control was drawn in Kashmir.

Problem-Solution

The ***problem-solution design*** is the organizational pattern to use if your material clearly falls into two main points: a problem and a solution. The first main point focuses on demonstrating to the audience that there is a problem and the implications of that problem, while the second main point centers on explaining a workable solution to the problem. While problem-solution speeches can be used in either informative or persuasive situations, they are primarily used in persuasive presentations. Chapter 9 in your textbook provides more information on the problem-solution speech design.

Specific Purpose: To persuade my audience to reduce utilization and waste of plastic shopping bags.

Thesis Statement: Discarded plastic bags create major problems for our environment and with some simple strategies, we can eliminate some of these problems.

Main Points:

I.   There are two major problems with the use of plastic bags: they are non-biodegradable and they negatively affect the ecosystem.

II.   There are three simple solutions we can employ to reduce our plastic bag waste.

Here is another example from another student on a speech about noise pollution.

> **Specific Purpose:** To persuade my audience to protect themselves from the dangers of noise pollution.
>
> **Thesis Statement:** Noise pollution leads to three primary problems but by following a few easy guidelines, we can reduce our exposure.

Main Points:

I. Noise pollution leads to three problems: annoyance, speech interference, and hearing loss.

II. Noise pollution can be prevented if we adhere to three easy guidelines.

Causal Pattern

Speeches using the ***causal design*** seek to establish a cause-effect relationship between two variables or events. Presentations arranged in this format have two main points. The first main point centers on the causes, while the second main point addresses the effects. It is important to understand that speeches of cause and effect can be arranged in either two ways: cause, then effect or effect, followed by cause. Here are examples:

Main Points:

I. Strong storms on the surface of the sun called solar flares release large amounts of magnetic energy toward the Earth.

II. Solar flares are so powerful they can damage satellites, cause power outages, and disrupt other electronic and magnetic equipment.

Or

Main Points:

I. The history of life on the planet Earth has been characterized by a series of major extinctions.

II. The cause of many of these extinctions has been traced to the impact of large meteors or comets.

Topical

Presentations that do not fall into one of the other organizational patterns described (spatial, chronological, problem-solution, or causal) usually fit within the ***topical pattern***. The topic is subdivided into smaller parts or subtopics that then become the main points of the speech. The key to using the topical pattern successfully is ensuring that your topic divides into a set of main points that are logical and consistent.

Consider the following topic that Nathan pursued last semester: controversies in men's professional golf.

Specific Purpose:	To inform my audience of the major controversies that have recently occurred in men's professional golf.
Thesis Statement:	Recently, men's professional golf has experienced controversies regarding race, disabilities, and gender.

Main Points:

I.   Professional golf has experienced controversies regarding race.

II.   Professional golf has experienced controversies regarding disabilities.

III.   Professional golf has experienced controversies regarding gender.

Heather gave an informative speech on the process of parents selecting the gender of their offspring.

Specific Purpose:	To inform my audience about the methods of gender selection.
Thesis Statement:	The two methods used for gender selection today are MicroSort and the timing method.

Main Points:

I.   MicroSort is the process of sorting the X and Y chromosomes through an instrument called a cytometer.

II.   The timing method is the process of using the woman's natural cycle to enhance the likelihood of conceiving a male or female child.

Characteristics of Good Main Points

Main Points Should Be Balanced

Balance means that you spend approximately the same amount of time addressing each of your main points. When you identify your main points, you are saying that these items are essentially equal in terms of importance. If that is true, you should spend roughly the same amount of time addressing each main point. If after examining your outline you notice that your speech breaks down like this:

> *You should spend roughly the same amount of time addressing each main point.*

MPI:	75%
MPII:	20%
MPIII:	5%

then you can determine one of two things: first, you may not have developed points two and three like they should have been developed. Perhaps you have focused too much energy and planning on the first main point. Second, perhaps you only have one main point. In this case, go back and look at your material and see if you can break it down differently. You may not have initially divided the material in the most effective way.

Your time allocation for each main point does not have to be equal. Spending roughly the same amount of time on each main point is sufficient. Here are a few breakdowns that give you an idea of how much time you might spend on each of your main points:

MPI:	30%	**MPI:**	30%
MPII:	45%	**MPII:**	30%
MPIII:	25%	**MPIII:**	40%

All organizational patterns contain main points that should be balanced.

Try to Use Parallel Wording

It is easier for an audience to follow your speech if you use ***parallel wording*** for your main points. What this means is using the same phrasing for your main points. For example, the following sets of main points demonstrate the difference between main points that are parallel in structure and those that are not. While both sets of points get the same ideas across, the first set of points will be easier for your audience to follow.

Effective

MPI: A good night's sleep helps promote healthy glucose processing.

MPII: A good night's sleep helps regulate a healthy weight.

MPIII: A good night's sleep helps promote cognitive health.

Less Effective

MPI: Glucose is converted to insulin more efficiently after a productive sleep period.

MPII: Leptin, a hormone that regulates feelings of fullness and therefore regulates weight, is produced after a good night's rest.

MPIII: Lack of sleep is associated with shrinkage in the right temporal lobe of the brain.

Of course, all materials will not allow themselves to be so easily organized into parallel structure; however, if you can use parallel wording, you should.

SUPPORTING EVIDENCE

The main points are just the skeletons of your presentation. The supporting evidence you provide for each of your main points will flesh out the body of your speech. One important aspect that beginning speakers often overlook is that the supporting material within each main point should also be organized into subpoints. This means that you should have an organizational pattern within each main point. So while your overall pattern may be topical, one main point and its supporting material or subpoints may be organized chronologically or spatially. Examine the organization of the main points and subpoints in the following excerpt. As you can see, the subpoints of main point one are arranged topically, while the subpoints of main point two are arranged spatially.

MPI: Dangerous traffic signs are characterized by one of the following attributes.

    A.   Sign lettering is illegible.

    B.   Sign is obstructed.

    C.   Sign is missing.

> **MPII:** West Lafayette has many dangerous signs and some of the most hazardous can be found at the following locations.
>
> A. At the intersection of 3rd and Main, there are three illegible street signs.
>
> B. In the older New Chauncey neighborhood, there are many obstructed signs.
>
> C. On roads adjacent to Purdue's on-campus housing, there are many missing signs.

(Although not noted here, the student then provided statistics and other documentation to further support this material.)

Another key to remember is to make sure that all of your main points are supported. Sometimes you will find that your material only supports a couple of your main points. That leaves some of your arguments completely unsupported. Although the material you have collected is related to your topic, it does not directly support all of your arguments. At this point, you may have to discard some of your research and go back to the library to collect more supporting material. One trip to the library or one massive search for supporting material is rarely enough.

> *Make sure that all of your main points are supported.*

Another mistake students commonly make is dividing their material incorrectly. There is a tendency to have too many main points and not enough supporting evidence or subpoints. Many times, the extra main points can be collapsed into subpoints that support two or three main points. Examine the following example.

> **MPI:** The media portray hackers incorrectly.
>
> **MPII:** The media describe hackers as males who lack social skills.
>
> **MPIII:** The media define hackers as overweight and unattractive.
>
> **MPIV:** The media describe hackers as inherently evil.

Although each of these main points supports the speaker's ultimate goal, to persuade the audience that the media misrepresent hackers, they do not stand alone. They can be collapsed into a more concise organizational pattern. It would make more sense to combine the speech the following way:

> **MPI:** The media portray hackers incorrectly.
>
> A. The media describe hackers as those who lack social skills.
>
> B. The media define hackers as overweight and unattractive.
>
> C. The media describe hackers as inherently evil.

TRANSITIONS

Transitions are words, phrases or sentences that show the relationship between ideas in your presentation. They are the elements that help your speech flow and allow listeners to follow you easily. Research suggests that the skillful use of transitions is essential to audience understanding (Meyer & Poon, 2001; Rickards, et al., 1997; Rowan, 2003). Students often work very hard to organize their main points and supporting material but still feel something is missing that could aid their audience in understanding their message. Just like Kelly in the opening story, usually, that key is transitions. There are four types of transitions: directional transitions, signposts, internal previews, and internal summaries. Transitions can be sentences, phrases and in some cases a single word. Let's discuss each of these types of transitions and strategies for using them effectively in your presentations.

Directional Transitions

Directional transitions are phrases that let your audience know that you are moving away from one idea and on to another. They contain two parts. First, they restate the information you are leaving and second, they preview the information that is coming. **You must use a directional transition between each of your main points.** Next you will find some examples of directional transitions.

> **Now that you understand** the causes of poverty, **let's examine the effect** on our nation's youth.

> **As you can see,** internships are an important step in attaining future employment, **so** the university has implemented a process to aid in the search of finding these opportunities.

> **After examining** some of the problems associated with e-waste, it is important that **we explore** some possible solutions.

The key to using directional transitions effectively is to remind the audience of what they have just heard and then preview the upcoming point. Directional transitions are primarily used between the major sections of the speech (e.g., the introduction, body, and conclusion)

Spotlight on Research

TRANSITIONS HAVE POSITIVE IMPACT

Researchers presented a lecture to 40 college students. The students were instructed to take notes during the lecture. When the lecture contained transitions such as directional transitions, signposts, and internal and external summaries, the students were able to take more notes than when the lectures did not contain transitions. Additionally, their notes recalled more ideas from the lecture.

As you can see, using transitions can have a positive impact on your audience. A well organized presentation that highlights transitions will improve your audience's ability to hear and understand the important points of your message.

Rickards, J. P., Fajen, B. R., Sullivan, J. F., & Gillespie, G. (1997). Signaling, notetaking and field independence-dependence in text comprehension and recall. *Journal of Educational Psychology, 89,* 508–517.

and between each of the main points. While it is necessary to include a directional transition between the major elements of a presentation, it can also be necessary to use directional transitions within main points.

Signposts

Signposts are transitions that mark the exact location in the speech. They tell the audience where they are within the presentation. Here are some commonly used signposts:

> The first point . . .
>
> The second cause . . .
>
> In conclusion . . .
>
> The most important point . . .

Signposts are extremely helpful for the audience. They help organize the material in a way that is easy to follow. Students often overlook the importance of signposting. This is one of the easiest ways to assist your audience in following the information in your presentation.

Internal Previews

Internal previews are just that, they preview material but within the body of the presentation or even within a main point. Internal previews are not always necessary. However, if your material is lengthy and contains many small components and subpoints, or is complicated, an internal preview will enhance your audience's ability to follow your message. Here is an example taken from a student presentation:

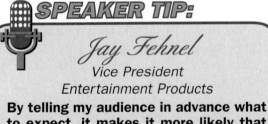

> In examining the effects of e-waste there are two problems: the use of landfills and the use of hazardous materials.

Sometimes you can combine a directional transition with an internal preview. Here is an example of how that might look:

> After understanding how DNA profiling works, let's move on to the techniques of DNA profiling (directional transition). I will examine two types of DNA profiling—PCR analysis and STR analysis (internal preview).

Internal Summaries

Internal summaries are similar to internal previews except they remind the audience of what was just covered. Like internal previews, they should be used when the material you just presented was complicated, lengthy, or important. Here is an example:

Transitions become even more important when your audience is distributed, as in this photograph.

As you have seen, there are many reasons plastic bags have become a problem for our environment. They are dispersed in large quantities, are disposed of carelessly, are cheaper and hold less than paper or cloth bags, therefore increasing our consumption.

Internal summaries are an excellent way to assist audiences in remembering your ideas. By restating key material, you are able to reinforce the main ideas of the presentation.

Just as you can combine a directional transition and internal preview, you can also combine an internal summary with other transitions. Here is an example:

> *" Internal summaries are an excellent way to assist audiences in remembering your ideas. "*

To reiterate, there are several problems with environmental tobacco smoke (internal summary). First (signpost), it has been proven to cause cancer. Second (signpost), it increases heart rate and blood pressure. Third (signpost), it increases the likelihood of Sudden Infant Death Syndrome among babies. Now that you have a thorough understanding of the problem, let's examine some possible solutions (directional transition).

CONCLUSION

Organization is vital to a successful presentation. Using the right organizational pattern (spatial, chronological, problem-solution, causal, or topical) is extremely important; not only does organization affect your audience's ability to process your information, it also has implications for the credibility of the speaker. The number of main points, the way they are worded, and the skillful use of transitions are all important elements of effective organization. Don't overlook the importance of organization. Your audience will appreciate it and your presentation will be more successful.

KEY TERMS

Balance

Causal design

Chronological pattern

Directional transitions

Internal previews

Internal summaries

Main points

Organizational pattern

Parallel wording

Problem-solution design

Signposts

Spatial pattern

Topical pattern

Transitions

EXERCISES

1. Identify the organizational pattern used in each of the sets of main points below.

Example A

I. Research in human-animal chimeras has generated medical concerns.

II. Research in human-animal chimeras has generated ethical concerns.

III. Research in human-animal chimeras has generated legal concerns.

Example B

I. Students' eating habits at school contribute to obesity among youths.

II. Students' eating habits at home contribute to obesity among youths.

Example C

I.   Studies show bad eating habits begin in very young children.

II. Teens continue to eat poorly at school or at college.

III. Adults often make poor eating choices because of busy schedules.

Example D

I.   Avian flu is a sometimes fatal disease that is spreading throughout Asia and Europe.

II. The flu is spreading rapidly because of a lack of a government-mandated inspection process in the poultry industry and the prevalence of wild birds in local cuisine.

Example E

I.   Purdue students, like most college students nationwide, don't eat healthy.

II. An "Eating Healthy" Web site could provide students with easy-to-make, healthy recipes; economical menu ideas; and highlight healthy eating options at campus dining facilities.

2. From the topic list below, select one topic. Then, organize possible main points for the topic in at least two different organizational patterns (spatial, chronological, problem-solution, causal, topical). What are the benefits of the various patterns you selected? Which one is best, and why?

- Applying to college
- Obtaining a driver's license
- Losing weight
- Animal adoption
- Fraternity/Sorority membership
- Financial aid
- Hybrid cars
- Cell phones
- Giving blood
- College housing options
- Identity theft
- Study abroad
- Music downloading
- Video games
- Computers

An example:

I.   Secondhand smoke is dangerous to the health of patrons and workers at the city's businesses.

II. Passing a citywide smoking ban in public places would help reduce health risks from secondhand smoke.

Or

I.   A citywide smoking ban in public places would have health benefits.

II. A citywide smoking ban in public places would have economic benefits.

3. Identify the following types of transitions and where they most likely appear in presentations.

a. Now that you understand why sleep is important, let's look at some of the reasons why we don't get enough sleep.

b. A second cause of sleep deprivation is work demands.

c. So sleep is important to us. But oftentimes, stress, poor eating habits, and a busy lifestyle can lead to us not getting the needed amount of sleep each night.

d. As you have seen, exercise is important to your mental well-being. Exercise produces endorphins, which have been proven to make people happier, and numerous studies show it reduces stress.

e. In conclusion, I have told you that cigarette smoking has both a negative physical and economic impact.

REFERENCES

Mayer, R. E., Bove, W., Bryman, A., Mars, R., & Tapangco, L. (1996). When less is more: Meaningful learning from visual and verbal summaries of science textbook lessons. *Journal of Educational Psychology, 88,* 64–73.

Meyer, B. J. F. & Poon, L. W. (2001). Effects of structure strategy training and signaling on recall of text. *Journal of Educational Psychology, 93,* 141–159.

Rickards, J. P., Fajen, B. R., Sullivan, J. F., & Gillespie, G. (1997). Signaling, notetaking and field independence-dependence in text comprehension and recall. *Journal of Educational Psychology, 89,* 508–517.

Rowan, K. E. (2003). Informing and explaining skills: Theory and research on informative communication. In J.O. Greene & B. R. Burleson (Eds.), *The handbook of communication and social interaction skills* (pp. 403–438). Mahwah, NJ: Erlbaum.

Sharp, H. J. & McClung, T. (1966). Effects of the organization on the speaker's ethos. *Speech Monographs, 33,* 182–183.

Thompson, E. C. (1960). An experimental investigation of the relative effectiveness of organizational structure in oral communication. *Southern Speech Journal, 26,* 59–69.

Towler, A. J. & Dipboye, R. L. (2001). Effects of trainer expressiveness, organization and trainee goal orientation on training outcomes. *Journal of Applied Psychology, 86,* 664–673.

Chapter 6

SUPPORTING EVIDENCE AND RESEARCH

CHAPTER OBJECTIVES

After reading this chapter, you should be able to:

- ▣ Explain why speakers need strong evidence.

- ▣ Identify types of supporting materials.

- ▣ Distinguish among types of examples.

- ▣ Distinguish among types of testimony.

- ▣ Understand how to evaluate supporting material.

- ▣ Identify sources for finding supporting evidence.

$\mathscr{A}$ former student, Carol, was very excited about the topic for her persuasive speech. Her sister had been a Peace Corps volunteer, and Carol said she had wonderful stories to share about the people her sister had helped and the rewarding work that the Peace Corps did. Carol wanted to give a speech encouraging her classmates to visit with the Peace Corps during an upcoming on-campus recruiting trip. On the day of her speech, Carol reported that: "In its 40 years, more than 170,000 Peace Corps volunteers have helped people have a better life in more than 136 countries." She continued with numerous statistics about the number of schools and hospitals built, acres planted, etc., that Peace Corps volunteers had helped achieve. After the speech was over, Carol was a little disappointed. She didn't think her speech delivered the emotional impact she had hoped, despite that fact that she had opened with a strong statistic to back up her point that the Peace Corps was a worthwhile organization. When her instructor asked Carol to recall her conversations with her sister and decide just what it was that convinced her that the Peace Corps was a worthy organization, Carol replied, "Well, her stories about the people she helped."

If it was the stories she heard that convinced Carol that the Peace Corps was a worthy organization, chances are those stories would have had the same impact on her audience of peers. The stories of real people might have been more persuasive to her audience than the numbers she chose to provide. Narratives make strong emotional appeals to audiences that have little knowledge about a subject matter, such as poverty in third-world countries. Carol should have used a combination of the compelling stories and statistics (Allen, et al., 2000).

The material or evidence you use to support your main points is actually the heart of your presentation. Without it, your thesis statement and all of your claims are just uninformed opinions. Depending on the presentation, you will need to use different types of supporting material in varying degrees to provide evidence for your main points or arguments. How much and what type of supporting material will depend on a variety of factors, including: audience knowledge of the topic (novice or expert), your own credibility with the topic (novice or expert), and the purpose of the speech (informative or persuasive).

For example, if a scientist were giving a presentation on the age of the solar system to other scientists in the field, the nature of the facts she discussed would most likely be the specific procedures and results of her own scientific studies. If the same expert was invited to give a presentation on this same topic to a lay audience, she would likely simplify the supporting material, focusing more on providing general information regarding her results. She would reduce the complexity of the statistics and procedures and use more narratives and explanative analogies regarding the formation of the solar system and why it is important to understand this subject in the first place. If a novice were to speak on this topic, it would be important for them to systematically document what specific experts in the field believe about the age of the solar system. This would bolster their own credibility as a speaker on this subject and demonstrate that they are basically summarizing and explaining the research and thoughts of experts on this topic. They are essentially borrowing the credibility of experts.

Each of these presentations would be very different, primarily because they used different types of supporting evidence to make claims about the topic. It is the supporting evidence, ultimately, that makes the difference between a believable and interesting presentation and one that is ultimately uninformative or unimportant to the audience (O'Keefe, 1998).

This chapter is designed to give you an overview of the types of supporting evidence you will likely use as you begin to construct your presentation. It will also provide you with information on where to find supporting material and how to evaluate it.

WHY SUPPORTING EVIDENCE IS IMPORTANT

Students often complain about including supporting evidence in their presentations. They simply don't understand why they need to cite somebody else when they know everything there is to know about a topic. Imagine you decide to speak on the benefits of Greek life. After all, you're an expert; you have been a member for over three years. While your audience will appreciate your own experiences and those of your house, they will also want to hear other evidence. After all, your own experiences and those of your brothers or sisters will be somewhat biased. You can bolster your claims by providing statistics and testimony from national sources. What are the national statistics, examples, etc., relating to Greek life and academic success, for example?

By incorporating outside evidence into your presentation, you strengthen your own arguments, but you also enhance your own credibility as a speaker. Studies have shown that citing evidence within a presentation can actually improve audience perceptions of a speaker's expertise and trustworthiness (O'Keefe, 1998; Reinard, 1988). Of course, perceptions of expertise and trustworthiness are only bolstered by high-credibility sources. Low-credibility supporting evidence does not generate this same effect. This chapter is also designed to help you determine the difference between the two.

TYPES OF SUPPORTING MATERIALS

STATISTICS

Statistics are an extremely powerful type of supporting evidence (Allen & Preiss, 1997). We hear and see them so often in our everyday lives that we expect them. They carry a great deal of power and can be extremely persuasive. Just think about the number of statistics you read or hear every day: Reports indicate that 15% of U.S. children between the ages of 6 to 19 are severely overweight; the film King Kong opened at number one at the box office, earning $50.1 million; 75 percent of American high school students report getting along well, if not very well, with their parents. We feel secure using numbers. Statistics are especially useful in demonstrating trends, explaining relationships, and quantifying information. By using statistics, you can summarize a large amount of material in a very concise manner.

Using statistics as supporting evidence in your presentations can be very compelling for an audience. Consider the following two statements:

Americans are throwing away large amounts of trash each day.

Or

According to Environmental Defense, Americans go through 2.5 million plastic bottles every hour. American consumers and industries throw away enough aluminum to rebuild our entire commercial air fleet every three months.

The second statement is much more compelling. It clarifies the point and adds strength to the argument. We have a much better idea of just how much trash Americans are disposing each day. By adding statistics to bolster the argument, audiences will more likely be persuaded.

TIPS FOR USING STATISTICS

Make Sure Statistics Are Representative

One common flaw in the use of statistical evidence is that the data can be collected in unscientific ways. Every time you hear statistics you should ask yourself the following questions: How was the data collected? How large was the sample size? Who were the participants in the study? Was the sample representative of the population it claims to represent? Who conducted the survey? When was it conducted?

Let us assume that you survey your peers in this class and then claim that 50% of the students surveyed at this university are dissatisfied with food services on campus. This is not a compelling statistic. The 28 students in your class are not a representative sample, and you cannot make this claim using the data you have collected. Using the criteria preceding, you can easily see the sample size is too small to be representative. Additionally, because the individuals are all drawn from the same class, there are likely peculiar characteristics of this sample that are unique to them. Because they are all drawn from the same required class, there are some characteristics that other students at the university would not have. For example, they come from a restrictive set of majors and they are primarily freshmen and sophomores. As an ethical speaker, it is up to you to ensure that your statistics truly represent what you claim.

> " *One common flaw in the use of statistical evidence is that the data can be collected in unscientific ways.* "

Understand What the Statistics Mean

It is important when using statistics that you have a reasonable understanding of what statistics are appropriate for making which types of claims. For example, if you have a relatively small sample size, a single **outlier**, or an extremely high or low figure, will influence the mean of the group more than it will the median. The mean and median are different ways of describing average tendencies within a set of data. They are often confused with each other. They both have their advantages and disadvantages, depending on the nature of the data being reported.

The **mean** is the arithmetic average of a collection of numbers, computed by adding them up and dividing by the number of cases in your sample. The mean can be very sensitive. For example, if you survey 10 people and find that one of them makes a million dollars a year but the other nine make around $50,000 a year, the mean salary will suggest that, on average, the sample makes approximately $145,000 per year. This statistic, while technically accurate, would lead audience members to conclude that the sample makes a whole lot more money than they really do.

The **median**, on the other hand, represents the middle value in a series of numbers. It is found by arranging a set of values in order and then selecting the one in the middle. (If the total number of values in the sample is even, then the median is the average of the two middle numbers.) In our example, the median income would be $50,500. This would provide a statistic that would show a much lower value than the mean and would give the audience a better picture of the earnings of this sample. Table 1 shows how you would calculate the mean and median for this set of data.

TABLE 1	
Mean	**Median**
$41,000	$41,000
$43,000	$43,000
$48,000	$48,000
$50,000	$50,000
$50,000	$50,000
$51,000	$51,000
$53,000	$53,000
$56,000	$56,000
$57,000	$57,000
$1,000,000	$1,000,000
Total:	Total:
1,449,000/10 = 144,900	50,000 + 51,000 = 101,000/2 = 50,500
Mean = $144,900	**Median = $50,500**

Explain the Statistics

It is extremely important that you explain what the statistics mean to your audience. In other words, you need to relate them to your audience and their particular context. One of the easiest ways to accomplish explaining statistics is through visual aids. It is hard for audiences to visualize large numbers. However, if you can relate the information to something that is easy to visualize, they will have a much easier time following your arguments.

Sometimes visual aids are not practical or aren't enough to explain a particular number. If that is the case, use analogies or examples that make those numbers have more meaning for your audience. Consider the following example: "Forty million U.S. adults have only rudimentary reading and writing skills." Forty million people—this is a hard number for an audience to visualize. Restate that number in terms they can understand. For example, you could say the following to explain the statistic: "Forty million people, this figure is equal to the populations of Illinois, Indiana, Ohio, and Michigan combined." By making this comparison for your audience, you have provided them

> " Sometimes, when numbers get very large, audiences have difficulty conceptualizing them. "

Using graphical representations of statistics is an effective way to utilize information in your presentations.

with a much better understanding of exactly how many people 40 million is. Sometimes, when numbers get very large, audiences have difficulty conceptualizing them (Sullivan & Smith, 2006). Provide them with some additional way to visualize them. It will add impact to your statistic.

Localize Statistics

Whenever possible, you want to relate your statistics directly to your audience and their lives. What does a particular statistic mean for your audience and their particular geographical area? As mentioned in Chapter 3, this is called **localizing**.

Here is an example of how you might localize a national statistic for your audience. "A survey by State Farm estimates that 1.5 million vehicles are involved in collisions with deer each year." You could stop there. This is a compelling statistic. Most audience members would be surprised to learn deer caused this much damage. But you can make the statistic even more meaningful by bringing it home to your audience. Imagine adding the next series of statistics to the State Farm figure. "Indiana is ranked 8th in number of auto-deer collisions. The Indiana State Police report that in 2004, over 14,800 deer-car collisions were reported in our state. Of those, 14,470 involved property damage to a vehicle, 404 resulted in injury to a driver, and 3 resulted in fatalities. In our own county, Tippecanoe, 355 total deer-car collisions were reported in 2004. Three hundred and forty resulted in property damage to cars, fifteen in injuries, and zero in fatalities."

> *By localizing your statistics like the example preceding, you make your material much more relevant.*

By localizing your statistics like the preceding example, you make your material much more relevant to your particular audience. While the first statistic from State Farm is alarming, it becomes much more compelling when we see how it affects us personally in our own state and even in our own county. Your statistics will carry more impact if you can relate them directly to your audience.

Limit Your Use of Statistics

Long lists of statistics get very tiresome for audiences to follow. Nothing will bore an audience faster than being bombarded with a list of statistics. Be strategic. Use statistics when you really need the added impact or the type of audience you will be addressing demands it.

Round Off Statistics

Processing large amounts of numerical data is taxing on an audience. One way to simplify large amounts of data is to round off your statistics; unless it is extremely important that your numbers be exact, round them off.

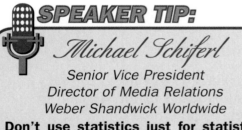

SPEAKER TIP:

Michael Schiferl

Senior Vice President
Director of Media Relations
Weber Shandwick Worldwide

Don't use statistics just for statistics sake. Those statistics which are surprising or counter to popular belief are sometimes most interesting to an audience.

EXAMPLES

Examples are another type of supporting evidence. They give life to your presentation. They are powerful tools that personalize or put a "face" on your message and your ideas. They help your audience see your ideas and they add vividness to the entire presentation. Often your message is abstract and by using examples, you make the concept more relatable to your audience. For example, poverty is a difficult topic to grasp without the aid of an example. Statistics alone cannot create a personal tie with your audience. The concept becomes more real when we hear the story of a family similar to ours who was separated due to homelessness and hunger. There are three different kinds of examples that you can use to add support to your presentation.

Brief Examples

Brief examples are specific instances. They are cases used to briefly illustrate an idea. Here are a couple of examples from student speeches:

> A new revolutionary AbioCor heart transplant system has given Robert Tools back his life. Tools was suffering from diabetes, kidney failure, and congestive heart failure. But within a month of his transplant, he could take trips outside of the hospital and was able to converse with others as he had not done in months.

Or

> Some fabrics protect from UV light better than others. For example, blue jeans provide more protection than cotton knits.

Extended Examples

Extended examples are longer stories or narratives. This is an excellent way to generate audience interest in your topic. Consider the example below from a recent student speech:

> Hugo Paulino was a UN peacekeeper who wanted to make a difference in the world. He was one of hundreds of Portuguese peacekeepers that were sent to Kosovo. In their time off, the peacekeepers bathed in the river, ate the local fruit, and wandered around the town that had been heavily bombed during the Kosovo War. At age 21, Hugo returned to Portugal on February 12, 2000. He came home complaining of headaches, nausea, and flu-like symptoms. Ten days later, Hugo had a major seizure, and was rushed to the military hospital where he remained until March 9, when Hugo died of leukemia. His case of leukemia was caused by exposure to radiation in Kosovo from the depleted uranium shells that were used previously during the war. Scientists predict that there will be 10,000 deaths among local residents, aid workers, and peacekeepers due to the use of depleted uranium in Serbia.

The speaker could have easily said that many peacekeepers in Kosovo experienced exposure to high levels of radiation. However, her story makes the presentation more compelling and adds a human component that the audience would not otherwise have experienced.

You don't have to know of the example firsthand. Many magazines and newspapers have these types of examples that you can use. As long as you cite your source, feel free to use the examples you find in the media.

Hypothetical Examples

Sometimes, the examples you use will be true or factual like the ones you have just read, and sometimes they will be hypothetical or imaginary. *Hypothetical examples* allow your audience to identify with the situation you are describing. Here is an example a student used in her speech on power blackouts:

> It's 3:00 a.m. and you are sitting in front of your computer putting the finishing touches on your final paper for your English composition course. Suddenly, you hear a buzzing sound and your power goes out. Your screen goes black. You can't remember the last time you saved your work. You start to panic as the power comes back on and you frantically wait to see just how much work you have lost.

By using this example, the speaker is able to draw her audience into her presentation. In a classroom presentation, most of her audience members are going to be able to identify with the scenario she has depicted. The example would have been even more powerful if the speaker had added statistics indicating how often power blackouts occur. It's a good idea to add facts or testimony to demonstrate that a hypothetical example is realistic.

One mistake speakers make is using outrageous hypothetical examples. You cannot ask an audience of college-aged students to picture themselves as 80-year-old men who have just lost their partner of 60 years. They simply will not be able to identify.

TIPS FOR USING EXAMPLES

Make Examples Vivid

Detail makes examples come to life. You want to paint a mental picture for your audience. Include details that help your audience envision the scenario you are describing. One way to enhance vividness is through the characters in your story. Make sure you mention the names of your characters. It is much easier to envision Mary, a Purdue freshman, than if you had just said a female student. These small details give your examples texture and help your audience relate to them.

Make Sure Extended Examples Have a Beginning, Middle, and End

Anytime you tell a story you want to ensure it has a beginning, middle, and end. You want your examples, especially extended examples, to be fully developed. Most of the time, you will not want to leave your audience hanging. Even if the final outcome of your story isn't essential, your audience will appreciate closure.

Practice Delivering Extended Examples

Not all of us are born storytellers. Some of us are naturally better at telling stories than others. So practice telling your examples. You would never want to read an extended example to your audience. You should maintain good eye contact and use delivery cues that will add impact to your story. You simply cannot accomplish this if you read to them.

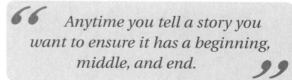

Anytime you tell a story you want to ensure it has a beginning, middle, and end.

By practicing you can also determine how long your story will be when delivered orally. Many speakers spend so much time telling a narrative that they run out of speaking time and fail to complete the entire presentation. Don't let this happen to you. Practice your extended examples so that they achieve your desired impact.

TESTIMONY

The third type of supporting evidence is testimony. *Testimony* is a quotation or paraphrase from an expert or knowledgeable source used to support an idea or point you are making in a presentation. Testimony can be very persuasive. Think about the following scenario: You have a sore tooth and are talking to your friend about it. You explain that you are not from Lafayette and so you don't have a dentist in the area. Your friend tells you that she has been seeing Dr. Browne, a local dentist, and finds him to be gentle, professional, and affordable. Based on your friend's recommendation, you schedule an appointment with Dr. Browne. You have been persuaded from the testimony of your friend. If you stop and think about it, many of the decisions we make in everyday life are based on the testimony of friends or co-workers.

Audiences are often swayed by testimony of individuals that they respect. Within the course of a presentation, you can use testimony to add strength to your claims. There are three types of testimony: expert testimony, peer testimony, and prestige testimony.

Expert Testimony

Expert testimony is evidence from people who have the experience or education to be recognized as authorities in their field. Since you will rarely be speaking on topics on which you are an expert in this class, expert testimony is a way to enhance your own credibility. By borrowing the ethos or credibility of an expert, you can add support to the claims you are making within your presentation.

In trying to persuade the class that DNA evidence is reliable, Jessie used the following testimony:

> According to Dr. Ian Findlay, a scientist involved in the human genome project at Queensland University, it is impossible to not leave behind traces of blood, semen, hair, or skin cells at crime scenes. He stated that someone would have to wear a spacesuit to avoid leaving DNA evidence at a crime scene.

Although Jessie is studying health sciences and has even worked in a crime lab, her credibility is greatly enhanced by providing the opinion of an expert.

Peer Testimony

Another type of testimony is peer testimony. *Peer testimony* is opinions from ordinary people, not experts, who have experienced the topic at hand. This type of evidence is compelling because it capitalizes on average experiences with which your audience can easily relate.

If you were delivering a speech on parking issues here on campus, it would be important that you share statements of opinion from students here on campus who actually own cars. Without hearing about their experiences, the speech would not have the impact you would want it to.

Prestige Testimony

Prestige testimony is the paraphrase or quotation of the opinion of a celebrity or famous individual. The individuals are not experts on the topic, but they carry a great deal of respect, and audiences often solicit their opinions. For example, millions of Americans tune in to hear Oprah Winfrey's opinions on fashion, literature, and a host of other topics. While she is not an expert on literature, as someone who has earned a Ph.D. or written best-selling novels, she does carry immense credibility. Millions of Americans buy books on her recommended reading list. Prestige testimony can be a strong source of evidence if you recognize the differences between it and expert testimony.

TIPS FOR USING TESTIMONY

Quote or Paraphrase Accurately

Make sure that you quote or paraphrase your sources accurately. So many times, individuals are misquoted. Often their statements are abbreviated so that we don't hear their entire statements, or their comments are taken out of context. It is your responsibility as an ethical speaker to ensure that you have used their words as your sources intended.

Use Testimony from Unbiased Sources

Make sure that the testimony you are citing is from an unbiased source. Suzy, a student in this course, read an article that claimed that canned vegetables were healthier than either frozen or fresh vegetables. After further investigation, she discovered the research presented in the article was conducted by the aluminum can industry, hardly an unbiased source. For all we know, the information in the article and the conclusions of the study may have been right on target—completely accurate. However, given the biased nature of the source, these results seem a little suspicious. Your audience will likely think so as well. Make sure your testimony is from credible, competent, and objective experts.

Cite the Credentials of Your Sources

When you introduce testimony, identify your source. Here are a couple of examples of how you would introduce this information within your presentation:

> Beth, a Purdue freshman and nursing major, had this to say about the Grand Prix . . .

> Dr. Browne, a cardiologist at M. D. Anderson Hospital in Houston, warns that obesity . . .

You owe it to your audience to let them know what the qualifications of your experts are. Your audience should be able to judge for themselves whether or not they find your expert credible.

GENERAL TIPS ON USING SUPPORTING MATERIAL

Use a Variety of Types of Supporting Material

As you begin to prepare your presentation, it will be important for you to include a variety of different types of supporting materials. As discussed in Chapter 2 of the textbook, certain audiences are more likely to be interested in and persuaded by different types of evidence. It is important that you use a variety of materials so that you can appeal to different members of your audience.

Use a Variety of Sources for Supporting Material

Even if you use a variety of types of supporting material, your audience may question your motives or your level of research if you use a limited number of sources for your support. By using different sources (newspapers, journals, interviews, etc.) and different types of material, you will enhance your own credibility, and, at the same time, increase the believability of your information.

Use Consistent and Complementary Supporting Material

Your supporting material is not a set of independent observations. They are all parts of a larger whole. They should work together to build a case or make a point. Ask yourself, "Does this evidence enhance the overall presentation?" Or, "How does this evidence or supporting material relate to other supporting material I am providing?" Often, novice speakers string together miscellaneous bits of information that do not, in totality, work together in meaningful ways.

 ## WHERE TO FIND SUPPORTING EVIDENCE

Students often cringe at the thought of going to the library to collect research. Many of them feel unfamiliar with the library and don't know where to go to get started. One of the best pieces of advice is to ask a reference librarian for help. That's what they are there for. You will find them extremely helpful, and you can find what you need in less time if you just ask for help when you need it. Purdue offers a variety of formats for seeking assistance. You can chat with a reference librarian 11:00 a.m. to 10:00 p.m. Monday through Thursday and from 6:00 p.m. to 10:00 p.m. on Sunday. You can also schedule an appointment through the Research Project Advisory Service to set up individual assistance with a project.

The undergraduate library provides an online tutorial called CORE (Comprehensive Online Research Education). This tutorial is extremely helpful in getting you started on the research process. The undergraduate library at Purdue also offers a 15-minute audio tour. You can check out the equipment at the circulation desk and find out where everything is. Both of these are excellent resources to assist you in becoming familiar with the material at the library.

There are many places to go in the library to find supporting material. You can visit the libraries at Purdue by going to their homepage at http://www.lib.purdue.edu. We have several libraries at Purdue, and you may have to visit several of them to locate all the materials you need.

Even with access to excellent libraries, libraries are not the only source for information. You may have to go elsewhere for information. For instance, you may need to actually interview experts, conduct polls, go to museums, visit organizations, or use other methods to get the information and supporting material necessary for your presentation. The library represents the most common source for gathering information, but your speech may require that you use more than the library to locate information.

SOURCES OF SUPPORTING MATERIAL

BOOKS

Books are a good place to begin your research for your presentations. They usually provide a thorough treatment of the topic that they address and, therefore, provide a substantial amount of material on a given topic. The primary limitation with books is that they become outdated rather quickly. It takes a book a good deal of time to reach the shelf, from the moment it is written to the time it is published, so even books with very recent copyright dates may have dated material. This may not be important for every topic, but for those topics where information is changing quickly, such as technological or scientific advancements, books may not be the best source of supporting evidence.

REFERENCE WORKS

Sometimes you need to check a quick fact when putting together your presentation. For example, you may need to know the date of an important historical event, the Gross National Product of a country, or the population of a particular geographical region. Answers to these questions can be found in a variety of common and respected reference resources. These may include encyclopedias, dictionaries, atlases, yearbooks, almanacs, and biographical aids, just to name a few. Here are two Web links of commonly accessed reference works that may be beneficial to you: the CIA World Factbook, http://www.cia.gov/cia/publications/factbook and the Encyclopedia Britannica online at http://www.britannica.com/. LexisNexis, an online database, also provides excellent reference works indexing the World Almanac, Roper polls, famous quotations, country profiles, state profiles and biographical profiles.

Look for the most current version of the print versions; they, too, can become dated very quickly and are often updated yearly. Online versions of these publications may be the most beneficial because they are continuously updated. While reference works are good places to find quick facts, they will not provide ample material for your presentation.

MAGAZINES AND NEWSPAPERS

Articles from magazines and newspapers will provide some of the best supporting materials for your presentations. These periodicals are published often (daily, weekly, or monthly), so they usually provide current and up-to-date material. One limitation with magazines and newspapers is that the authors are usually journalists and not experts on the topic on which they are writing. It is important that you keep this in mind as you evaluate the material you consult for the presentation.

One of the best indexes to help you search these materials efficiently is LexisNexis. This index is an invaluable source for finding information. The Purdue library offers this database online. You can access it from any computer on campus or even from home. All of the articles it indexes are in full-text. This means the entire content of every article indexed is provided within the database, not just the abstract, so you can do some of your research from the comfort of your own home.

To access the database, go to the Purdue library site at **http://www. lib.purdue.edu**. From the "Articles and Databases" on the menu at the top of the screen, chose "Databases by Title" from the dropdown menu. Click on the "L" in the menu, and then "LexisNexis Academic."

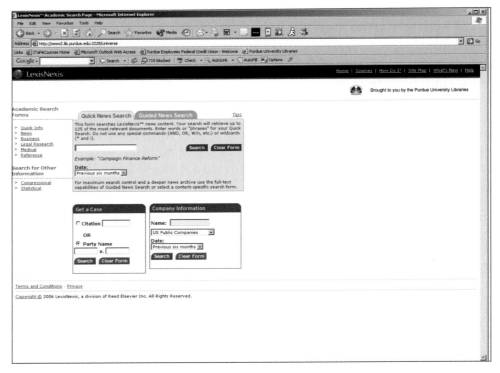

LexisNexis "Quick News Search" page

On the opening screen, you have several options for searching. If you choose the "Quick News" search on the opening page, LexisNexis will display the results of your simple search based on the 125 documents it judges most pertinent in its database from the last six months. (This is the default setting. With the dropdown menu, you can change the date to narrow the search to within the last few weeks, or expand it to within the last two years.) This means your search results will include not just articles from mainstream newspapers but any materials from the various sources LexisNexis indexes. For instance, type in the search term "hurricanes" in the "Quick News" search box, and contained in the top 125 results are results from such sources as U.S. Federal News, National Public Radio, CNN, the Federal Document Clearing House, and the *Miami Herald*. Clicking on any of the results will produce a full text copy of the article.

There are limitations to the "Quick News" search. First, you cannot narrow your search very effectively. The search field will only accept one word or a combination of words that would appear together. You cannot use special commands, such as "And" or "Or," to narrow your search. Also, the "Date" box will only allow you to search for sources within the last two years. To get access to information published before that, you will have to do a more specific search.

To get a more specific search, you must choose one of the search fields on the left-hand side of the opening page. Clicking on one of the fields will bring up a "Guided News" search page that allows you to narrow your search by specific categories and source type, multiple keywords that are not adjacent in the copy, and more extensive dates. For instance, you can limit your search to only major newspapers and popular magazines by clicking on the "News" search. From the "Guided News" search page you can select a news category, such as "General News"; select a news source, such as "Major Papers"; and enter search terms of "hurricanes" and "damage" and "total." All of the results will be articles from major newspapers and contain each of your search terms somewhere on the page; they do not have to appear together. Note you also had the option in the "Date Range" box to extend your search to more than 10 years ago. Other specific search categories in LexisNexis include business, medical, reference, legal and congressional news.

Newspaper Source is another database you can use to easily locate newspaper articles This database provides abstracts and full-text articles for over 150 U.S. and international newspapers from 1994 to the present. This collection includes major newspapers such as *The New York Times, The Wall Street Journal, USA Today* and international papers such as the *Kyodo News International,* a Japanese publication. Visit the Purdue libraries' home page for information on finding this database.

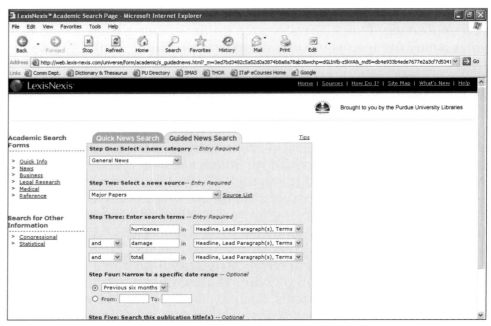

LexisNexis "Guided News Search" page

GOVERNMENT DOCUMENTS

Government documents are generated by federal, state, and local governments. The purpose of these documents is keeping records and statistics. They are also key in helping keep the public informed on government activity and policy. Some good sites for governmental statistical information are: http://www.census.gov/statab/www/ and FedStats at http://www.fedstats.gov/.

You can visit the Purdue libraries for a list of many additional Web sites that can facilitate the search of government documents. The following site will give you more information on what is available to Purdue students, and it is sorted by subject: http://www.lib.purdue.edu/govdocs/subjguides.html.

ACADEMIC JOURNALS

Academic journals are written for scholars or individuals who do research in a particular area. They distribute original research to a particular scientific or scholarly community. They contain the latest developments in the field. Sometimes they are difficult for students to decipher because they are full of technical jargon particular to a specific subject area. However, they are a highly credible source of information.

A good place to search for academic journals is Academic Search Premier. This database indexes over 3,000 academic journals, magazines and newspapers. ArticleFirst, another database, indexes articles from over 12,000 journals in a variety of disciplines. Proquest Research Library is a database well suited for finding academic publications as well. This database indexes over 2,350 magazines, academic journals, and newspaper articles in many different subject areas. Some are even available in full-text versions. JSTOR, the Scholarly Journal Archive, has full-text articles from over 450 journals, including disciplines such as the social sciences, humanities, economics, and mathematics. All of these databases can be found at the Purdue library at **http://gemini.lib.purdue.edu/eresource/result2.cfm?filter=1**.

WEB SITES

Web pages can be beneficial as supporting evidence, if you understand what you are dealing with. Anyone can put up a Web page. Unlike print resources, there is no editorial process. In other words, no third party is checking to make sure the material is truthful like they do at *The New York Times*. Although the ability to publish your own material makes the Web a powerful tool, it also brings about limitations. Therefore, it is important that you know exactly what you are dealing with when you choose to use supporting evidence that comes from a Web page. Personal Web pages carry the most danger. While they don't necessarily contain erroneous material, you should examine them critically and use them with extreme caution. In this course, it is highly recommended that you

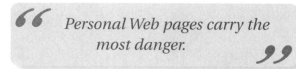

Personal Web pages carry the most danger.

avoid personal Web pages. If you feel that you simply must use some information from a personal page, get your instructor's approval beforehand.

As previously stated, when you use Web pages as supporting evidence, you are taking a risk. By following some of the guidelines outlined in the following section, you can minimize some of these risks.

Examine the Site's Credentials

One of the first steps in this process is to examine the credentials of the author. The Johns Hopkins University Libraries suggest that this may be the most important criteria to consider. Do the authors have the credentials necessary to make claims or give the advice they are recommending? If not, be leery of the information on the page. If the authors include their credentials, it is probably a sign that something could be amiss. If you still find the page valuable and author credentials aren't posted, you may be able to find them elsewhere. If contact information is included, contact the authors directly and inquire about their background. If the Web site doesn't include good bibliographic information, look up the author in Google to find out more about him/her.

In addition to the author of specific information, the publisher of the site should be evaluated as well. If the site belongs to an organization, it may not include the name of the author of each section or page. If not, who is the publishing body? Is the organization recognized in the field it represents? Does the organization presenting the information have a stake in the material presented? Does it have its own agenda? This could mean that the material presented on the site is biased. Is it trying to sell something or is it trying to get you to do something? Is it a corporate organization? Carefully, examine the site and answer all of these questions. You cannot assume that biased Web sites will be obvious.

Carefully examine the contents of Web pages thoroughly before relying on them for information.

Examine the URL

Even sites that appear legitimate may not be. Look at the URL carefully. The URL or Web address contains valuable information about who owns the domain, what kind of server it belongs to, etc. For more information on dissecting the URL, visit the following Web site at the Johns Hopkins libraries: **http://www.library.jhu.edu/ researchhelp/general/evaluating/ url.html**.

One of the most important questions you can ask is does the URL make sense for the claims the page is making? If the page claims to represent the U.S. Department of Agriculture, for example, and USDA doesn't appear anywhere in the URL, something is wrong. If the page claims to be created by a government entity, examine the URL for the proper domain type. Does it end in .gov, .mil, or .us? If so, it is probably a legitimate site. If not, there is a problem.

Another resource available to examine a URL is alexa.com. Simply go to this site and paste in the URL in question to get some added information. This site provides information on the level of traffic the site receives, reviews, contact/ownership information for the domain name, and a list of sites that link to the page. All of this information may enable you to make a better judgment about the quality of the site.

Examine External Links

Examine the sites that the page links to. These can be informative as well. Questions to consider about links are: Are they well respected links or are they suspect? Do the links work? Do the links offer other viewpoints on the subject? Do the links represent a bias?

A Web site found at www.martinlutherking.org seems like a legitimate site, on first glance, offering information on Martin Luther King and his life. However, a quick click on the external links offers another interpretation. The site links to white supremacist groups and other sites that promote hate and racism.

Examine Citations

The evidence a particular page cites can be important as well. Who are they citing? Are they reputable and respected sources? Can you find the material the page references? Sometimes individuals fabricate sources. Check them out for yourself to examine their validity.

Examine Timeliness of Information

Examine the most recent date the page was updated. For some topics timeliness will be extremely important.

Reputable directories such as Librarians' Index, Infomine, or AcademicInfo evaluate Web content and may be helpful in determining the value of a particular site. These sites index few pages in comparison to the number of Web pages out there and so inclusion on one of the sites may be a good sign. However, make sure you review all of the comments the site makes about a particular page before deciding to use it.

EVALUATING SUPPORTING MATERIALS

Even though Web pages carry the most risk, all sources should be evaluated. The following guidelines apply to all reference materials.

Is It Relevant?

Sometimes we can find fascinating material that is only tangentially related to our topic. Perhaps you have found an interesting statistic that you would like to include just because you think your audience might find it fascinating. If it isn't directly related to the goal of your presentation, do not include the material. Only include that information that directly helps you achieve the goal of your presentation. Doing otherwise may distract your audience and distract from your message.

Is It Credible?

As an ethical speaker, you owe it to your audience to find information that comes from sources that are credible. Many times as a speaker, you will be asking your audience to make changes that may affect their lives. Asking them to base their decisions on material that is less than reliable is unethical. Your supporting material should come from respected sources.

Is It Current?

In addition to being credible, your supporting material should be current. We are living during a time when scientific advancements are being made daily. So, how current is current? Well, it depends on your topic. Some subject areas are experiencing changes in knowledge daily, while others have had little advancement in several years. For most topics, you will need to consult the most recently published evidence.

Have You Consulted a Variety of Resources?

Ethical speakers consult a variety of resources hoping to validate their research in multiple places. Make sure you look at a variety of types of information, ranging from scholarly journals to newspapers. Each publication has its own strengths and weaknesses. By drawing supporting materials from a variety of sources, you will compensate for any weakness a particular source may have.

◆ CITING YOUR EVIDENCE DURING THE PRESENTATION

As you will read in Chapter 9 in your textbook, citing your sources within your speech will enhance your credibility as a speaker and can even make your presentation more persuasive (O'Keefe, 1998). As an ethical speaker, it is also important that you cite your sources to avoid plagiarism. The following examples demonstrate methods for citing sources orally during your presentation. One thing that is important to keep in mind when orally citing your material is variety. Don't introduce each piece of supporting evidence with, "According to . . ." Use variety when introducing these elements into your presentation.

> ❝ *Citing your sources within your speech will enhance your credibility as a speaker.* ❞

BOOKS

When citing a book, you need to cite the author, his or her credentials (if it will enhance your credibility), the title of the book, and the date it was published. Here is an example:

> In his 1988 book, "Influence: Science and Practice," Robert Cialdini, a professor of psychology at the University of Arizona, says that there are seven weapons of influence.

JOURNAL OR MAGAZINE ARTICLES

You should include the name and date of the publication. You may also want to include the name of the author or the article.

> According to an August 3, 2003, article in *Time Magazine*, urban cities, or centers, "not only endure bad weather, they help create it."

> Jeffrey Kluger writes in an August 3, 2003, article in *Time Magazine* titled, "How Cities Make Their Own Weather," that urban cities, or centers, "not only endure bad weather, they help create it."

NEWSPAPERS

For newspaper articles, include the name of the newspaper and the date of the article.

> According to an August 6, 2003, article in *The New York Times*, hotels in New York City are charging less for rooms than they did last summer.

INTERVIEWS

To cite information from an interview that you conducted, cite the person's name, their credentials, and when the interview took place.

> In a November 23, 2003, interview with Professor Steven R. Wilson, Ph.D., a family violence researcher at Purdue University, he stated, "Child abuse is an interactional phenomenon; that is, parents do not strike their children at random moments, but rather at predictable times that grow out of larger daily interactions."

MORE INFORMATION ON EVALUATING WEB SOURCES

Visit these sites for more information regarding criteria for evaluating resources on the Web.

- http://www.lib.berkeley.edu/ TeachingLib/Guides/Internet/ Evaluate.html
- http://www.library.cornell.edu/ olinuris/ref/research/webeval.html
- http://www.library.jhu.edu/ researchhelp/general/evaluating/ index.html

Style Guide for APA Formatting
Based on APA Style Manual—5th Edition

Interview

Last name, First initial. Second initial. (personal communication, date)

Example:

Smith, J. E. (personal communication, August 31, 2007).

Periodical

Author, A. A. (Year). Title of article. *Title of periodical, volume number,* pages.

Example:

Smith, J. E. (2007). Speaking strategies for business presentations. *Presentational Speaking Quarterly, 21,* 35–47.

Newspaper

Author, A. A. (Date of publication). Title of article. *Title of newspaper,* page(s).

Example:

Smith, J. E. (2007, August 31). Speaking strategies for business presentations. *The Daily Times,* C14.

Online Periodical/Article

Author, A. A. (Date of publication). Title of article. *Title of periodical or journal, volume number,* Retrieved Month Day, Year from http://Web address.

Example:

Smith, J. E. (n.d.). Speaking strategies for business presentations. *Presentational Speaking Quarterly, 21,* Retrieved August 31, 2006 from http://www.com114rocks.org.

Internet Website

Author, A. A. & Author, B. B. (Date of posting). Title of work. Retrieved month, day, year from URL.

Example:

Smith, J. E. & Smythe, W. A. (2006, May). Speaking strategies for business presentations. Retrieved August 31, 2006 from http://www.presenterstraining.edu/comrocks

Internet Web Site with No Author/No Date

Title of web page. (n.d.). Retrieved month day, year from Organization Web site:
    URL.

Example:

Purdue Convocations. (n.d.). Retrieved August 31, 2006 from
        Purdue University Web site: http://www.purdue.edu/convos/.

Tips:

- "References" should appear, centered, at the top of your reference page (without quotation marks)
- The reference page should be double-spaced
- The reference page should be alphabetized by last name
- The 2nd, 3rd, etc. lines should be indented five spaces using a hanging indent (see above)

CONCLUSION

The use of supporting evidence is crucial to an effective presentation. Without supporting material, your information is just your opinion. There are a variety of types of material that you can use to bolster your assertions and arguments. These include statistics, examples, and testimony. Each of these types of supporting evidence has strengths and weaknesses. You should evaluate your speaking situation thoroughly in order to determine what evidence is best suited to your particular needs. Regardless of what you choose, using a variety of types of supporting material that is cited effectively will help ensure that your presentation is successful.

KEY TERMS

Examples

Expert testimony

Extended example

Hypothetical example

Localizing

Peer testimony

Prestige testimony

Statistics

Testimony

EXERCISES

1. Complete the Purdue library's CORE (Comprehensive Online Research Education) training module, located at http://core.lib.purdue.edu. CORE guides you through each step of the research process, from selecting a topic, to finding support, to evaluating supporting materials.

2. Each of the statements contains at least one error in rules for correct and effective citations. Identify the error or errors.

   a. The chances of developing a potentially fatal illness simply by checking into a British hospital ward are among the lowest in the world, says a report from the British Medical Association.

   b. And *Time* magazine reported that two new major studies found that daily calcium supplements provide little or no benefit against osteoporosis and colorectal cancer.

   c. A 1978 report by the U.S. Food and Drug Administration said artificial sweeteners cause cancer in humans.

   d. Purdue sophomore Bill Smith said a proposed smoking ban would lead to drastic financial losses for many local businesses.

e. In a recent interview, Dr. Howard Smith said the prevention of heart disease needs to begin early in life, because by age 50, the damage has already been done.

f. According to ILOVEENGLAND.com, most British residents oppose the Euro dollar and would like to see a return to the English pound.

g. According to an article in *The New York Times*, more than 500,000 Americans have home security systems.

h. A recent survey of students in the Purdue Union Starbucks showed that most Purdue students think the economy is the biggest issue in upcoming elections.

i. Most college students will graduate with lots of debt.

REFERENCES

Allen, M., Bruflat, R., Fucilla, R., Kramer, M., McKellips, S., Ryan, D. J., et al., (2000). Testing the persuasiveness of evidence: Combining narrative and statistical forms. *Communication Research Reports, 17,* 331–336.

Allen, M., & Preiss, R. W. (1997). Comparing the persuasiveness of narrative and statistical evidence using meta-analysis. *Communication Research Reports, 14,* 125–131.

Barker, J. (2005). Evaluating Web pages: Techniques to apply and questions to ask. Retrieved March 14, 2006, from University of California at Berkeley, UC Berkeley Library Web site: http://www.lib.berkeley.edu/TeachingLib/Guides/Internet/Evaluate.html.

Campbell, A., Kirsche, I.S., & Kolstad, A. (1992). *Assessing literacy: The framework for the national adult literacy survey* (NCES No. 92113). Washington, DC: U. S. National Center for Education Statistics.

Goncalves, E. (2002). The secret nuclear war. *The Ecologist, 29,* 2.

Kirk, E. (1996). Evaluating information found on the internet. Retrieved March 14, 2006, from Johns Hopkins University, The Sheridan Libraries Web site: http://www.library.jhu.edu/ researchhelp/general/evaluating/index.html.

O'Keefe, D. J. (1998). Justification explicitness and persuasive effect: A meta-analytic review of the effects of varying support articulation in persuasive messages. *Argumentation and Advocacy, 35,* 61–75.

Reinard, J. C. (1988). The empirical study of the persuasive effects of evidence: The status after fifty years of research. *Human Communication Research, 15,* 3–59.

Reinard, J. C. (1998). The persuasive effects of testimonial assertion evidence. In M. Allen & R. W. Preiss (Eds.), *Persuasion: Advances through meta-analysis* (pp. 69–86). Cresskil, NJ: Hampton.

Sullivan, C. & Smith, C. M. (2006). 5 TIPS for writing popular science. *Writer, 119,* 23–25.

Thagard, P. (1992). Analogy, explanation, and education. *Journal of Research in Science Teaching, 29,* 537–544.

Chapter 7

OUTLINING THE PRESENTATION

CHAPTER OBJECTIVES

After reading this chapter, you should be able to:

- ☐ Explain why outlining is important to an effective presentation.

- ☐ Explain the differences between a preparation outline and a speaking outline.

- ☐ Construct a preparation outline following the guidelines presented in this chapter.

- ☐ Construct a speaking outline following the guidelines presented in this chapter.

$\mathcal{O}$ne complaint students often make about speech preparation is the process of writing the outline. Students often find this step challenging and feel it can be time consuming. This chapter is designed to walk you through each of the steps of preparing both your preparation outline and your speaking outline. After reading this chapter and working through the guidelines, you will find that outlining is not as difficult as you may have initially thought.

The outline is the blueprint of your entire presentation and is the tool that ensures your decisions in the planning process have been adequate. The outline lays the foundation for everything you want to accomplish during the speech. If something is wrong in this initial design, your presentation will likely suffer. Zach, a former student in this course, realized this lesson the hard way.

Zach, who took this class a few years ago, landed a fabulous job at ESPN after graduation. Within a couple of months at the broadcasting network, he was asked to deliver a presentation to some clients. Zach had done well in this class and felt confident in his ability to speak effectively. After preparing a slick PowerPoint slide show, which included digitized video, and conducting numerous interviews with leading authorities on his subject, Zach thought he was thoroughly prepared.

After the big event, Zach was very disappointed with the way the presentation had gone. He felt the speech was flat, and it was obvious to him from the questions the audience asked that they didn't understand and follow all of the points in his presentation. His audience seemed confused and unable to follow the main ideas in his presentation. The organization of the presentation had not been clear, and Zach felt embarrassed and humiliated.

After processing what went wrong during the presentation and not being able to discern where he had lost his audience, he became frustrated and decided to seek advice. Zach called his public speaking instructor, and she agreed to meet with him to talk about the presentation. She asked him to bring in all of the materials he used to prepare and deliver the talk. As they started to go through the material, she asked him if she could see his outline. Zach replied that he didn't write one because he thought he had passed that stage and didn't need to do that anymore. Well, that was Zach's fundamental error. The outline is the tool speakers of all levels use to envision and critique their entire presentation. It helps ensure the organization of the presentation is clear and balanced, that transitions are natural and smooth, that the flow is logical and progressive, that content is supported by evidence from credible sources, that the amount of material reflects the time you will have, and that you will be able to adapt flexibly to the moment if so required. This was the one crucial mistake Zach made in preparing his presentation and explains why his audience was unable to follow the presentation. Without a blueprint, Zach's presentation inherently lacked a structure and his audience became lost.

Zach learned the hard way that he skipped over the most important step. The outlining stage of the speech preparation process is crucial. Without drafting a blueprint, it is hard to envision a speech, which can lead to many unexpected events. As we will discuss in this chapter, the outline stage determines if all the decisions you have made thus far in the presentation will work together.

WHY OUTLINING IS IMPORTANT

Once you have selected your topic, purpose and thesis; determined your main ideas; conducted your research; and begun crafting the introduction and conclusion of your presentation, you are ready to test this plan by examining the design through a preparation outline. The outline is the initial representation of your content. It allows you the first opportunity to adapt the presentation to the audience. If you skip this step, you will have missed a vital opportunity to analyze your speech in terms of the audience. Through the outline, you will organize what you will say in the presentation, how you will introduce the material, how you will arrange main points, how you will support those points, and how you will conclude the presentation. It can be best thought of as a tool to determine whether the choices you have made thus far in the planning process are effective and whether you will need to resolve any problem areas.

ENSURES ORGANIZATION

One of the most important functions of the outline is to ensure clear organization. By examining the way the main points and supporting material work together, you can determine whether the organizational pattern you have selected is the most appropriate for the material, the audience, and the goal of your presentation. Clear organization often characterizes a well-received presentation, since audiences perceive organized speakers as more credible and become frustrated by those presentations that lack organization (Sharp & McClung, 1966).

BALANCES THE PRESENTATION

The preparation outline is a mechanism that ensures **balance**. In other words, it prompts you to make sure all your main points are complete and that they are adequately developed. Each main point should be covered in approximately the same amount of detail. For example, you would want to avoid a lengthy explanation of main point number one and cursory coverage of main point number two. From a preparation outline, even a brief glance will provide basic visual clues about how balanced your presentation will be. If your second main point fills up half a page and your third main point runs just two sentences, you quickly will have identified a problem with balance.

> *A commonly used guideline is that introductions should take up about 10 percent of the presentation time, while conclusions take about 5 percent.*

From your outline, you can also measure the length of your introduction and conclusion relative to the body of the speech.

IDENTIFIES EVIDENCE

The outline also provides an opportunity for you to check and see whether each point has been supported with appropriate research material. If your main points do not have research supporting the claims you make, you will lose credibility and find it difficult to achieve the goals of your presentation. The outline also allows you to ensure that your research has been adequately cited within the presentation. A good guideline is that every point or subpoint should have at least one type of supporting evidence.

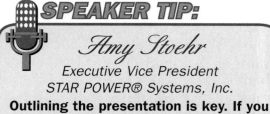

SPEAKER TIP:

Amy Stoehr

Executive Vice President
STAR POWER® Systems, Inc.

Outlining the presentation is key. If you have a solid outline, then you are able to make adjustments on the fly for time constraints. Outlines ensure that key points get communicated.

ASSESSES QUANTITY

One of the most restrictive factors of the presentational situation is the time constraint to which the speech must adhere. The outline can roughly indicate how much material you have and how long it will take you to cover it. With experience, you will be able to use the outline as a very precise gauge of how long your presentation will run. It is important to note here that it is a speaker's ethical obligation to understand how much time they have to speak and to fill that time appropriately. Audiences place a high value on their own time and expect to get their "money's worth" when listening to a speaker. They may become resentful when speakers take advantage of the situation by speaking longer or shorter than expected.

ALLOWS FOR FLEXIBILITY

One of the most important benefits to speaking from an outline rather than a manuscript or from memory is the flexibility an outline provides. When the presentation isn't committed to an exact stream of words, sentences, and paragraphs, it affords you the adaptability needed to make adjustments during the presentation. This flexible nature of an outline will afford you with the ability to adapt to the specific needs of the audience and the situation.

ALLOWS FOR INSTRUCTIONAL FEEDBACK

In the classroom situation, the outline is the only chance you will have to get feedback from your instructor before you deliver the actual graded presentation. In an English course, you can submit various versions of your actual paper and get feedback before your final draft is due. Presentations don't lend themselves to this same process. There is simply not enough time during the course of the semester for students to present "rough drafts" of their presentations. Although this situation would be ideal, there simply isn't enough time. Therefore, the more detail you can provide on your outline, the more feedback you can get on how to improve the content of your presentation. This means showing where you cite material, where and what you will use for a visual aid, internal summaries and previews, as well as a complete bibliography. Now that you know the importance of the presentational outline, let's examine its format and features.

FORMATTING THE PREPARATION OUTLINE

The *preparation outline* is a very detailed representation of the speech. It is carefully constructed and has a variety of features. The following sections identify each of the features that needs to be included in your presentation outline.

Full Sentences

The preparation outline is written in full sentences. Every aspect of the outline is written in complete sentences: main points, subpoints, sub-subpoints, and transitions. This forces you to be specific about the claims you will make in your speech and ensures that your presentation will be more focused and to the point. One maxim worth heeding in this situation is, "If you can't say it, you don't know it." In other words, if you have trouble articulating your ideas in your outline, it will be impossible to do so in the presentation. If you can't outline it, you simply do not have a solid grip on your material. **One sentence per point is adequate.** The point is not to write out the entire speech word for word, but to clearly state your main ideas. Let's look at an example:

Ineffective:	I. Sleeping habits
Better:	I. Sleep is being widely neglected among individuals aged 18 to 35 in today's society.

The ineffective main point doesn't tell us much. What about sleeping habits? Whose sleeping habits? This main point doesn't have focus or direction. It has not been clearly articulated.

> *Do not write more than one sentence per entry on the body of the outline.*

The more effective example has been expressed as a complete sentence. Notice the difference in clarity from the ineffective example. The direction of this main point is clear and more precise. The complete sentence tells us exactly what direction the main point is heading. The ineffective version would likely result in a rambling, imprecise speech. Writing your outline in complete sentences will help alleviate this problem.

Appropriate Symbolization

The format for the outline follows the common alphanumeric system. You will designate main points with Roman numerals (I., II., III.), supporting points with capital letters (A., B., C.), subpoints with Arabic (regular) numbers (1., 2., 3.), and sub-subpoints with lowercase letters (a., b., c.). Basically, you will proceed from the most important ideas to the least important. The structure for the body of the presentation looks something like this:

I. **Main Point One**
    A. Supporting Point
        1. Subpoint
        2. Subpoint
    B. Supporting Point

II. **Main Point Two**
    A. Supporting Point
        1. Subpoint
           a. Sub-subpoint
           b. Sub-subpoint
        2. Subpoint
    B. Supporting Point
    C. Supporting Point
        1. Subpoint
        2. Subpoint

EFFECTIVE SUBORDINATION

One of the primary reasons for preparing the outline is to examine and critique the relationship between your claims and your supporting evidence. This makes sure that you have sound reasoning and helps the audience follow your presentation. Each claim you make should be supported by evidence. Simply stated, the idea of **subordination** means that all the first level points or main points are supported by supporting points, called **subpoints**. And subpoints are supported by sub-subpoints so that each subordinate point supports the idea under which it is indented. Basically, it is a method of physically indenting material so that the relationship among ideas becomes clear and becomes visually apparent. Let's examine the example below.

   I. Childhood obesity is an epidemic in the United States (The Morning Call, March 3, 2002).
      A. According to a December 12, 2001, article in the Journal of the American Medical Association, "Being overweight is the most common health problem facing U.S. children" (pg. 2845).
      B. 15.3% of U.S. children are overweight (American Obesity Association, 2005).
      C. Obesity in children has increased for all age, race and sex groups since 1970.
         1. The biggest increase in obesity, however, is among African American and Hispanic children, up 120%.
         2. There was a 50% increase in obesity among white children.
      D. Not only did the number of children who were overweight increase, but also the severity of the obesity increased as well.

As is demonstrated in this excerpt of a sample outline, each of the subpoints serves to support or further illuminate or explain the point above. Take, for example, subpoint C. This statement supports and further explains the obesity epidemic for children in the U.S. It provides further clarification by explaining that this is an epidemic for all age and race groups. Subpoint C is further supported by sub-subpoint 1 by the explanation that this statistic has increased most for African American and Hispanic children.

COORDINATED POINTS

In addition to subordination, it is important that your outline follow the rules for coordination. ***Coordination*** means that the ideas at the same level of importance should use the same series of symbols and, therefore, be indented at the same level. Consider the main points in the following example in a speech about food safety:

    I.   Wash hands and cooking surfaces often.
    II. Don't cross contaminate various food products.
    III. Cook and store foods at proper temperatures.

This particular example outlines guidelines to follow for managing food safely, and each of these steps is as important as the next in terms of preventing food borne illness. Each of these main points is equal in terms of importance. Violating any one of these rules for food safety could result in food poisoning. Therefore, they should all be at the same level in the outline.

The next step in preparing this outline would be to add supporting material. If we add supporting material to each of these main points, it is important that we insert it at the appropriate level. We would not want subpoint A under main point one "Hands should be washed with soap. . . ." to be a separate main point. It serves to support main point one by providing a specific example of how to wash hands properly. It is supporting material and should therefore be inserted at the appropriate spot—subordinate to main point one.

    I.   Wash hands and cooking surfaces often.
        A. Hands should be washed with soap for a minimum of 20 seconds.
        B. Use paper towels instead of kitchen towels to clean cooking surfaces.

   II. **Don't cross contaminate various food products.**

      A. Separate raw meat from other food in the shopping cart.

      B. Use one cutting board for meat and another for vegetables.

  III. **Cook and store foods at proper temperatures.**

      A. Make sure there are no cold spots in food where bacteria can hide.

      B. Leftovers should be refrigerated within two hours of use.

Each of the supporting material adds to the main point it follows by further elaborating on the ideas it presents.

SPECIFIC PURPOSE AND THESIS STATEMENTS

It is important to include your specific purpose statement and your thesis statement at the top of your outline. After all, these are the over-arching goals of your speech. Every decision that you make about what to include in the presentation should enhance these goals. So when thinking about including a point or a piece of supporting material, refer back to the specific purpose and thesis statement. If the material will assist in achieving these goals include it; if not, leave it out.

Good presentations rely on thorough research.

TRANSITIONS

Transitions are the elements that make your speech flow and enable your audience to follow your presentation. **Directional transitions** are used between main points to let the audience know that you are moving from one idea to another (e.g., Now that we have discussed the causes of eating disorders, let's examine some of the treatments.). **Signposts** mark the exact place in the speech by alerting the audience to their exact location in the presentation (e.g., The first cause . . .; The most important point . . .; In summary . . .;). ***Internal previews*** are transitions used within main points and alert listeners of what lies ahead (e.g., There are many different causes of eating disorders: media representations, concern with body image, and issues of self-esteem. Let's begin by focusing on media representations.). ***Internal reviews*** or summaries are also located within main points and simply restate the main ideas of a main point (e.g., We have examined three causes of eating disorders: media representations, concern with body image, and self-esteem.). Remember, internal previews and reviews are only necessary when a main point is extremely complex or there are a lot of ideas for the audience to keep up with. It is important to include all transitions, regardless of type, in your preparation outline. You are more likely to include your transitions in your actual presentation when they are part of your outline.

BIBLIOGRAPHY

A ***bibliography*** or reference list comprised of the sources you consulted to construct the outline makes the preparation outline complete. The bibliography will include any books, magazine articles, newspaper articles, pamphlets and brochures, personal interviews, and Web resources. (Check with your instructor to see if Web pages are appropriate supporting material.) Use ***APA style*** (American Psychological Association) to format your bibliography or reference list. It is important that the citations are complete and consistent. You can go to the following Web sites for advice on using APA: The American Psychological Association style site **http://www.apastyle.org/elecref.html** or Purdue University's Online Writing Lab **http://owl.english.purdue.edu/**. A complete example of a bibliography is provided at the end of the chapter.

 PUTTING THE OUTLINE TOGETHER

The next few paragraphs will walk you step by step through the process of creating an outline that follows the appropriate format.

Step One: Start by writing your specific purpose statement and your thesis statement at the top of your outline. It will look something like this:

Specific Purpose Statement: To inform my audience about the origins of photomicrography.

Thesis Statement: Photomicrography is an intriguing type of photography with interesting origins in biology and photography.

Step Two: Begin by labeling your introduction, body, and conclusion. This ensures that each of these components will be included in your presentation.

Introduction

Body

Conclusion

Step Three: Go back and add Roman numerals for all of the components of each of these elements (introduction, body, conclusion).

Introduction

I.   Attention Getter

II. Credibility Statement

III. Relate Topic to Audience

IV. Thesis Statement

Body

I.   Main Point One

II. Main Point Two

III. Main Point Three

Conclusion

I.   Restatement of Thesis

II. Clincher

Step Four: Next, go back and outline the body of the presentation. The body should always be constructed before the introduction or conclusion, since your introduction and conclusion will reflect the body of the presentation, once you are certain of it.

Begin by adding the appropriate subpoints to your main points. Use capital letters to insert the subpoints. Recall that a subpoint is content that supports a main point. Sometimes it may also be necessary to add sub-subpoints in a presentation. If you need this extra level of detail, simply add Arabic numbers (1., 2., 3.). It is important that you recognize that at this step you are dividing your main points into subpoints.

> **"** *The rule is, if you divide, you need at least two parts. Therefore, you cannot have an A without a B. If you have a 1, you must have a 2, also!* **"**

Step Five: Add transitions between each of your main points. If you have internal transitions such as internal summaries or previews, mark those as well. Adding the transitions into the preparation outline increases the likelihood that you will use them during the presentation.

Step Six: Once you have arranged your main points and transitions into the standard format, you are ready to go back and add your external source citations. This ensures that you cite appropriately during your presentation.

Step Seven: Write out your introduction and conclusion. Once the body has been finalized, you are in good shape to finish these important elements. Simply insert the material into the appropriate place in the outline. Speakers feel the most anxious during the introduction of a presentation (Behnke & Sawyer, 2001; Finn, Sawyer, & Behnke, 2003; Freeman, Sawyer & Behnke, 1997). Therefore, it is perfectly acceptable to write out the introduction word for word. This way if your anxiety is heightened, you won't be required to think on your feet by speaking extemporaneously. Sometimes, it can actually reduce anxiety to memorize the introduction of the presentation.

As explained in Chapter 4, the conclusion is a vital element in the success of the presentation. Research has shown that the information an audience hears last can have a powerful impact on them (Kahana & Howard, 2005). This impact is called the recency effect. Because of the power of the recency effect, you should also write out your conclusion word for word as well. Don't leave your final comments to chance; plan an ending that will make an impact on your audience.

Step Eight: Create your bibliography. Recall that the bibliography completes the outline. Use a consistent style of citation. For this class it is required that you use the APA style.

Step Nine: Once you have completed your outline, you are ready to finalize the entire presentation. Check for each of the following components:

- ◇ Audience Analysis-Relevance
- ◇ Symmetry
- ◇ Balance
- ◇ External Sources/Supporting Material
- ◇ Requirements of the assignment

Step Ten: If you are asked to provide a title for your presentation, do this last. You probably won't need one for classroom presentations. Titles often are important if your presentation will be listed in a program or announced in some way. Titles should be brief, yet encapsulate the major idea of your presentation.

THE SPEAKING OUTLINE

After finalizing your preparation outline, you are ready to begin constructing the speaking outline. The ***speaking outline*** consists of the notes you will actually use to deliver your speech. It is important to remember that the speaking outline is merely a tool to jog your memory. By the time of your presentation, you will have rehearsed your speech so many times that you will know the material cold. The speaking outline will function primarily as a memory aid and as a gauge to remind you of where you are during the presentation.

At this point, you are probably wondering exactly what you should include in your speaking outline and how it should look. Speaking outlines are very idiosyncratic. Each individual has certain items they like to include, and those they prefer to omit. As you gain more experience making presentations, you will develop a style that works best for you. Until you gain this experience, here are some guidelines that will help you get started.

Notice the extemporaneous style of the speaker allows him to adapt and identify with his audience.

GUIDELINES FOR THE SPEAKING OUTLINE

Be Brief

In order to maintain extemporaneous delivery, it is important to keep the speaking outline brief. Unlike the preparation outline, the speaking outline consists of key words, phrases, and abbreviations. If your notes are too detailed, you will have trouble making eye contact and, therefore, connections with your audience. Most beginning speakers use too many notes, leaning on them as a psychological crutch that ends up interfering with the delivery of the presentation. However, if you have practiced the speech adequately, you will only need the memory cues contained in a well-written speaking outline to get you through the presentation.

Follow Structure of the Preparation Outline

For the speaking outline, it is important to use the same outline style used in your preparation outline; this means you will want to use the same exact symbols and indentation as you used in the preparation outline. However, because the speaking outline must be brief, you will want to replicate only a brief version of the presentation outline. The example at the end of the chapter on pages 174–175 demonstrates these guidelines.

> **CHECKLIST FOR A PREPARATION OUTLINE**
> ◉ Use full sentences
> ◉ Use a consistent indentation and symbolization system
> ◉ Include transitions
> ◉ Include internal citations
> ◉ Include a complete bibliography in APA

Include Supporting Materials

You will also want to include any references you will need to cite during the presentation. This will enhance your credibility as a speaker and deter plagiarism. Also consider adding any direct quotations you plan to present. Lengthy quotations and statistics should be written out verbatim so that you can cite them completely and accurately.

Be Legible

One of the most important aspects of the speaking outline is making sure that you can read it while you are delivering your presentation. Write or type in large letters so that you can see them easily while you are speaking. Write on only one side of the note card and number each one. If the stack of cards falls on the floor, you will want to be able to recover quickly and easily!

Provide Delivery Cues

Delivery cues are the stage directions that add emphasis to your presentation. Dramatic pauses, repetition, rate, and volume are all examples of important delivery aspects. A well-polished and effective presentation depends not only on what you say, but how you say it. Including delivery cues in your speaking outline will remind you to use these types of special features to add impact.

Delivery cues can be added to the speaking outline in a variety of ways. Perhaps you would like to highlight certain portions of the speech or maybe you want to write in specific directions. Whatever choice you make, insert your delivery cues clearly and legibly so that they do not interfere with your ability to read the outline. Here are some example cues you might add to your speaking outline:

- ◇ slow down
- ◇ pause
- ◇ make eye contact
- ◇ move from the podium
- ◇ walk to the other side of the room

Usually Use Note Cards

One common question that speakers often ask is whether they should write their speaking outline on note cards or a sheet of paper. Most experts agree that note cards are sturdier and more adaptable. For example, note cards work with either a lectern or without one. They also tend to be less distracting and easier to rearrange. One guideline regarding this question is simple: if you do not have access to a lectern, use note cards. They will be less distracting than sheets of paper. Regardless of which you decide to use, it is important to write on only one side of the card or paper. Additionally, you should number each of your cards or sheets of paper.

> **GUIDELINES FOR AN EFFECTIVE SPEAKING OUTLINE**
> - Be brief
> - Print large enough to read easily
> - Write legibly
> - Write out quotations and statistics
> - Number your index cards or pages
> - Write on only one side of the index card or paper
> - Unless you are using a lectern, use index cards

CONCLUSION

Outlines are extremely important. Even experienced speakers cannot afford to take shortcuts at this step in the process. A great outline increases the likelihood of a successful speech, and a flawed outline translates into a flawed presentation every single time. This chapter presented two types of outlines that play different roles during different parts of the preparation of the presentation.

The preparation outline is the major outline you prepare that enables you to see your entire presentation in a highly structured and detailed way. It affords you the opportunity to critique your presentation's organization, level of detail, use of evidence, etc. The speaking outline is what you actually use during the presentation. It prompts you to cover your main points, to read exact quotes, to express transitions, to gauge your timing, as well as to include other vital information during the presentation. However, the overall level of detail is considerably less than the presentation outline.

By taking the information in this chapter seriously, you can learn from Zach's mistake. Snazzy PowerPoints might look good and help make a point, but they do not constitute adequate preparation for a presentation. And they cannot compensate for a weak outline. Outlining is fundamental.

KEY TERMS

APA style
Balance
Bibliography
Coordination
Delivery cues

Directional transitions
Internal preview
Internal review
Preparation outline
Signpost

Speaking outline
Subordination
Subpoint
Transitions

EXERCISES

1. Using the outline on page 169–173, construct a speaking outline that you may use to deliver this speech. Make sure that you follow the guidelines suggested in this chapter when constructing your speaking outline.

2. Each of the following statements comprise the body of a speech about family mealtime. Unscramble the parts to assemble an outline that is coherent and organized.

Family mealtime improves children physically.

Second, eating meals as a family improves self-esteem.

Jerry Harris, a marriage and family therapist who works at LDS Family Services, reported in a September 2004 article that dinner time not only benefits parents in being able to get better acquainted with current issues in their children's lives, but also provides children with a closer and stable relationship with family members. The attentiveness of parents help children feel cared for and loved.

According to a May 2005 article published in The New York Times, studies suggest that eating as a family improves children's consumption of fruits and vegetables, grains, fiber and vitamins and minerals.

According to a May 2005 article in The New York Times, studies have shown that children eating with both parents are stimulated through advanced language.

Family mealtime improves children mentally.

The same study showed that teens who do not eat regular meals with family are 72% more likely to turn to addictive substances.

It was reported in a September 2004 article published in Deseret News that research conducted by The National Center on Addiction and Substance Abuse at Columbia University consistently found that children who eat dinner with their family are 31% less likely to smoke, drink or use illegal substances.

First, eating meals as a family promotes healthy eating.

Developed relationships with family members help children make better decisions in which friends to have. According to the May 2005 article published in The New York Times, the more often teens have dinner with their parents, the less likely they are to have sexually active friends, less likely girls were to have boyfriends two years older, and the less time teens spent with boyfriends or girlfriends.

Family mealtime improves children socially.

Second, eating meals as a family prevents substance abuse.

According to the May 2005 article in The New York Times, studies have also shown that children who eat with family on a regular basis are less likely to become depressed and to generate suicidal thoughts.

According to the same article, children have shown great advancement in vocabulary and receive higher grades than those who rarely eat with family.

First, eating meals as a family improves intelligence.

According to an October 2004 article published in Work & Family Newsbrief, college students with eating disorders were found to have fewer family meals growing up.

According to the same New York Times article, children who have family meals also eat less fried food, saturated fat, and soda.

REFERENCES

Behnke, R. R., & Sawyer, C. R. (2001). Patterns of psychological state anxiety in public speaking as a function of anxiety sensitivity. *Communication Quarterly, 49,* 84–94.

Finn, A. N., Sawyer, C. R., & Behnke, R. R. (2003). Audience-perceived anxiety patterns of public speakers. *Communication Quarterly, 51,* 470–481.

Freeman, T., Sawyer, C. R., & Behnke, R. R. (1997). Behavioral inhibition and the attribution of public speaking state anxiety. *Communication Education, 46,* 175–187.

Kahana, M. J., & Howard, M. W. (2005). Spacing and lag effects in free recall of pure lists. *Psychonomic Bulletin & Review, 12*(1). 159–164.

Sharp, H. Jr., & McClung, T. (1966). Effects of organization on the speaker's ethos. *Speech Monographs, 33,* 182ff.

Uncovering the Solace of Sleep

General Purpose: To inform

Specific Purpose: To inform my audience about the role of sleep in our everyday lives.

Thesis Statement: In order to understand the role of sleep in our daily lives, it is important to recognize the effects of sleep on health, typical sleep profiles of Americans, and factors that interfere with our ability to get enough sleep.

INTRODUCTION

I. **Attention Getter:** In 2001, the National Highway Traffic Safety Administration estimated that more than 100,000 automobile accidents are related to driver fatigue. In fact, 1,500 deaths and tens of thousands of injuries and disabilities are related to drowsy driving. This problem impacts drivers age 25 and younger more than any other age group. (National Highway Traffic Safety Administration, 2002)

II. **Credibility Statement:** After falling asleep at the wheel many times myself, I became curious about sleep's role in our day-to-day activities and would like to share some of the interesting information I have uncovered.

III. **Relating to the Audience:** As college students, we all know how precious time is and sleep is one of the first things we cut from our schedules.

IV. **Thesis Statement:** In order to understand the role of sleep in our daily lives, it is important to recognize the effects of sleep on health, typical sleep profiles of Americans, and factors that interfere with our ability to get enough sleep.

Transition: First, I'll discuss the effects of sleep on health.

BODY

I. Generally, sleep is necessary for our health.

    A. First, sleep is necessary for physical health.

        1. According to the 2001 Chicago Tribune article "Waking Up to the Danger of Sleep Deprivation" by Ronald Kotulak, when people do not get enough sleep their insulin has a harder time converting glucose from food into energy. (Kotulak, 2001)

           a. As a result, the body produces 2 to 3 times the normal amount of glucose, which is called insulin resistance.

           b. This puts a person at a much higher risk of getting diabetes and/or suffering from obesity.

169

2. The lack of sleep influences production of leptin, a hormone that tells the brain you are full or no longer hungry.
   a. The less you sleep, the less leptin is produced in your body.
   b. People who do not sleep enough may eat more because they do not feel full due to the lack of leptin, which can put them at risk for gaining weight.

B. Second, sleep is necessary for cognitive health.
   1. The lack of sleep influences levels of learning.
      a. A 2001 Chicago Tribune article by Ronald Kotulak cites an experiment done by Robert Stickgold of Harvard University showing a connection between sleep, learning, and retaining information. (Kotulak, 2001)
      b. The results indicate that the ability for people to learn and retain information is best if they had received an adequate amount of sleep.
   2. The lack of sleep also influences the structure of the brain.
      a. A study by Kwangwook Cho published in the June 2001 Nature Neuroscience concludes that sleep deprivation due to intense traveling and regular jet lag can change the structure of the brain. (Cho, 2001)
      b. Brain scans done in this research showed that part of the patients' brains, specifically the right temporal lobe, had shrunk due to the lack of sleep.

Transition: Now that you know the effects of sleep on our health, next I will discuss the typical sleep profiles of Americans.

II. The sleep profiles of Americans indicate that they do not get the recommended amount of sleep.
   A. According to the 2002 National Sleep Foundation brochure, "When You Can't Sleep: The ABCs of ZZZs," the majority of healthy adults need an average of eight hours of sleep per night. (National Sleep Foundation, 2002)
   B. In 2001, the National Sleep Foundation published a "Sleep in America Poll," an opinion poll involving telephone interviews with 1,004 adults that examines the sleep profiles of Americans. (National Sleep Foundation, 2001)
   C. The results of this poll indicate Americans' sleep profiles differ based on age, gender, region of residency, family status, and weight status.
      1. Age influences the sleep patterns of Americans.

      a.   18 to 29 year olds report getting an average of 7.1 hours of sleep on weekdays and 65% have driven while drowsy.

      b.   30 to 64 year olds report getting an average of 7.0 hours of sleep on weekdays and 51% have driven while drowsy.

2. Gender influences the sleep patterns of Americans.

      a.   Males get an average of 6.9 hours of sleep a night.

      b.   Females get an average of 7.1 hours of sleep a night.

3. Region of residency influences the sleep patterns of Americans.

      a.   Individuals from the Midwest get an average of 6.8 hours of sleep.

      b.   Individuals from the Northeast get an average of 7.1 hours of sleep.

      c.   Individuals from the West get an average of 7.2 hours of sleep.

4. Family status influences the sleep patterns of Americans.

      a.   Individuals married with children get an average of 6.7 hours of sleep.

      b.   Individuals married without children get an average of 7.2 hours of sleep.

      c.   Individuals single without children get an average of 7.1 hours of sleep.

5. Weight status influences the sleep patterns of Americans.

      a.   Individuals who are overweight get an average of 6.9 hours of sleep.

      b.   Individuals who are underweight get an average of 7.1 hours of sleep.

Transition: Now that you know the sleep profiles of Americans, finally I'll tell you about factors that interfere with our ability to get enough sleep.

III. According to the 2002 National Sleep Foundation brochure titled "When You Can't Sleep: The ABCs of ZZZs," there are various "sleep stealers" that make it difficult to get the recommended eight hours of sleep a night. (National Sleep Foundation, 2002)

  A. First, factors related to stress serve as sleep stealers.

    1. Stress is the number one cause of short-term sleeping difficulties.

    2. Stressful situations that trigger sleep problems include school or job pressures, family or marriage problems, and a serious illness or death in the family.

    3. In most cases, sleep problems disappear when the stressful situation disappears but if not managed correctly the problems may persist.

B. Second, lifestyle behaviors serve as sleep stealers.

1. Things that may interfere with a good night's sleep include drinking alcoholic beverages in the afternoon or evening, having an irregular morning and nighttime schedule, and doing mentally intense activities before or after getting into bed.

2. In a 2001 Sunday Times (London) article, Helen Kirwan-Taylor argues exercising near bedtime, eating spicy foods, and drinking carbonated or caffeine beverages anytime after 4:00 p.m. makes it difficult to fall asleep. (Kirwan-Taylor, 2001)

C. Finally, physical factors serve as sleep stealers.

1. Physical conditions that cause pain, backache, or discomfort, such as arthritis, make it hard to sleep comfortably.

2. Sleep apnea, a condition involving snoring and interrupted breathing, causes brief awakenings and excessive daytime sleepiness.

3. Disorders that cause involuntary limb movement interrupt normal sleep patterns, such as Restless Leg syndrome.

4. Women can experience physical factors that intrude on normal sleep patterns such as pregnancy, hormonal shifts, premenstrual syndrome (PMS), or menopause.

Transition: In closing, I have shared with you the important role sleep plays in our everyday lives.

CONCLUSION

I. Restate Thesis: Specifically, I have discussed the effects of sleep on health, typical sleep profiles of Americans, and factors that interfere with our ability to get enough sleep.

II. Closing Statement: Thousands of automobile deaths each year aren't "just random"; rather, they occur because we fail to recognize the power of a fundamental part of human life we almost never think about—the solace that is sleep.

REFERENCES

Cho, K. (2001, June). Chronic 'jet lag' produces temporal lobe atrophy and spatial cognitive deficits. *Nature Neuroscience*, 4, 567–568.

Kirwan-Taylor, H. (2001, May 13). Snooze control. *Sunday Times (London)*, p. A12.

Kotulak, R. (2001, June 12). Waking up to the danger of sleep deprivation. *Chicago Tribune*, p. A4.

National Highway Traffic Safety Administration. (2002). *Drowsy driving and automobile crashes* [Brochure]. Washington, DC.

National Sleep Foundation. (2001, January). *Sleep in America Poll.* Washington, DC.

National Sleep Foundation. (2002). *When you can't sleep: The ABCs of ZZZs* (2nd ed.) [Brochure]. Washington, DC.

SAMPLE SPEAKING OUTLINE

The following note cards provide a speaking outline for the introduction, conclusion, and main point one for the sample outline.

1

INTRO   **Make Eye Contact!!!!!!**

  I. 2001, NHTSA est. more than 100,000 auto, 1500 deaths, 10s of 1000s injuries, drivers 25 & ↓

  II. Falling asleep myself . . .

  III. Sleep first thing cut

  IV. Preview, effect on health /// sleep profiles /// factors that interfere

Transition: First, discuss effects of sleep on health

2

I. Sleep necessary for health

  A. First, physical health

    1. 2001 Chic Tribune—Kotulak
       Waking up Dangers of Sleep Depr.
       Insulin harder convert glucose

      a. 2 to 3 more glucose

      b. diabetes/obesity

    2. Production of leptin

      a. less sleep = less leptin

      b. eat more-gain weight

3

B. Second, cognitive health
   1. Levels of learning
      a. Previous Kotulak article Stickgold–Harvard–
         connect sleep, learning, retain info
      b. retain info if enough sleep
   2. Structure of Brain
      a. Cho 6/01 Nature Neuroscience Jet lag change
         structure brain
      b. scan show rite temporal lobe shrinkage

7

Transition: In closing share importance of sleep
CONCLUSION
   I. Specifically, effects on health//sleep profiles//factors that
      interfere
   II. 1000 accidents not random, rather occur fail to recognize
       fund part of life—solace of sleep

Good Hand Hygiene

General Purpose: To persuade

Specific Purpose: To persuade my audience to practice better hand hygiene.

Thesis: Practicing good hand hygiene and washing your hands regularly provides a simple solution to many health issues we face today. Today I am going to explain just how dirty we really are, why washing your hands can help you stay healthy, and the proper techniques to use when washing your hands.

INTRODUCTION

A. **Attention Getter:** According to Jill Max in her book, Germ Warfare In Public, the average American touches 300 surfaces every 30 minutes, picking up millions of germs and bacteria along the way.

B. **Relevance:** As we enter into the winter season, it seems that sickness and colds are inevitable during this time of year. You might feel like there is no way around your annual winter cold. However, I am going to provide you with some tips to keep you well this flu season.

C. **Credibility:** Since I have been at college, I have been getting one cold after another. Becoming frustrated with all these illnesses, I jumped on the Internet to see if there was anything I could do. I was surprised to learn that one of the most effective things we can do to prevent illness is something we do every day.

D. **Thesis:** Practicing good hand hygiene and washing your hands regularly provides a simple solution to many health issues we face today. Today I am going to explain just how dirty we really are, why washing your hands can help you stay healthy, and the proper techniques to use when washing your hands.

Transition: Now that you know what can solve our dilemma, I am going to give you the dirt on just how filthy our hands are at any given moment.

BODY

I. There are many dangerous, illness-causing germs people come in contact with every day.

A. First, I want to give you an idea of just how many germs you have on you when you begin the day.

1. Even at your cleanest moment in the day, the CDC estimates that you have between 2 million and 10 million bacteria just between the tip

of your fingers and your elbow on only one arm. (Centers for Disease Control and Prevention)

    2.   Now figure in the rest of your body's surface area, and you are talking about hundreds of millions of germs.

    3.   Millions of germs hide under watches and bracelets. (Mayo Clinic)

    4.   Under one ring alone, there could be as many germs as there are people in Europe. (Centers for Disease Control and Prevention)

B.   Now that you know roughly how many germs you face the world with each morning, the second thing you should know is where you pick up germs during the day.

    1.   We are all aware of the fact that there are germs in public places such as restrooms, offices, and restaurants.

    2.   What most of us are not aware of, however, is where the most harmful germs are hiding.

    3.   The most harmful germs we come into contact with on a daily basis are found on credit cards, gas nozzles, calculators, library books, computer keyboards, treadmill keypads, refrigerator handles, and even hand soap dispensers. (Purell)

C.   Thirdly, it is important to recognize that because of other people's poor hand hygiene, the number of germs each one of us comes into contact with each day multiplies by millions.

    1.   Up to one half of all men and one quarter of all women fail to wash their hands after going to the bathroom. (Centers for Disease Control and Prevention)

    2.   After using the restroom, the number of germs on your fingertips doubles. (Centers for Disease Control and Prevention)

    3.   This means if you double the number of germs any one person has come into contact with in a given day, that is what you are touching when you touch the door handle after them, or you shake their hand.

    4.   Now I am going to show you a little clip from a movie that is a perfect example of how we encounter germs every day and don't realize it. The facts presented are actually true.

Directional Transition: Now that you know the facts of just how dirty our everyday life is, I'm going to tell you how washing your hands can wash away your worries.

II.   Washing your hands is the simplest and the most effective way to protect yourself from our dirty world. (Mayo Clinic)

A.   Washing your hands and practicing good hand hygiene drastically lowers your risk of catching a serious illness. (Mayo Clinic, Clean)

1. Hand washing kills even the most harmful bacteria, including E Coli, Salmonella, Shigellosis, Hepatitis A, and several others. (Clean)

2. Researchers have proven that washing your hands thoroughly helps to stop the spreading of the common cold, the flu, and even more harmful viruses. (Mayo Clinic)

3. Here is an example: there are around 76 million food born illnesses each year in America, and 25% of these could be prevented by people simply washing their hands. (Hospitality, Mayo Clinic)

B. Experts at England's Queen Mary's School of Medicine conducted a study to find the most effective ways of preventing illnesses such as the flu, food poisoning, and the common cold, and hand washing was determined to be the most effective way to prevent illness, as this is how it works. (Vital Health, Max, Mayo Clinic)

1. Let's say someone with a cold sneezes into their hand and then gets on the City Bus, holds on to the bar for support, and then exits.

2. You get on, hold the bar and then scratch your eye, thereby exposing yourself to that person's germs, which increases your chance of catching their cold.

3. Washing your hands before scratching your eye would have killed most of those germs, reducing your chance of getting sick.

C. A study in Detroit showed that people who thoroughly wash their hands at least four times a day miss 24% less school or work days for respiratory illness and 51% less for upset stomachs than those who do not. (Vital Health)

1. Washing your hands has been proven to be the best way to avoid getting sick this winter.

2. You can protect yourself from millions of germs each day just by washing your hands more often.

Directional Transition: So you know now that you need to wash your hands more often, but if you do not do it the right way, it is not going to help.

III. It is estimated that 90% of all adults do not properly wash their hands, so let's look at the right way to do it. (Vital Health)

A. Proper hand washing techniques could be the difference between a healthy and an unhealthy winter.

1. First, you should spend at least 20 seconds washing your hands every time you wash them. (Max, Clean)

2. Secondly, most right-handed people wash their left hand better and vice versa, so make an effort to wash them evenly. (Max)

3. Thirdly, wash under your fingernails! This is where most germs hide. (Max)

4. Finally, when you turn off the faucet, use a paper towel because you just touched it with dirty hands when turning on the water. (Max)

B. There are also some simple ways to help avoid spreading germs to others.

   1. Keep hands moisturized because dry, cracked hands offer more spaces for bacteria to climb into, which also makes them harder to get rid of. (Vital Health)

   2. Dry your hands well, because damp hands transfer 1,000 times more germs than dry hands. (Vital Health)

Directional Transition: Now that you know the common mistakes we make, you can think about them the next time you go to wash your hands.

CONCLUSION

A. **Review of Thesis:** I have told you today how dirty we really are, why washing your hands can help, and common mistakes to avoid when washing your hands.

B. **Review Statement:** We live in a dirty world. Washing your hands often has proven to be the most effective way of reducing your risk of getting sick. Therefore, we need to wash our hands more often and more thoroughly.

C. **Clincher:** Thousands of people will avoid sickness this winter by washing their hands more often. Will you be one of them?

REFERENCES

Centers for Disease Control and Prevention Fact Book 2004. (2004). New York: Centers for Disease Control and Prevention.

Clean Hands First Defense Against Diseases. (2006, July 30). *The Pakistan Newswire* (Pakistan), n.p.

Hospitality Institute of Technology and Management. (2005, September). Food Poisoning. *Hospitality Institute Of Technology and Management*. Retrieved October 26, 2006, from http://www.hi-tm.com/ Documents2000/Hand-poster.html

Max, Jill. (2005). *Germ Warfare In Public*. New York: ScienCentral, Inc.

Mayo Clinic. (2005, December). Hand Washing: A Simple Way to Prevent Infection. *CNN.com*. Retrieved October 24, 2006, from http://www.cnn.com/HEALTH/ library/HQ/00407.html

Purell. (2006, May). 99 Places Where Germs are Likely to Lurk. *Purell*. Retrieved October 25, 2006, from http://www.purell.com/germs

Vital Health and Statistics. (2000). New York: National Center for Health Statistics.

Chapter 8

INFORMATIVE SPEAKING

CHAPTER OBJECTIVES

After reading this chapter, you should be able to:

- ☐ Explain the differences between informatory and explanatory presentations.

- ☐ Understand and explain the components of news presentations.

- ☐ Understand and explain the states of instructional presentations.

- ☐ Understand the strategies for using elucidating explanations.

- ☐ Understand the strategies for using quasi-scientific explanations.

- ☐ Understand the strategies for using transformative explanations.

In 1999, the Mars Polar Orbiter was deployed to Mars to collect information on the planet's climate and atmosphere. The orbiter was never able to collect this information, however; it disintegrated in the Martian atmosphere because of a communication error (Perlman, 1999). Lockheed engineers in Colorado transmitted the orbiter's final course and velocity to JPL Mission Control in Pasadena using the English term of pounds per second of force. Almost all space scientists and engineers use the metric system. Therefore, their computers used the metric term newtons, or grams per second of force, to send final course and velocity commands to the orbiter. This mistake caused the orbiter to fly too close to Mars and disintegrate. This small communication error cost $125 million (Rowan, 2003).

As you have seen from the previous example, our ability to explain information to an audience is extremely important. While students enrolled in this course readily see the benefits of persuasive speaking and look forward to those presentations all semester, they often overlook the importance of the informative presentation. Providing information to an audience, however, is one of the most important skills you can develop as an effective speaker. College graduates report that informational speaking is actually more common in their careers than is persuasive speaking (Johnson & Szczupakiewicz, 1987). The ability to share information effectively and increase audience understanding has extreme consequences. Just consider the example in the opening of this chapter. The failure to clarify a simple measurement devastated the entire mission.

While poor informative skills can be costly and dangerous, as you have just seen, there is a good deal of research on how to present information effectively so that our audiences can understand us and mistakes such as these can be avoided. This chapter will present some of the latest theories and research to help you excel at this important communicative skill. There are two types of informative speaking that we will address in this course. The first is called informatory and the second, explanatory. The remainder of this chapter discusses these two types of informative presentations, their differences, and strategies for using each effectively.

INFORMATIVE SPEAKING

Informative speaking is the process of enhancing the understanding of your audience in relation to some important term, object, event, process, etc. This can be achieved through instruction, explanation, description, demonstration, clarification, or correction. Informative presentations include speeches about objects, events, or persons. They include "how to" or instructional presentations. Presentations about concepts or complex processes, academic lectures, and even analyses of events are all considered informative presentations.

> " *Informative speaking is the process of enhancing the understanding of your audience in relation to some important term, object, event, process, etc.* "

TYPES OF INFORMATIVE SPEAKING

Kathy Rowan, a communication professor and researcher, has described two types of informative speaking. The first type is informatory speaking, while the second type is explanatory speaking.

Informatory speaking seeks to create awareness on the part of an audience regarding a specific issue. This type of speaking assumes that there is a need for new information on a topic for a specific audience. For example, we know that animals are being trained to help in the fight against terrorism. Dogs are used to detect bombs and other potentially hazardous situations. A student from a past semester took this same topic and put a spin on it using new information. He delivered a presentation informing his audience that bees are now being trained to detect bombs. He described the program and its components. This was a fascinating presentation. The topic was novel and almost every audience member was interested in hearing new developments related to detecting and, therefore, preventing terrorism.

Explanatory speaking, on the other hand, takes the presentation a step further. This type of speaking assumes that an audience has some knowledge of the topic but lacks sufficient understanding of the process. Therefore, the goal of this type of presentation is to deepen an audience's understanding of a specific issue (Rowan, 2003). For example, a former student in this course gave an explanatory presentation explaining how banks process our checks. While many of us have some awareness of this process, we don't know all the details and specifics that occur. Another student explained the process the FDA uses to approve drugs. Each of these presentations went beyond presenting new information and actually deepened our level of understanding of the phenomena under question. Now that you know the difference between informatory and explanatory speaking, let's examine each in more detail.

INFORMATORY PRESENTATIONS

There are basically two types of informatory presentations: news and instructional. Each of these presentations enhances an audience's awareness of a topic. Informatory presentations are primarily delivered when an audience is interested in the latest information on a particular issue (news), or desires the necessary steps to complete a task (instructions).

NEWS PRESENTATIONS

News presentations present interesting information to an audience on a new topic or a topic that they are already familiar with and interested in. They can be presentations about objects, events, or even people. The goal of a news presentation is to create awareness of the latest information on a topic. The speaker may provide an update on some topic, present a progress report, describe an unpredictable recent event, or share information that is completely new to an audience.

In this photo the teacher is presenting information to her students on a field trip. It is a good example of an informatory presentation.

A key component in news presentations is that the information presented needs to be *relevant* to the audience. It would be senseless to deliver a presentation on developments in the technology used in treating diabetes when no one in the audience had the disease or any connection to the disease. While they might find the topic interesting, the topic has little relevance to this audience and their everyday lives.

Sometimes in a news presentation, you really have to emphasize the relevancy for your audience. Informative presentations can sometimes be a bit pedestrian for both the speaker and the audience. Just think about some of the topics you would need to address in a presentation as a manager in an organization. Imagine having to explain to your employees the details of the new policies regarding e-mail privacy. On the face of it, this topic may not be very exciting. This is where the relevance statement becomes particularly important (see Chapter 4). By explaining why the information is valuable and important to your employees, you can increase their motivation to listen to the information.

According to research in this area, news presentations should have the following components: surprise value, factuality, and comprehensiveness (Rowan, 2003). ***Surprise value*** is the amount of novel or new information relative to the information already known by the audience. Since the goal of the presentation is to make your audience aware of "news" in this area, most of the information you present should be new to your audience. You want to spend very little time describing elements of the topic that the audience is already aware of—spend your time on the new information.

Factuality is the extent to which the material presented in the speech actually corresponds to the research in this area. Here, it is important that you verify your information through several different sources and make sure that you report this information accurately to your audience. As an ethical speaker, it is your responsibility to make sure your information is true and presented in a straightforward manner.

Comprehensiveness simply refers to the thoroughness or completeness of the information in your presentation. As an ethical speaker, you want to ensure that you adequately address the information in your presentation. You will need to consider your time constraints and may only be able to address a small portion of the latest developments thoroughly. The key here is to make sure that you present enough detail on the topic so that your audience has adequate information on which to base decisions regarding the material in your presentation.

While all three components (surprise value, factuality, and comprehensiveness) are extremely important to an effective news presentation, the real motivation for audience involvement comes from the surprise value. So you really want to highlight this aspect of the presentation. Since this is what will be most captivating for your audience, you don't want to save the surprise value or "news" for the end of the presentation. Present this information early so you can get your audience involved right away.

In order to plan an effective news presentation, there are three major skills you should keep in mind. First, you must have a clear understanding of your audience and what types of information are likely to both surprise and be relevant to your audience. Second, you must also be a good researcher and have the skills necessary to verify the factuality of that information. Finally, you must present the information in such a way as to provide your audience with a contextual frame with which to interpret the information (Rowan, 2003). What this means is that you have to present the big picture for your audience. For example, suppose you deliver new information on your organization's e-mail privacy policy. You must contextualize this new information for your audience. In other words, what does this information mean to your audience? Should they manage their e-mail differently? Should they limit all personal e-mails? Should e-mail only be used for specific types of communication within the organization? Answering these questions can help ensure you achieve the goals of a news presentation.

Emily, a former student in this class, presented a news presentation on the new services provided by Purdue's Center for Career Opportunities (CCO). Here is an abbreviated version of her outline.

Emily uses a compelling statistic or fact to get our attention and highlight the effectiveness of the CCO.	The 2003 edition of Kaplan's "The Unofficial, Unbiased Insider's Guide to the 320 Most Interesting Colleges" listed Purdue as having one of the best career placement services, says a 2002 Purdue news release.
Here, she establishes relevance for her student audience by explaining that there are services they can use right now even if they aren't looking for a job. These services will help prepare them for a job when they begin their job search. So, it is important they that learn what some of these are.	As current students, you have access to these phenomenal services right now. Although you may not be currently searching for a job, the Center for Career Opportunities, or CCO, offers many programs that you can take advantage of now. These services will prepare you for the workforce so that you will be more marketable when that time comes.
Here Emily states her credibility. She not only uses the services but has also worked at the CCO.	I have used many of the services myself and have even served as a student ambassador at the CCO.
Emily states her thesis and previews her main points in this step.	While the CCO provides many valuable services for students, there are two new services: talk with a pro and a state-of-the-art job listing service that I think you will want to take advantage of.
She uses a transition to indicate to the audience that she is moving to the first main point.	Let's begin with Talk with a Pro.
In main point one Emily describes the talk with a pro service. This is novel information and therefore has surprise value.	I. Talk with a Pro is a new service implemented by the CCO to help students learn about different careers. A. It is staffed with volunteer alumni and non-alumni who represent a variety of careers across the country. B. The volunteers provide information to students about their careers, the industry, and market conditions.

Emily uses a directional transition to indicate that we are leaving one main point and moving to the second.

The second main point describes the new job posting service. Again, the novel information has surprise value.

Through the use of a transition, Emily indicates to her audience that she is moving to the conclusion of her presentation.

She restates her thesis.

She ends with a clincher by referring back to her attention getter.

Talk with a Pro can give you a perspective on a career, but if you are looking for a job, you need to visit the new job listing service.

II. The new job posting system helps students find jobs and internships in a struggling economy, says director Tim Luzader.
   A. The Web-based service allows employers to reduce recruiting costs by posting jobs free of charge.
   B. Students and potential employers can exchange information over the Internet in a secure environment, which reduces the cost of the selection process.

In closing, I hope you will find these two additional resources useful.

The CCO provides many wonderful opportunities. Talk with a Pro and the new job listing service are just two of them.

This commitment to excellence and meeting student needs is what makes our CCO one of the best in the nation.

INSTRUCTIONAL PRESENTATIONS

Instructional presentations are concerned with giving audiences directions on performing a particular task. Sometimes these types of presentations are called "how to" presentations, or demonstration presentations. In this type of presentation, your goal is to move an audience from their current level of knowledge (wanting to build a PC) to a desired state of knowledge (having the ability to build a PC).

> Instructional presentations are concerned with giving audiences directions on performing a particular task. Sometimes these types of presentations are called "how to" presentations.

According to the research on instructional or demonstration presentations, there are four states that must be addressed in an effective "how to" presentation (Farkas, 1999). First, you must explain to your audience the ***desired state***. What is the goal you are hoping they will be able to accomplish? Perhaps it is registering for classes online. In this example, you must explain to your audience exactly what you want them to be able to achieve at the end of your presentation. Secondly, you must address any ***prerequisite states***. What do they need to have or need to have completed so that they can achieve this desired goal? Continuing with our example, if you are explaining to your audience how to register for classes online, you should explain all of the things necessary to begin that process. First, they need to know their career account ID and password. They must have paid all fees and currently have a zero balance in their university account. And finally, they will need to have met with their counselor to discuss their degree plan and received their special registration code.

Once all the prerequisites have been explained, you can begin to address the process of registering online. This is called the ***interim state***. The interim state is comprised of all the steps you move through as you proceed toward your goal. In our example, these steps may include "Locate a computer with Internet access and locate a Web browser (such as Internet Explorer). Type the following URL: http://purdue.registrar.edu." These directions would continue until you had walked your audience through each of the steps necessary to get enrolled electronically.

The final state that must be addressed is ***unwanted states***. These are things you want the audience to avoid. These would include errors that could impede their ability to effectively register online. For example, you will notice on the URL used to locate the registration site that there is no "www." You might want to point this out to your audience. Many are accustomed to supplying this information when typing in a Web address in their browser. Simply telling them that they should type in the address without the "www" should help them avoid ending up at the wrong Web site. By including each of these four states, you have a better chance of reaching your audience and ensuring they are able to perform the task you are trying to explain.

> **FOUR STATES OF EFFECTIVE INSTRUCTIONAL PRESENTATIONS**
> - Describe the desired state
> - Describe prerequisite states
> - Describe the interim state
> - Describe the unwanted states

So how should you organize this type of presentation? Historically, we have told students to use a chronological or spatial pattern. However, simply placing your material in these types of patterns overlooks some of the important states that we have just discussed. While you may be able to effectively use one of these two patterns, you should examine the complexity of the states you need to address and choose a pattern that will best address your informational needs.

EXPLANATORY PRESENTATIONS

The focus of this section of the chapter is on developing strategies for making explanatory presentations. As previously discussed, an explanatory presentation is a type of informative speaking that deepens the audience's understanding. The explanatory presentation requires that you go beyond simply making the audience aware of a particular phenomenon and actually create understanding on the part of your audience. For example, a speech on how to fax a document creates awareness, whereas, a speech on how that fax machine works increases an audience's understanding (Rowan, 1990). For help choosing a topic for this assignment, ask yourself, "Why?" or "What does that mean?" Answers to these questions make good challenging or explanatory topics.

Explanatory presentations introduce unique problems for the speaker. Not only must you deal with the issues of organization and support, but they also present special challenges in terms of audience analysis. As mentioned in other chapters in this book, all good presentations require thorough audience analysis. However, when faced with presenting difficult information, we must step back and analyze our audience in different ways. We must ask the following questions:

- What type of educational background does this particular audience bring to this situation that may enhance or impede their ability to process the material?
- What obstacles (e.g., previously held ideas) may interfere with this audience's ability to process this information?
- What are the challenges inherent in this information that might make it difficult for an audience to understand (e.g., vocabulary, amount of material, etc.)?

In order to be an effective speaker in this complex situation, you must have a thorough understanding of just what it is about the information you are presenting that may make it difficult for an audience to understand it. The goal for you when presenting an explanation is to anticipate what difficulties it may present for your audience and then to design a presentation that overcomes those obstacles. By answering these questions, you have better insight into the needs of your audience.

There are several obstacles that may interfere with an audience's ability to understand a difficult presentation. These difficulties are inherent in the material itself. Audiences experience difficulty understanding ideas or topics for three reasons:

1. Difficulty Understanding the Use of a Concept or Term

For example, your audience may be unfamiliar with the idea of nanotechnology. What does this concept mean, and how is it used? Other problems in understanding the use of a concept or term may surround the misuse of terminology. For example, many people outside of the world of information technology do not understand the difference between a server, an ISP, and the Internet. We often misuse these terms to describe our activities on the computer.

2. Difficulty Understanding a Phenomenon, Structure, or Process

Some presentations are difficult to understand because they describe processes or structures that are hard for an audience to envision. Either the amount of the material is difficult to process, or the relationship between elements in the presentation is hard for the audience to see. For example, audiences may have difficulty understanding how food is genetically engineered. This is a complicated process with many facets. Picturing and following all of the components in this process is difficult for an audience with limited understanding of genetic engineering. Therefore, laying this presentation out in such a way that the audience can follow and grasp the essential parts in the process is imperative.

3. Difficulty Understanding Particular Phenomena That Are Hard to Believe

Sometimes information is hard to understand because the ideas surrounding the information are counterintuitive to our experiences. Audiences may have trouble understanding that the Earth is weightless or how forest fires could be good for a forest (Rowan, 1992). Each of these three difficulties or obstacles has unique strategies that can help illuminate your ideas for an audience. The remaining portion of this chapter will discuss in more detail each of the three difficulties followed by a discussion of the specific strategies that will help increase audience understanding.

DIFFICULTY UNDERSTANDING THE USE OF A CONCEPT OR TERM

Sometimes the difficulty in understanding information comes in understanding the concepts or the definitions that surround a particular phenomenon. We often misuse certain terminology in ways that make it difficult for us to understand larger issues. For example, imagine that you are planning to present material concerning schizophrenia, a type of mental illness. Schizophrenia is a very complex disease of the brain that is misunderstood by a large majority of society. After conducting your research, you have decided that your audience's primary obstacle in understanding your presentation will surround their ideas about what schizophrenia is and what it is not. Now that you understand what obstacle your audience may face in thoroughly understanding your topic, you can plan to overcome this hurdle.

Research has shown that in order for audiences to understand content in which concepts or definitions may be difficult, it is best to use an ***elucidating explanation***. Elucidating explanations simply explain a concept's meaning or use. It is helpful if you can explain to the audience what is essential in the definition and what is not essential. Let's consider the example of schizophrenia. Many people think individuals suffering from schizophrenia are dangerous, psychotic individuals (NIMH, 2001). In fact, the media perpetuates images of violent and dangerous serial killers suffering from schizophrenia. Schizophrenia, however, is defined as a brain disorder accompanied by some or all of the following symptoms: hallucinations, delusions, thought disorder, altered sense of self, depression, lack of motivation, and social withdrawal (Health Canada, 2001). So as you can see, violence and aggression are not essential elements of the definition. Although in very rare circumstances a person with schizophrenia may become violent, it is more common for the person to withdraw socially. Therefore, being violent and dangerous are nonessential elements of schizophrenia.

When making a presentation that uses the elucidating explanation, it is best to follow these steps.

Step One: **Provide a Definition of the Concept**

Provide the audience with a definition that lists all of the essential characteristics and essential features of the definition. Let's examine the following example of dietary fiber. "The term dietary fiber refers to the parts of plants that pass through the human stomach and small intestine undigested—ranging from the brittle husks of whole wheat, to the stringy pods of green beans, to the gummy flesh of barley grains" (Murray, M., 1990, p. 78). This definition becomes very clear for the audience. We know exactly that dietary fiber is the part of a plant that passes through the stomach undigested. The essential characteristics of the definition are made clear.

Sometimes concepts have associated meanings that make truly understanding the definition difficult. For example, members of an audience often consider radiation dangerous. However, all radiation is not harmful. Radiation is simply the process of emitting radiant energy in the form of waves or particles. The term radiation refers to the electromagnetic radiation that includes radio waves, X-rays and even the energy from sunlight, lightbulbs and candles. By addressing the associated meaning—dangerous—along with providing a definition, the audience gets a much better understanding of the concept radiation (Rowan, 1990).

Step Two: **Provide Examples**

While it may seem obvious to provide an example of the definition you are presenting, research on explaining information suggests that you should provide several examples. Continuing with the example on fiber, the speaker should also provide us with the following examples that further illuminate the definition: apples, carrots, oranges, bran, oats, whole wheat, peas, kidney beans, and lentils are all examples of dietary fiber.

Step Three: **Provide Nonexamples**

Your audience's understanding will be further enhanced by using varied examples and nonexamples of the concepts you are explaining. Often your audience may have difficulty deciding what examples fit the definition of your concept. By presenting examples and commonly held nonexamples, you can enhance understanding. Nonexamples resemble the concept by sharing some aspects of the criteria but fall short of having all of the criteria. By presenting some of these nonexamples to the audience, they will clearly understand the difference. Continuing with the fiber example, you may explain the following nonexample, "It is a common belief that tough meat is also a good source of dietary fiber. However, as previously explained in our definition, animal protein is not a source of fiber because only plant materials are classified as fiber."

Sometimes the entire goal of your presentation is to explain the definition of a concept or term. If this is the case, use a topical organizational pattern utilizing all three of the steps. For example, if the entire goal of your presentation is to explain to your audience exactly what is and what is not considered schizophrenia, you would simply use a topical pattern.

Other times, explaining a concept or definition may be a smaller part of a larger topic or purpose. Imagine that you have been asked to address your neighborhood concerning information on a halfway house

> **ELUCIDATING EXPLANATIONS**
> ◉ Provide definition of the concept
> ◉ Provide examples
> ◉ Provide nonexamples

being planned for your community. This program will provide transitional housing for individuals who have schizophrenia and are learning to live on their own. As you can see, understanding the disease itself is a smaller part of the overall goal. If this is the case, simply use the appropriate organizational pattern for your material and weave the three steps for elucidating explanations in at the appropriate time.

UNDERSTANDING COMPLEX STRUCTURES OR PROCESSES

Often, what makes a particular topic difficult is the structure or the processes inherent in the topic. It is, therefore, difficult for an audience to picture the phenomenon in question. For example, individuals have difficulty picturing genetic mutation, understanding how global positioning systems know where we are, how bar codes are assigned to products, or even how the state's ISTEP testing works. In each of these examples, the audience struggles to envision the processes or structures that accompany these processes. Complex structures or processes can best be explained using *quasi-scientific explanations*. Effective quasi-scientific explanations have two important characteristics. First, they help audiences attune to important features of the message. Secondly, they help organize the information so that audiences see relationships in the material. There are some simple devices you can use to achieve solid quasi-scientific explanations: organizing analogies, visual aids, repetition, and transitions.

> *There are some simple devices you can use to achieve solid quasi-scientific explanations: organizing analogies, visual aids, repetition, and transitions.*

The first tool is an analogy or metaphor (Rowan, 2003; Sullivan & Smith, 2006). It is one of the best ways to organize the information for your audience. Organizing analogies take your material and relate it to something with which the audience is already familiar. Ongoing research programs in various disciplines from science to marketing have indicated that individuals understand unfamiliar concepts better when the material is presented through the use of an analogy (Thagard, 1992).

Here is an example that recently appeared in a *Popular Science* magazine article that explained how viruses such as smallpox and Ebola are filtered from blood.

> Infected blood flows into the Hemopurifier through a tube extending from one artery. **The toxin filters work like a colander, allowing small viruses through but not large red and white blood cells.** The filter, which is made from biocompatible plastic called polysulfone, is coated with special plant-derived antibodies that hold fast to the pathogens, ensuring that they don't reenter the bloodstream (p. 37).

This speaker uses a diagram to illustrate the dance steps to his audience in the quasi-scientific explanation.

Members of the audience are familiar with the workings of a colander. The comparison of the Hemopurifier to this simple kitchen gadget makes the process much more clear to your audience.

Another example of an organizing analogy was used by a former student in this course and explained the way the working memory operates by comparing it to a computer. He continued using this analogy throughout his entire presentation. Because his audience was familiar with the workings of a computer, the analogy made the explanation of the process more clear. One thing to remember with analogies or metaphors is to tailor the comparison to your own audience. If your audience isn't very familiar with beekeeping, using this analogy to explain a concept won't be very effective (Sullivan & Smith, 2006). Make sure the analogies you use will resonate with your audience members.

Diagramming the process for your audience is the second tool that you will find useful. Diagrams, charts, and visual representations aid audiences in processing this information. Visual aids become particularly important with quasi-scientific explanations and are absolutely necessary. Whether the difficulty results from the amount of information or the relationship between the information, visual representations help the audience organize the material and see relationships.

Repetition is the third important device in a quasi-scientific explanation. As explained throughout this text, audiences do not have the luxury of going back to hear what you said previously like they do when reading a text. So, remind them of what you told them. They will appreciate it, and it increases the likelihood that your explanation will be effective and that it will be retained by your audience.

The final device is the transition. Transitions are essential in quasi-scientific explanations. Although they are important in any presentation (see Chapter 5), quasi-scientific presentations

QUASI-SCIENTIFIC EXPLANATIONS

◉ Relate the material to something the audience already understands
◉ Use visual aids
◉ Use repetition
◉ Use numerous transitions

will require you to use them more frequently. Directional transitions are the tools
that link ideas and concepts together for
your audience. Signposts help your audience focus on the elements that are most
important to the presentation. Internal
reviews and previews help with repetition.
All four types of transitions should be utilized in a quasi-scientific presentation.

SPEAKER TIP:

Jay Fehnel
Vice President
Entertainment Products

**Clear organization of a complex topic
isn't just important, it's mandatory. If
you think your audience may not understand a concept, try to find an analogy
that will help.**

Research shows that when the types of
devices just discussed (organizing analogies, diagrams, transitions, and repetition)
are used, audiences are better able to envision the processes discussed, and their
problem-solving abilities regarding the material are improved
(Rowan, 1992). All four of these strategies are necessary in an effective
quasi-scientific presentation.

Organization of quasi-scientific presentations can take any form.
Problem-solution, cause-effect, topical, spatial and chronological are
all equally viable options. The important thing to remember is to
choose the right pattern for your information and employ the four
devices previously discussed.

HARD TO BELIEVE PHENOMENA

Occasionally, a topic is difficult for an audience to understand
because the theories or ideas that encompass that topic are hard for
an audience to believe. The difficulty with the material isn't related to
any particular term, or a complex collection of information, but rather
the idea itself is counterintuitive to a particular audience.

People develop lay theories around events and experiences that
are familiar to them. They do not develop lay theories around phenomena that do not hold personal importance. Thus, people do not
hold lay theories about new findings regarding nanotechnology or
mathematical Knot Theory. They do hold lay theories about house-
hold safety, disease management, and nutrition (Rowan, 2003).

Lay audiences struggle to understand
how the Earth could be weightless, or why
getting a chill doesn't cause a cold. With each
of these ideas, we have developed lay theories that we use to explain our world. Some
of these theories are passed down from generation to generation, so they are deeply
ingrained. In many cases, these lay theories
are wrong. In fact, these nonscientific or lay

TRANSFORMATIVE EXPLANATIONS

⊚ State the lay theory
⊚ Acknowledge the reasonableness of
the lay theory
⊚ Show limitations with the lay theory
⊚ Explain the scientific theory or
positions

theories are the source of our confusion and often lead to dangerous consequences. If you believe the material you are presenting to your audience is hard to understand due to some preconceived notion or lay theory the audience holds, you will want to use a ***transformative explanation***.

An effective transformative explanation contains four elements. First, the explanation should contain a statement of the lay theory to which the audience currently subscribes. Secondly, the strengths or reasonableness of the lay theory are acknowledged in the explanation. Thirdly, transformative presentations create dissatisfaction with the current lay theory by explaining its weaknesses. Finally, the scientific explanation is presented, and a justification is provided as to why it better explains the phenomenon under question. Each of these steps is further explained along with an illustrative example about hypothermia (Rowan, 2003).

Step One: **State the Lay Theory**

At this step, present the lay theory that the audience holds or currently believes to be true. Here is an example, "Usually, we think of hypothermia as something that happens to people outdoors in extremely cold temperatures." The speaker simply states what the audience currently believes regarding hypothermia.

Step Two: **Acknowledge the Reasonableness of the Lay View**

At this step, you want to show that the current view does have some merit for explaining the current situation. You don't want to offend your audience by attacking their current beliefs. So, at this step, explain why their current views are plausible. Continuing with our hypothermia example, one might say, "Sometimes this is true. However, hypothermia is defined as a sudden loss of the core temperature of your body to below 95°F or 96°F (National Institute on Aging, 2005). This is just a two-degree drop in temperature." Here the speaker acknowledges that yes, normally, things must be very cold, but sometimes this may not be the case.

Step Three: **Show Dissatisfaction with the Current View**

Here you want to show them what is wrong with their current view. For example, you might state, "Did you know that some older adults have had a dangerous drop in body temperature while sitting inside their own homes? As people age, they may lose their ability to keep themselves warm in the cold, but even a young healthy individual can suffer hypothermia in temperatures as warm as 60°F. Bill Wately, an experienced hiker, took off for a run in the foothills of Southern California. He left wearing a T-shirt and shorts due to the 65°F day. After about an hour, a group of hikers found Bill sitting down along the trail. His complexion was pale and he was complaining of being dizzy. They called for medical assistance only to learn that Bill was suffering from hypothermia."

These two examples have demonstrated that people can get hypothermia inside of their homes and in temperatures as high as 60°F. Problems with the nonscientific or lay view have been pointed out to the audience.

Step Four: **Explain the Scientific Theory or Position**

In step four you must lay out the true explanation for the audience and provide them with the evidence that will help them accept the orthodox notion. Continuing with the example, "According to health officials, heavy exertion (such as running), wet clothes, and wind exposure can easily lead to hypothermia, even in 60°F

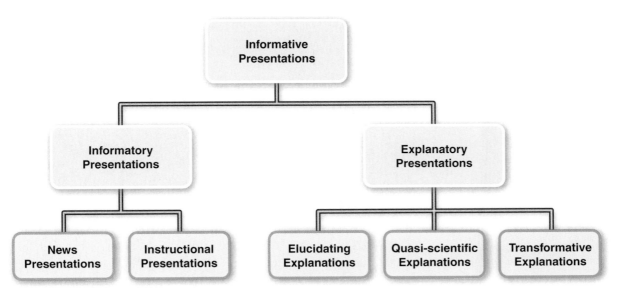

(Adapted from Rowan, 1992)

weather, in a healthy person. Body temperature in mammals is maintained by both the heat energy individuals generate within their bodies and the environmental conditions they experience. Wind and wetness lead to heat loss." Here you have explained why individuals can get hypothermia even in moderate temperatures. By providing your audience with this information, you may have prevented them from experiencing this condition because of their erroneously held beliefs.

One important factor related to transformative explanations is that the steps do not have to be presented in order within your presentation. As long as all four steps are present and adequate, your presentation will be effective.

CONCLUSION

Informative speaking is a vital skill for you to develop. As this chapter has demonstrated, informative speaking is just as important, and can be as challenging for the speaker, as persuasive speaking is. Informative speaking consists of both informatory speaking and explanatory speaking. Each of these two types of presentations contains its own set of challenges and recommendations for overcoming those challenges.

KEY TERMS

Comprehensiveness

Desired state

Elucidating explanation

Explanatory speaking

Factuality

Informative speaking

Informatory speaking

Instructional presentations

Interim state

News presentations

Prerequisite states

Quasi-scientific explanation

Relevant

Surprise value

Transformative explanation

Unwanted states

EXERCISES

1. Presenting an explanatory presentation that includes material your audience might find hard to believe due to some preconceived notion or lay theory will require you to use a transformative explanation. For this activity, pick one of the following common misconceptions. Then, construct a simple transformative explanation that states the lay theory, acknowledges the reasonableness of the lay view, shows what is incorrect about the lay theory, and then provides the audience with the evidence that will help them accept the correct view.

   • Eating turkey makes people sleepy
   • Eating celery results in negative calories
   • Drinking alcohol in cold weather warms you up
   • Using your fireplace in winter will help warm your house and thus lower heating bills
   • You will get sick if you go out in the cold with wet hair
   • If you cut a worm in half, each half will grow back into a complete worm

2. One of the most important elements in an informative news presentation is the "surprise value." This is the amount of novel or new information relative to the information already known by the audience. For this activity, scan the various news articles on any news site (Yahoo news, Google news, CNN). Pick three articles that contain novel or new information

about an existing situation (technology, health issue, political issue, education, etc.) and prepare a short presentation that highlights the new information.

3. During an instructional presentation, the speaker is concerned with giving audiences directions on performing a particular task. To practice this skill, pick one of the following situations. Prepare a short instructional presentation, keeping in mind the audience's knowledge of the topic and the four states that must be addressed in order for your presentation to be successful.

- Show a new driver how to parallel park
- Show a person who drives an automatic how to drive a car with a manual transmission
- Show a 4-year-old how to tie a shoe
- Instruct novices on CPR
- Instruct novices on the Heimlich maneuver
- Instruct someone unfamiliar with downloading music how to download a song at iTunes
- Show a novice how to tie a tie
- Instruct a novice on how to use AOL's instant messenger
- Instruct your grandmother on how to program a DVD recorder

REFERENCES

Farkas, D. K. (1999). The logic and rhetorical construction of procedural discourse. *Technical Communication, 46*(1), 42–54.

Johnson, J. R. & Szczupakiewicz, N. (1987). The public speaking course: Is it preparing students with work-related public speaking skills? *Communication Education, 36,* 131–137.

Kohn, D. (2006, April). The blood cleaner. *Popular Science*, 36–37.

Murray, M. (1990). Confused about fiber? *Reader's Digest,* 76.

National Institute of Mental Health (April, 2006). Schizophrenia. Retrieved April 4, 2006, from http://www.nimh.nih.gov/healthinformation/schizophreniamenu.cfm.

National Institute on Aging (December, 2005). Hypothermia: A cold weather hazard. Retrieved March 27, 2005, from http://www.niapublications.org/agepages/hypother.asp

Health Canada (1991). Schizophrenia: A handbook for families. Retrieved April 4, 2006, from http://www.phac-aspc.gc.ca/mh-sm/mentalhealth/pubs/schizophrenia/index.html.

Perlman, D. (1999, Oct. 1). Simple error doomed Mars Polar Orbiter: Computer confused pounds, grams when determining its course. San Francisco Chronicle, p. 1.

Rowan, K. E. (1990). The speech to explain difficult ideas. *Speech Communication Teacher, 4,* 69–71.

Rowan, K. E. (1992). Strategies for enhancing the comprehension of science. In B. V. Lewenstein (ed.) *When science meets the public* (pp. 131–143). Washington, D.C. American Association for the Advancement of Science.

Rowan, K. (2003). Informing and explaining skills: Theory and research on informative communication. *The handbook of communication and social interaction skills* (eds.) J. Greene & B. Burleson, Mahwah, NJ: Erlbaum.

Sullivan, C. & Smith, C. M. (2006). 5 TIPS for writing popular science. *Writer*, 119, 23-25.

Thagard, P. (1992). Analogy, explanation, and education. *Journal of Research in Science Teaching, 29*, 537-544.

Chapter 9

THE PERSUASIVE PROCESS

CHAPTER OBJECTIVES

After reading this chapter, you should be able to:

- ▣ Explain the differences between informative and persuasive speaking.

- ▣ Explain persuasion as a process and its implications for delivering a presentation.

- ▣ Clarify the differences between beliefs, attitudes, and behaviors.

- ▣ Differentiate between the different types of persuasive speaking.

- ▣ Understand and apply principles of the Elaboration Likelihood Model.

- ▣ Understand and apply principles of Social Judgment Theory.

*E*ach day we deliver numerous persuasive messages to our friends, family, and acquaintances. We may try to convince friends to go to the movie we want to see or eat at our favorite restaurant. We may try to convince a professor to give the class an extension on the class project. We usually have to convince a boss of the need for time off to study for an exam or to travel out of town.

All of us engage in numerous persuasive attempts like those above each and every day. Some of these attempts at persuasion are successful, and some don't turn out as well as we might have liked. Persuasion is one of the most important skills you can develop as a communicator. To help ensure success in this arena, it is imperative that you have a firm understanding of the persuasive process and its underlying principles. Persuasion, however, is a difficult task. When crafting a persuasive message, there are many things to consider and employ. This chapter is designed to lay out some of the basic issues of the persuasion process so that this task may seem a bit more manageable.

 ## DIFFERENCES BETWEEN INFORMATIVE AND PERSUASIVE PRESENTATIONS

Before we discuss persuasive strategies and theories, it is important that you understand the differences between informative and persuasive speaking. This will enable you to choose the best set of strategies for your speaking situation.

PERSUASIVE SPEAKING ASKS THE AUDIENCE TO CHOOSE BETWEEN TWO OR MORE ALTERNATIVES

As was mentioned earlier in the text, in an informative speech, a speaker acts as a teacher. As a teacher, a presenter simply explains a particular point of view or presents information on a topic. In persuasive speaking, the task becomes more complex. In addition to illuminating the topic, the presenter must also act as a leader. You are asking your audience to do more than just learn and understand issues on a specific topic; you are also asking them to adopt a position on the issue. For example, there isn't much controversy on a speech about the history of reproductive rights in the U.S. However, a speech advocating human cloning as a choice for reproduction is highly volatile. In this example, a persuasive speaker's primary goal is to convince the audience to agree with his or her position.

Notice how the speaker is trying to identify with his audience in this persuasive presentation by dressing down and wearing jeans. In this way, he is hoping that his audience feels similar to him and hopefully his ideas.

PERSUASIVE SPEAKING DEMANDS MORE THOROUGH AUDIENCE ANALYSIS

Because persuasion relies so much on attitudes, beliefs, and behaviors, it is imperative that a persuasive speaker know as much about how a particular audience feels about an issue as possible. If you are a sales representative for Microsoft pitching your proposal on incorporating a new computing system into an organization, you need to know what types of attitudes and beliefs the organization holds about Microsoft prior to the presentation. If the company had invested substantial time and money in a competitor's products, then the presentation should have a different focus than if it had experience with Microsoft products. This might further be complicated by how positive or negative those experiences had been. Persuasive speakers simply must know their audience well and prepare their presentations accordingly.

PERSUASIVE SPEAKING MAKES MORE DEMANDS OF AN AUDIENCE

Whereas informative presentations ask audiences to understand something, persuasive presentations go a step further. The persuasive speech asks audiences to do or change something as a function of that understanding. This is more difficult. People are often skeptical and resistant to change. They often do not see reasons to change their behavior or beliefs. Because of this, they have to process your information more carefully, evaluating the arguments and appeals in your message against the information and beliefs they hold. When it becomes apparent that your goal is to change their beliefs, they will need to take more time than otherwise evaluating your message.

PERSUASIVE SPEAKING HAS A HIGHER ETHICAL THRESHOLD

When asking the audience to change a behavior or to support a particular position, you are assuming an important responsibility. If you encourage your audience to vote for a particular candidate for student government, you must really know that this candidate will be the best person for the job. Another part of your responsibility is to ensure that your supporting evidence is of the highest quality. Are your experts qualified? Are your statistics up to date? Have you verified your information in more than just one source? Asking your audiences to make changes or commitments based on questionable evidence is unethical. As an ethical speaker, it is your responsibility to ensure that the appeals you make are reasonable and in the best interest of your audience.

Now that you have a firm grasp of the characteristics of persuasive speaking, let's examine the process of persuasion and how you can apply it to your presentation.

WHAT IS PERSUASION?

> *Persuasion can be defined as the process of changing, creating, or reinforcing an attitude, belief, or behavior.*

In order to be successful at persuasive speaking, it is important to examine the definition of persuasion itself. For the purposes in this course, ***persuasion*** can be defined as the process of changing, creating, or reinforcing an attitude, belief, or behavior.

THE PROCESS OF PERSUASION

One of the most important aspects of this definition is that persuasion is a process (Miller, 1972). People are rarely persuaded in one shot. It usually takes multiple messages and multiple exposures to a message in order to persuade a particular audience. The following example will illuminate this feature of the definition.

Imagine that you are a sales representative making a pitch to an important client. A sales rep rarely has only one chance at persuading the client. Usually, your company will make multiple presentations, send backup documents, and engage in multiple conversations with key players within that organization before a decision is reached. Each of these communication efforts with the client is a persuasive attempt. While we will focus on the persuasive presentation itself, it is important for you as a speaker to recognize that this presentation is just one of many tools you or your organization will be using to persuade the client.

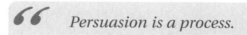

Persuasion is a process.

In addition to having multiple opportunities to persuade a given audience, the definition also implies that persuasion is accomplished incrementally. You will have little success if you push for your ultimate goal on the first persuasive attempt. You have to lay the groundwork and move slowly toward your ultimate goal. Seeking too much in one persuasive attempt will backfire. Consider how this works in real life. Imagine that you are trying to persuade your parents to buy you a new car. Simply coming down to dinner one evening and saying, "Dad, will you buy me a car?" will probably result in less-than-a-successful outcome. However, if you gradually build the arguments for why you need a new car, your parents will be more likely to hear your case and think about what you are requesting.

These realizations can help you develop strategies for creating more effective presentations. Recognizing that you don't have to cover everything in one persuasive attempt ensures that the presentation can be more targeted and strategic.

TARGETS OF PERSUASION

One of the most important elements to consider when constructing a persuasive message or presentation is your *target*. Just exactly what do you want the audience to think, feel, or do? As a speaker, you must decide if your persuasive presentation will target your audience's beliefs, attitudes, or behaviors. Each of these targets interacts with each other in complex ways. Beliefs underlie attitudes, and attitudes underlie behaviors (Fishbein, 1967; Kim & Hunter, 1993). In order to increase the likelihood of achieving your persuasive goal, it is important to understand how these three relate to each other. Let's examine each of these targets in more detail.

Beliefs

A **belief** is a cognition held by an individual concerning the truth or falsity of a claim or the existence or reality of something (Perloff, 2003). For example, some individuals in the medical community believe a series of vaccinations given in early childhood is leading to an increase in autism. On the other hand, there are many individuals in the medical community who think this claim is false. There is evidence that can be presented for both sides of this claim.

> " *A belief is a cognition held by an individual concerning the truth or falsity of a claim or the existence or reality of something.* "

One important feature about beliefs is that they cannot be proven or disproven for certain. There is always a degree of uncertainty associated with beliefs. Other points of view are possible and defendable. Consider this claim: Violent video games are causing our country's youth to become more violent. There is evidence that could be presented both for and against this claim. Some experts think that the increased violence in these games affects the behavior of children and has led to events like the Columbine shootings. Other experts say these games have a minimal effect. Each of these respective experts has research to back up the claim. An audience's belief concerning this claim will rest with the side they find most convincing. Here are some examples of beliefs:

◇ The MMR vaccine causes Autism.
◇ Aliens from outer space visit Earth on a regular basis.
◇ Listening to Mozart's music will make you smarter.

Beliefs are usually well-established and difficult to change. In order to change an audience's belief on any particular topic, you will have to present convincing evidence (Fishbein, 1967).

Attitudes

As discussed in Chapter 2, an **attitude** is an individual's evaluation of an object, event, person, policy, etc. (Fishbein & Ajzen, 1975). Attitudes attach a positive or negative evaluation onto a belief. So, our beliefs underlie our attitudes. Attitudes are learned and enduring evaluations of things that affect our behavior. People are highly motivated to act in ways that are consistent with their attitudes toward those things (Festinger, 1957). Because people want their attitude toward something to be consistent with their behavior, they will change their attitude to accommodate the behavior (Eagly & Chaiken, 1993).

> " *Attitudes attach a positive or negative evaluation onto a belief.* "

The woman in this crowd is reinforcing the attitudes, beliefs and behaviors of this supportive audience.

Here are some statements that reflect attitudes:

◇ The MMR vaccine is a dangerous vaccine.
◇ Space aliens are dangerous to the human species.
◇ Mozart is the best composer of the Classical Period.

While we are ambivalent toward some attitudes, others are extremely important to us. For instance, while most people may prefer to drink either Coke or Pepsi, they will often drink the other if their favorite is unavailable. However, most people are not so lackadaisical about their attitude toward an issue like abortion. When persuading people to change their evaluation of something, speakers need to factor in how important or strongly held an audience's existing attitudes are (Sherif & Sherif, 1967). Also, people do not always behave in ways that are consistent with attitudes. Although they may be motivated to do so, there may be obstacles that prevent them from achieving attitude-behavior consistency. For instance, a person may hold the attitude that Mercedes automobiles are the best cars to own, yet only be able to afford a Ford Focus.

Behaviors

Behaviors are observable actions. The behaviors we choose to enact are largely based on the beliefs and attitudes we hold. As mentioned previously, there is a strong link between beliefs, attitudes, and behaviors. We try not to engage in behaviors that we do not value or that are in opposition to the beliefs and attitudes we hold (Festinger, 1957).

Most of our persuasive attempts target behavior. We are bombarded by messages that attempt to persuade us to alter our behavior, for example, to buy a particular product or vote for a specific candidate. The daily attempts you make at persuasion are primarily targeted toward behaviors. You might try to persuade your parents to contribute toward your spring break vacation or persuade your roommate to go on a blind date.

> *Behaviors are observable actions.*

Although your primary goal may be to achieve some behavioral outcome, you may not be able to achieve this goal in a single persuasive presentation. Sometimes we have to focus on one of the underlying beliefs or attitudes first, and incrementally build toward a behavioral change in an audience. As a speaker, you cannot underestimate the important relationship between our beliefs, attitudes, and behaviors.

GOALS OF PERSUASION

Once you have selected a target for your persuasive presentation, you must decide on the best goal for your particular needs. There are three primary **goals** you can have in a persuasive message: you can seek to create, reinforce, or change an attitude, belief, or behavior. Let's further examine each of these goals so that you can get a better understanding of the process.

Creating

Sometimes an audience will have no established beliefs, attitudes, or behaviors regarding a particular issue. For example, Americans had few attitudes or behaviors concerning terrorism on U.S. soil before September 11, 2001. However, after that day, President Bush worked diligently to create attitudes and behaviors consistent with his plan for increased homeland security. Today, American's attitudes, beliefs, and behaviors toward security are much stronger and more sophisticated than in the past.

The goal of many advertising campaigns usually involves ***creating*** new beliefs, attitudes, and behaviors. Several years ago, Procter & Gamble introduced the Swiffer duster. Initially, I had no beliefs, attitudes, or behaviors concerning this new product. After watching commercial after commercial, being bombarded with coupons, and overhearing people in the grocery store talk about how great this new product worked, I bought a Swiffer and all of the supplies necessary to make it work. The advertisers had been successful. They capitalized on beliefs I already had, such as "My home should be clean." They convinced me that their product would help achieve a cleaner home and thus created a new behavior—buying their product.

Reinforcing

Sometimes it is important that we ***reinforce*** the beliefs, attitudes, and behaviors that people already hold (see Chapter 2). Consider Sunday sermons. The purpose of these messages is usually not to change or create, but to make the audience more devout and to strengthen those beliefs, attitudes, and behaviors they already hold. You have likely heard of the phrase "Preaching to the choir." Politicians are well aware of this phenomenon. Every rally and fundraising event they hold is primarily concerned with reinforcing their followers' commitment. This particular goal highlights the incremental nature of persuasion. Audiences are rarely persuaded in one single attempt. They have to be exposed to the persuasive attempt again and again before persuasion occurs.

Changing

Changing a persuasive target is usually what we associate with persuasion: getting PC computer users to switch to Macintosh computers, getting Republicans to vote Democrat, getting pro-lifers to become pro-choice.

When I teach this course, students always get excited about the persuasive assignment because they want to change the way the audience thinks or behaves. While changing persuasive targets is important, it is not always realistic. Some beliefs and attitudes are held very strongly by individuals, and they are very resistant to change. After conducting a thorough audience analysis (see Chapter 2 for these methods), you will be able to determine your audience's attitudes, beliefs, and behaviors. You may even be able to discern how strongly they hold these attitudes and beliefs. Given this information, you may be able to determine how much latitude a particular audience has for movement in the direction you are advocating.

Any of the goals discussed above are appropriate for your classroom presentations. You need to be cognizant of your situation and your audience, and choose those goals that you might be able to accomplish in the amount of time allotted for your presentation. These types of situational constraints should influence the decisions you make about targets and goals.

Now that you have a better understanding of just what persuasion is, there are two persuasive theories, The Elaboration Likelihood Model and Social Judgment Theory, that can add insight as you begin to plan your persuasive presentation. Let's take a look at each one of these perspectives.

THE ELABORATION LIKELIHOOD MODEL

Richard Petty and John Cacioppo, two social psychologists, have developed a way for us to better understand persuasion by examining an audience's motivation and knowledge concerning a given topic. The ***Elaboration Likelihood Model (ELM)*** proposes that there are two "routes" to persuasion, depending on how motivated and able the audience is to process the information in your presentation (Petty & Cacioppo, 1984).

Elaboration relates to the extent an audience will think about your message, while ***Likelihood*** refers to the probability that they will or will not think about or elaborate on the ideas you present. So in a nutshell, the theory's primary concern is determining how much your audience will think about the ideas you present. In order for this to happen, two things must be present: your audience must be motivated to process your message, and they must be able to process your message. If your audience members don't understand the major tenants of nanotechnology, it really doesn't matter how motivated they are by your topic. They simply won't be able to think or elaborate on your message in sophisticated ways because they don't have the knowledge necessary to do so.

> " *There are two "routes" to persuasion, depending on how motivated and able the audience is to process the information in your presentation.* "

According to the ELM, there are two "routes" or avenues to persuasion. There is a central route and a peripheral route. The ***central route*** is characterized by high levels of critical thinking. Messages are carefully analyzed, and your material will be related to information the audience already knows. Audiences engaged in the central route think about the implications of your messages and are extremely thorough in their analysis of your material.

The ***peripheral route***, on the other hand, is characterized by less elaboration. Your messages will be evaluated quickly, and your audience will rely on simple cues or decision rules to evaluate your argument or message. ***Decision rules*** are mental shortcuts. When an audience lacks the ability or motivation to carefully examine your ideas they rely on decision rules. So, instead of carefully critiquing your argument or ideas, they rely on all or some of the following:

- ◈ Your credibility on the issue.
- ◈ Your likeability as a speaker.
- ◈ The number of arguments you use.
- ◈ The length of your arguments.
- ◈ The perception of other audience members toward the presentation.

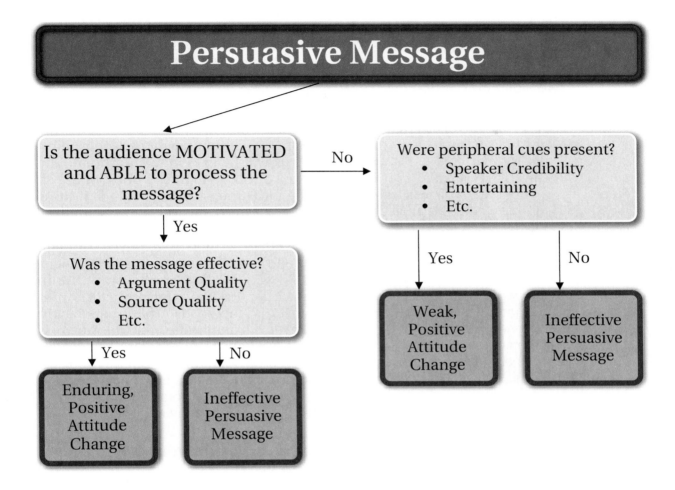

Persuasive Message

Is the audience MOTIVATED and ABLE to process the message?

No → Were peripheral cues present?
- Speaker Credibility
- Entertaining
- Etc.

Yes ↓

Was the message effective?
- Argument Quality
- Source Quality
- Etc.

Yes ↓   No ↓

Enduring, Positive Attitude Change   Ineffective Persuasive Message

Yes ↓   No ↓

Weak, Positive Attitude Change   Ineffective Persuasive Message

Central Route to Persuasion   **Peripheral Route to Persuasion**

(Adapted from Petty & Cacioppo, 1984)

An example that we used in Chapter 2 can help illustrate the ELM more clearly. Imagine that you are in an audience where the need for menu changes in the cafeteria of West Lafayette High School is being presented. The school board is recommending that all vending machines be removed from the premises. Although you attended this high school, you are now a freshman at Purdue. You aren't highly motivated to critically think about the arguments being presented because the changes won't affect you. While good logic and arguments are important, you are more likely to be persuaded by emotional appeals, the speaker's credibility and the rest of the audience's reaction.

Spotlight on Research

ONE-SIDED VERSUS TWO-SIDED MESSAGES

A one-sided message simply presents your position on a particular topic, while a two-sided message presents your position along with your opponent's position on the issue. Therefore, a two-sided message presents a very balanced view of the issue. A spin on the two-sided message is the two-sided rebuttal message. It presents your position, your opponent's position, and then refutes your opponent's position. But, which of these three approaches is most effective or most persuasive? Several meta-analyses have been conducted exploring this issue. This research has determined that two-sided refuted messages are the most persuasive types of messages. That is, presenting your own arguments along with your opponents and then refuting your opponent's position is the most persuasive strategy you can employ. Therefore, the refutational pattern suggested in this chapter is optimal.

However, time constraints and other environmental factors sometimes get in the way, and it isn't always feasible to present both sides of an issue plus a rebuttal. If this is the case, simply present your own position. A one-sided message is a more persuasive strategy than a two-sided message with no rebuttal. So if you have the option, always present a two-sided message with a rebuttal. If this is not possible, simply present the one-sided message.

Allen, M. (1991). Meta-analysis comparing the persuasiveness of one-sided and two-sided messages. *Western Journal of Speech Communication, 55*, 390-404.

O'Keefe, D. J. (1999). How to handle opposing arguments in persuasive messages: A meta-analytic review of the effects of one-sided and two-sided messages. *Communication Yearbook, 22*, 209-249.

Your neighbor, who is a senior at the local high school, would feel differently. Because the menu changes would directly affect him, he is highly motivated to be critical of the messages. The speaker will want to take the central route with an audience full of involved, motivated members, like your neighbor. Good logical appeals will be extremely important. The audience will be mentally questioning all of the ideas the speaker presents. If these questions aren't answered, it is unlikely that the audience will be persuaded.

Persuasion that is achieved through the central route is enduring. This means that it will last. It is not susceptible to counterpersuasive attempts. Another important factor is that persuasion achieved through the central route is highly predictive of behavior. Persuasion achieved through the peripheral route, on the other hand, is less enduring. It is susceptible to counterpersuasion, and it is not predictive of behavior.

APPLYING THE PRINCIPLES OF THE ELM

One aspect of using the ELM effectively is good audience analysis. You must have a thorough understanding of your audience's motivation and their ability to think critically on the given issue. If they are both motivated and able to think critically, the central route to persuasion would be the most appropriate. Good sound logic would be essential. Evidence from highly credible sources would also be important. Another key factor would be presenting two-sided messages with rebuttals (see spotlight on research).

If you suspect that your audience is less motivated and able to process your material, take the peripheral route. Focus on building and enhancing your credibility and likeability. Use emotional appeals and extended narrative examples.

If you face an audience that is mixed, meaning it is made up of both motivated and unmotivated members and those who will think critically and those who won't, it may be important to identify which of these two audiences is more important and tailor your message to them. If that is not possible, deliver a presentation that takes both the central and peripheral routes. This way both types of audience members will get the information they need.

> *Members of an audience evaluate messages in terms of the attitudes they already hold.*

Another consideration to make when using ELM is the goal of the presentation. Really analyze your goal and ask yourself the following questions: Are you seeking long-term commitment from your audience? Is the target of your persuasive appeal behavioral? If you answer yes to both of these questions, you want to encourage your audience to use the central route when processing the information in your presentation. As mentioned earlier, this route is more predictive of long-term change and behavioral changes (O'Keefe, 2002). Utilize those strategies that will encourage your audience to take that path (i.e., quality arguments).

SOCIAL JUDGMENT THEORY

Another theoretical perspective that helps us understand how persuasion works for an individual is **Social Judgment Theory**. This theory explains that members of an audience evaluate messages in terms of the attitudes they already hold and then make a decision whether to embrace a particular message or to reject it (Sherif & Sherif, 1967). According to this perspective, our attitudes fall along a continuum. At one end is the **latitude of acceptance**. Any message that falls into this place on the continuum will be accepted because it is viewed by the individual as consistent with attitudes they already hold. At the other end is the **latitude of rejection**. Messages that fall into this area will be rejected, because they are not consistent with an audience's attitudes. In addition to latitudes of acceptance and rejection is the **latitude of noncommitment**. This is that gray area that a person may not be sure about. It may be that they simply have not made up their mind or that they lack enough information about an issue to have a decisive attitude.

The size of these three latitudes depends on **ego-involvement** or how committed a person is to a particular idea. The more ego-involved an individual, the more difficult it will be to change their attitudes, beliefs or behaviors. If, for example, a person was an active member in the NRA and had firm attitudes on the right to bear arms, he or she would have a large latitude of rejection regarding any argument for gun control. Additionally, the latitude of noncommitment would be small. This person is not unsure or undecided on this issue. If Sarah Brady, a gun control activist, had to address an audience made up of individuals who hold these attitudes, she would have difficulty delivering any messages that would fall into their latitudes of acceptance or noncommittment. The size of these latitudes would be an important consideration when planning the presentation.

APPLYING SOCIAL JUDGMENT THEORY

From this discussion of social judgment theory, it should be evident that a speech topic on an extremely controversial issue such as abortion would be insurmountable in a public speaking course such as the one you are taking. On a topic such as this, your audience would have very decisive areas of acceptance and rejection and very small areas of noncommitment. On average, you have roughly seven minutes to make your presentation. It is impossible to change anyone's opinion on the topic within that time frame. Because the area of noncommitment is so small, there is just nowhere for an audience member to move.

On topics that are less controversial, it is important that you understand the attitudes of your audience and present a position that is close to their attitude of acceptance. For example, if you and your audience both agree that we need more social activities on campus, but disagree on how to pay for the programs, start where you agree and slowly move to points where you disagree. Don't start right off the bat pushing for a position where you know there is disagreement. Start in the latitude of acceptance and slowly move to areas of noncommitment.

Now that we understand all of this theory surrounding persuasion, we'll discuss how to take all of these ideas and turn them into meaningful and effective presentations.

 ORGANIZING THE PERSUASIVE SPEECH

This section is designed to help you organize your persuasive presentation. It presents each of the three types of persuasive speeches and discusses the appropriate way to organize each type.

PRESENTATIONS CONCERNING QUESTIONS OF FACT

If you decide to deliver a speech targeting an audience's beliefs, you will be giving a speech regarding a question of fact. Persuasive speeches regarding **questions of fact** are concerned with what is true or false, what happened or did not happen, or what exists or does not exist. If you think about it for a moment, there are very few questions for which we have definitive answers. We

> " *Persuasive speeches regarding questions of fact are concerned with what is true or false, what happened or did not happen, or what exists or does not exist.* "

know for example, that it is 190 miles from West Lafayette, Indiana, to Louisville, Kentucky. We know that Ford makes the Explorer SUV. These are simple questions to which we have concrete answers. Everyone would agree that these are true. There are other questions of fact, however, that are not so easily answered but are often debated. Consider the following examples:

- ◇ Do other intelligent life-forms exist?
- ◇ Did Lee Harvey Oswald act alone?
- ◇ Was Princess Diana's death an accident?
- ◇ Does eating a low-calorie diet lengthen the lifespan?

We have no definitive answers to any of the preceding questions. There are many experts who believe that Lee Harvey Oswald acted alone in shooting President John F. Kennedy, and many experts who believe that he did not. We have no definitive answer to this question. We might have a definitive answer at some point in the future, but right now we do not know for certain. Questions of fact surround a controversy. It is important to remember that if there is no controversy surrounding your claim, you are not delivering a persuasive presentation concerning a question of fact.

Organizing the Presentation

The speech regarding a question of fact can be organized in many different ways. The most common way is the topical design. Another design that is appropriate for presentations concerning questions of fact is the **causal pattern**. This particular pattern is most appropriate for those speeches where you are trying to establish a causal relationship between two variables.

Here is an example thesis statement that would follow the causal pattern of organization:

Specific Purpose: To persuade my audience that television causes Attention Deficit Disorder in young children.

| Thesis Statement: | Television viewing by young children affects neurological development and leads to attention deficit disorder in later years. |

In this presentation, the speaker would need to argue that early exposure to television (the cause) leads to changes in brain chemistry that trigger Attention Deficit Disorder (the effect).

| I. Main Point One: | Early exposure to television causes changes in brain chemistry. |
| II. Main Point Two: | These changes in brain chemistry lead to disorders such as Attention Deficit Disorder. |

Another type of pattern to use when making a presentation regarding a question of fact is the refutative pattern. It is one of the most effective designs you can use when making a persuasive argument because it presents both sides of an argument along with a rebuttal of opposing ideas (Allen, 1991; O'Keefe, 1999; see spotlight on research for more information). While the topical and causal design patterns are appropriate for informative speaking as well, the refutative pattern is unique to persuasive speaking.

The **refutative pattern** seeks to accomplish two goals: to deflate the opposition's arguments and to bolster your own. In order to accomplish this task, you must point out flaws in the opponent's argument. They may have weak evidence or problems in reasoning. The key to using this design successfully is a clear understanding of the opponent's position. You must have a thorough understanding of their purpose, arguments, and evidence.

The refutative pattern is particularly effective when addressing an audience that is hostile or unfavorable to your position. The design works with hostile audiences because you acknowledge your opponent's arguments first and then show the weaknesses in those arguments before presenting your own position.

There are four steps in the refutation pattern:

Step One:	State the argument you are going to refute.
Step Two:	State and list the errors of the opposing argument. At this step you must present facts, figures, examples, and/or testimony to support your refutation.
Step Three:	State and deliver evidence to support your alternative argument. Again, at this step you must present evidence that the audience will find credible and persuasive in order to support your position.
Step Four:	Explain how your argument or position disputes that of the opposition.

These steps can be arranged in many different ways within the body of your presentation. Let's look at one way a student organized her arguments for a classroom presentation.

Main Point I: According to the Atkins Center, high-protein diets contribute to weight loss and, therefore, to good health and disease prevention.

    A. Individuals who follow these diet plans do lose weight in the short term by eating high-protein foods, which lowers their caloric intake. (Explain the basics of the diet.)

    B. While individuals will lose weight in the short term, they are unlikely to continue with these diets for the long term and quickly return to unhealthy eating patterns.

    C. A diet high in protein and low in fruits and carbohydrates is risky even in the short term, and recent research shows it can lead to diseases such as diabetes, heart disease, and kidney disease. (Cite some of the recent studies.)

    D. When we examine the recent research in healthy eating, it becomes obvious that high-protein diets will not lead to good health or disease prevention.

Main Point II: In order to reach optimum health through healthy eating, one must make lifestyle changes.

    A. Lifestyle changes, not high-protein diets, lead to prolonged weight loss. (Cite some of the recent research.)

    B. Fruits, vegetables, and whole grains are the optimal base for a healthy diet and have been shown to lead to a decrease in diseases such as diabetes and heart problems. (Again, cite some of the research.)

    C. As you can see, adopting and maintaining a healthy lifestyle change by eating a well-balanced diet is the road to better nutrition.

In this design the student combined steps one and two in the first main point and steps three and four in the second main point. She addressed the opposition's arguments and showed why they are flawed. There are other combinations that could have worked. You could take each of the four steps and make each a main point. There is flexibility in how you arrange the four steps. As long as all the steps are included for all of the arguments you are refuting, you will be in good shape.

PRESENTATIONS CONCERNING QUESTIONS OF VALUE

The persuasive presentation concerning a question of value involves the audience's attitudes on a particular topic. **Questions of value** argue that positions are good or bad, ethical or unethical, moral or immoral, or right or wrong. Here are some examples of questions of value:

◈ Is hunting unethical?
◈ Is bullfighting inhumane?
◈ Is solar energy the ideal form of power?
◈ Is the space program a good use of taxpayer money?

One important key to handling a question of value effectively is to remember that questions of value are not opinions. Simply stating, "I think solar power is wonderful," is an opinion. This is your opinion, and no one will question you about it. You do not have to supply supporting evidence for your opinion. If, however, you make the claim, "Solar power is the ideal form of power," you have gone beyond stating your personal opinion and are now making a claim about a question of value.

> ❝ *Questions of value argue that positions are good or bad, ethical or unethical, moral or immoral, or right or wrong.* ❞

When you go beyond personal opinion, you must justify your claim through the use of supporting evidence. You must build a case for your position. One way to build the case for your position is to set the standards for the claim you are making. What makes an ideal power source? Define those standards first. Then show how your claim meets those standards.

Organizing the Presentation

Persuasive presentations on questions of value are usually organized topically. If you have a topic that requires you to set a standard against which to judge your argument, you will want to begin by laying out your standards. The second main point demonstrates how your argument measures up against the standards you have set. The following is an example of a speech positing that solar power is the ideal form of power:

Specific Purpose: To persuade my audience that solar energy is the ideal form of power.

Thesis Statement:　Solar power is the ideal form of power because it is clean, cost effective, and sustainable.

Main Point I:　An ideal form of power should meet the following criteria:

    A.　It should be clean.

    B.　It should be cost effective.

    C.　It should be sustainable.

Main Point II:　Solar energy meets all of these criteria for an ideal form of power.

    A.　Solar energy produces no by-products that pollute the environment, making it the cleanest form of power currently available.

    B.　Current advancements in solar panel construction have radically increased their efficiency, making them more cost effective than they have been in the past.

    C.　Unlike other fuels, solar power relies on a source of energy that will not be exhausted over time and through use.

You do not always have to follow the guidelines of setting up your criteria in the first main point and using the second main point to demonstrate how your claim meets the criteria. The following is another way you might organize a speech of value:

Specific Purpose:　To persuade my audience that spanking children is morally wrong.

Thesis Statement:　Spanking children is morally wrong because it demeans our children and devalues human integrity.

Main Point I:　Spanking our children is an immoral practice that demeans our youngest citizens. (Speaker provides supporting evidence.)

Main Point II:　Spanking young individuals devalues the worth of human beings. (Speaker provides supporting evidence.)

It is important to keep in mind that speeches of value may often be the catalyst that moves people to action. If someone becomes moved by your presentation on the unethical nature of hunting to get involved in an organization such as People for the Ethical Treatment of Animals (PETA), it is just the end result of your speech. Presentations on questions of value only argue the right and wrong of a particular issue. They do not concern themselves with what should or should not be done. Once you ask your audience to do something, you have targeted a behavior and crossed the line between questions of value and policy. Make sure that if your assignment asks you to make a persuasive presentation on a question of value, you stick to that goal. Do not make the mistake of asking your audience to take action. The action step moves you into questions of policy, which we will discuss next.

PRESENTATIONS CONCERNING QUESTIONS OF POLICY

The persuasive presentation concerning a *question of policy* targets behaviors or what we should or should not be doing—as an individual, a community, or even a nation. Here are some examples of questions of policy:

◇ Should we ban smoking in all public buildings, including restaurants and bars?
◇ Should physical education be mandatory at every grade level in our nation's schools?
◇ Should our community engage in curbside recycling?
◇ Should the United States change its immigration policies?

When you think about making a persuasive presentation, most of us think about speeches on questions of policy. We usually want to persuade someone or a group of people to do something related to some policy. We might want them to vote for our candidate for homecoming court, protest a recent Purdue administration decision, or take up exercising. If you are trying to get your audience to do something, you are talking about a question of policy.

It is important to note that questions of policy almost always include questions of fact or value. While the question of policy would be the primary goal of the presentation, secondary attention would have to be paid to questions of fact or value. Remember, attitudes and beliefs underlie behaviors, so they may need to be addressed in order to reach a behavioral goal or policy change. Questions of policy, however, always go beyond questions of fact and value and advocate that something should or should not be done.

> *The persuasive presentation concerning a question of policy targets behaviors or what we should or should not be doing—as an individual, a community, or even a nation.*

When making a speech concerning a question of policy, careful attention must be paid to the **need**, **plan**, and **practicality** of the proposals being presented (Lucas, 2006). First of all, you must demonstrate to your audience that there is a problem or a need for your proposed policy. Why should we ban smoking in all public buildings in our community? You must present evidence to show that smoking in public buildings is a problem for individuals in your community. The evidence you present must be compelling enough to convince your audience that some change in policy should be adopted.

Sometimes you are trying to change a policy and, other times, you might be arguing that some policy should remain the same. In other words, you are simply reinforcing the attitude that the current policy is adequate or reasonable. Consider the following topic: The U.S. should not change its

> **"** *When making a speech concerning a question of policy, careful attention must be paid to the need, plan, and practicality of the proposals.* **"**

ORDER OF ARGUMENTS

One of the most common questions students ask is which argument should be put first and which last? Should I spring my strongest argument on my audience first (***primacy effect***), or wait until the very end to use my strongest evidence (***recency effect***)? The research at this time is inconclusive (O'Keefe, 2002). One thing is for certain: never sandwich your best or strongest piece of evidence in the middle of your presentation. It is better to end or begin with a bang.

One aspect to consider is the situation in which you are speaking. If you know that you are likely to run out of time during the presentation, do not save your best argument for the end of the presentation because you may not get to it. In a situation where time is limited and you are worried about your ability to finish the presentation, use your strongest evidence or argument first, so that you can adequately explain and present that material. However, if you know that you will have plenty of time to address all of the points of your presentation, you may be able to build to your strongest piece of evidence. You will also want to think about how motivated your audience is to process the arguments you will present. If they are less motivated, their attention may wane as the presentation continues, so you may want to present your strongest argument first. As with every stage in the process of developing a presentation, you must consider the situation and audience when making these types of decisions.

O'Keefe, D. J. (2002). *Persuasion: Theory & Research.* Thousand Oaks, CA: Sage.

immigration policies. In this speech you would argue that changing the current policies would cause more harm than good, and advocate that the U.S. continue doing what it is already doing. You are still advocating a course of action.

In addition to convincing your audience that a problem or need exists, you must also demonstrate that you have a clear plan that will address the cause or causes of the problem. You must convince your audience that your solution will be able to alleviate the problem.

Once you have established a need to change current policy and presented your plan or solution, you must demonstrate that your plan is practical. Although you may have done an incredible job convincing your audience that there is a problem with current policy, unless you can also persuade them that your solution for alleviating the problem is feasible, you will be unsuccessful. The bottom line is that the audience wants to believe your plan is workable. They must believe that your plan will alleviate problems without causing new ones. While you may propose a wonderful plan to clean up the Wabash River, the price tag associated with your proposal may be too much for the community to absorb. The expense of the proposal would create problems in other areas for the community, perhaps increases in taxes and cutbacks in other community-funded programs.

Sometimes when speaking on a question of policy, a speaker's only goal is to get an audience to agree that, indeed, a change in policy does need to be made. However, the speaker may not be asking anything else from the audience. In this case, the speaker is seeking passive agreement. ***Passive agreement*** is gaining acceptance for your position from your audience without asking them to take action. Perhaps you persuade your audience that a change needs to be made, but you don't suggest what that change might be. Alternatively, you might seek to gain agreement from your audience, but that may be all you are seeking. You don't want them to take any further action, just agreement. If this is the case, you are seeking passive agreement.

Sometimes a speaker is seeking more than just passive agreement. That is, a speaker is asking for more than just an agreement that the proposed policy change should be made. The speaker seeks what we call active agreement. ***Active agreement*** requires both agreement and action on the part of the audience. In this case, the speaker needs the audience to get involved in order to achieve the change in policy. Perhaps the speaker asks the audience to sign a petition, buy a raffle ticket, vote for a proposition in an upcoming election, or sign a donor registration card. Regardless of the behavior the speaker advocates, the audience is being asked for more than just agreement. The audience has to become actively involved in order to achieve the ultimate goal of the presentation.

Organizing the Presentation

There are many ways to organize presentations concerning questions of policy. The problem-solution and the problem-cause-solution designs are organizational schemes for the presentation regarding the speech of policy. The following is an example of the ***problem-solution*** speech structure.

Specific Purpose:	To persuade my audience that action is needed to deal with the problems created by ineffective design and placement of street and road signs in Lafayette.
Thesis Statement:	Ineffective design and placement of street signs in Lafayette causes many traffic problems in our city, and there are steps we can take to improve the situation.

Main Point I: The ineffective design and placement of street and road signs in Lafayette is very dangerous. (This is the problem.)

    A. It is estimated that nearly one-third to one-half of all street signs in Lafayette are missing.

    B. More than one-half of the street signs in Lafayette are not clearly legible.

    C. Many local accidents are a result of mistakes drivers make due to ineffective or absent signs.

Main Point II: The problem with our road signs can be solved in a three-step process. (This is the solution.)

    A. First, all of the road signs in Lafayette must be replaced with signs that meet national safety recommendations.

    B. Second, the road signs must be relocated to appropriate locations within intersections.

    C. Finally, missing signs must be replaced.

The ***problem-cause-solution*** design simply adds a third step. After outlining the problem, you add a second main point, which lays out the causes of the problem. The final or third main point in this design is the solution. The design looks like this: Main point one, the problem; main point two, the causes of the problem; and main point three, the solution. I have found that when speakers use the problem-cause-solution design, their solutions are often more practical. Addressing the causes helps ensure that you propose a solution that is more feasible. This arrangement usually results in a tighter overall argument. The following is a brief example of an outline using the problem-cause-solution design.

Specific Purpose:	To persuade the audience that they should recycle as a way of combating the waste disposal problem in our area.
Thesis Statement:	Our landfills are overflowing and our failure to recycle is exacerbating this issue.

Main Point I: Waste disposal is a significant problem. (This is the problem.)

Main Point II: Why isn't our community recycling? (This is the underlying cause or causes.)

    A. There is a lack of knowledge about current recycling programs.

    B. Another reason has to do with the inconvenience of recycling.

Main Point III: There is an easy two-part solution that will make recycling both easier and more convenient. (This is the solution.)

    A. First, we need to implement promotional campaigns that clarify proper recycling procedures.

    B. Second, city sanitation departments must be expanded to provide curbside pickup and their hours must be increased.

In addition to these options is Monroe's motivated sequence, an adapted version of the problem-solution design. It was created at Purdue University by Professor Alan Monroe in the 1930s and is still prominently used in marketing and advertising today. **Monroe's motivated sequence** is primarily used when a speaker wants to move an audience to immediate action. While all of the other organizational patterns presented in your textbook have provided ways to organize the main points of a presentation, the motivated sequence provides a design to organize the entire presentation. There are five steps in this pattern: attention, need, satisfaction, visualization, and action.

> ❝ *The motivated sequence provides a design to organize the entire presentation.* ❞

Step One: **Attention**
This step is exactly like the first step in any other presentation you make. You must gain the audience's

attention. You can accomplish this through a variety of strategies.

Step Two: **Need**

Once you have grabbed your audience's attention, you then must convince the audience that there is a need for change. You must persuade them that the current product, policy, or candidate (for example) is problematic. You establish this need through the use of evidence. It is important that you have conducted a thorough audience analysis so that you can use the type of evidence that will convince your target audience that a need exists.

Step Three: **Satisfaction**

Now that you have generated a sense of need in your audience, you provide them with your solution, or satisfaction, to this need. Explain your plan. Remember, it is important at this point in the presentation that you demonstrate to your audience that the plan you are proposing is practical.

Step Four: **Visualization**

At this point, ask your audience to visualize your plan. You want to paint a mental picture of the solution. You want to show the audience the benefits of enacting your solution and the consequences if they do not. You must also be able to demonstrate to your audience how they will benefit directly from your proposed solution.

Step Five: **Action**

Once you have convinced your audience that there is a need, and you have proposed a workable solution, it is time to call them to action. Tell the audience exactly what they need to do and how to do it

---

USING MONROE'S MOTIVATED SEQUENCE

Introduction

I.   Attention Step

II.   Credibility Statement

III.   Relevance Statement

IV.   Thesis Statement

Transition

Body

MPI   Need Step

Transition

MPII   Satisfaction Step

Transition

MPIII   Visualization Step

Transition

Conclusion

I.   Restate Thesis

II.   Action Step

in order to ensure the activation of your plan. If you want them to send an e-mail to their representative, provide the e-mail address. If you want them to write a letter to the city commissioner, provide the address. If you want them to vote in the upcoming election, give details about where and when to vote. The clearer and easier you make the action step, the more likely your audience will respond to your call for action (O'Keefe, 1997). This means using a visual aid to reinforce the address, phone number, etc. It is insufficient to deliver these type of small details without the use of a visual aid. You really need that added impact. Finally, end the speech with a resounding appeal to action that will motivate your audience to get involved.

Here is an example of an abbreviated speech that utilizes Monroe's motivated sequence. Although it is not noted here, you must have all of the elements of the introduction and the conclusion that are required for any presentation. There is also a transcript of a speech employing Monroe's motivated sequence, with commentary, presented at the end of this chapter.

Introduction:

I.   Attention: Have you ever dreamed about being a hero or heroine? Have you ever wished you could do something great, something that would really make a difference in our world? I'm here to tell you, you can, if you're willing to give just three hours a week. (Put the rest of the elements of the introduction in here.)

Body:

II. Need: Our community needs volunteers to help take care of homeless and abandoned animals. The Humane Society of Lafayette has a program designed to care for these pets, but only volunteers can make the program work. The program needs at least 80 volunteers to work. At this point we only have 58.

III. Satisfaction: Volunteering at the Humane Society will help to ensure that this worthwhile program continues and flourishes. Being involved in this program will also make you a hero in the eyes of some neglected animal.

IV. Visualization: Maybe you can have an experience that will be as rewarding as mine has been. Last year I worked with a 4-year-old black Labrador mix. Her name was Reba and two afternoons each week, I bathed her and took her for a walk. She had been abandoned by her previous owners when they vacated their apartment. When I started volunteering at the shelter, she was extremely shy and nervous. But a couple of months after my visits began, she started to exhibit quite a personality. This program was remarkable. Not only was I able to help Reba adapt to her new environment and learn some important social skills, but I received the benefit of having a pet in my life. In my current situation, I can't have a pet of my own. Reba was adopted by a loving family, and I have to think that some of my love and attention enabled her to make that transition more easily. But what would have happened to Reba if I had not volunteered and the program could not continue?

Conclusion:

V.   Call for Action: Won't you join me and become one of the unsung heroines or heroes at the Humane Society? You can make a difference in just one or two afternoons each week. I've got the applications with me and will be waiting for you to sign up after class. There are many animals at the shelter that need a little love and companionship while they wait for the right family. Won't you help make a difference?

CONCLUSION

Although persuasion is something that we engage in every day, it is a very complex process. Persuasive presentations ask the audience to choose between two or more alternatives, demand a thorough analysis of the audience, make more demands of the audience, and have a higher ethical threshold than informative speaking.

In order to be effective, the persuasive speech must have a strong sense of purpose. The persuasive process begins with an understanding of what you are going to target in a persuasive attempt—attitude, belief, or behavior—and what your goal is, whether changing, creating, or reinforcing that target. Once this decision has been made, you must determine whether your presentation concerns a question of fact, value, or policy and organize it accordingly. Additionally, you will want to consider additional persuasive factors such as speaker credibility and message characteristics.

KEY TERMS

Active agreement
Attitude
Behavior
Belief
Causal pattern
Central route
Changing
Creating
Decision rules
Ego-Involvement
Elaboration
Elaboration Likelihood
  Model (ELM)

Goals
Latitude of acceptance
Latitude of noncommitment
Latitude of rejection
Monroe's motivated
  sequence
Need
Passive agreement
Peripheral route
Persuasion
Plan
Practicality

Primacy effect
Problem-cause-solution
Problem-solution
Questions of fact
Questions of policy
Questions of value
Recency effect
Refutative pattern
Reinforce
Social Judgment Theory
Target

EXERCISES

1. Monroe's motivated sequence is a common organizational pattern chosen for persuasive presentations, including the popular "infomercials" seen on television. For this activity, go to the Web site "I Saw it on TV" at http://www.isawitontv.info/ and choose one of the infomercials. As you watch/read the infomercial, identify how the commercial achieved each of the five steps necessary for a successful presentation using Monroe's.

2. As you read in this chapter, persuasive presentations are concerned with questions of fact, value or policy. For this activity, choose one of the topics below. Then, come up with three specific purpose statements, one each for a speech of fact, value and policy, on the topic.

West Lafayette smoking ban   **Nanotechnology**   **Generic drugs**
Parental Internet controls   **Redlining**   **Financial aid**

3. As you read in this chapter, persuasive presentations target audiences' beliefs, attitudes or behaviors. Each of these can interact with each other, as witnessed in the advertising world. For this activity, flip through advertisements in newspapers, magazines, or archived advertisements on such sites as adflip.com (http://www.adflip.com). See if you can determine the attitude, belief and/or behavior targeted. Why do you think this target was chosen?

4. Analyze the following speech "Three Ways of Helping Habitat." How well do you think the speech employed the guidelines suggested by this chapter? What suggestions might you make for improvement?

Three Ways of Helping Habitat
Student Speech with Commentary
(Monroe's Motivated Sequence)

Suzanne begins by gaining the attention of her audience. This fulfills the attention step of the sequence.

She's never had a home of her own. She's worked hard, but it just seems that she can never save enough for a down payment and closing costs to make owning her own home a reality. She really wants to provide the stability that owning her own home offers for her two children. She is tired of moving from one apartment to another because of noise, inconsiderate neighbors, and landlords who promise to fix things, but who never do. She wants the children to have the feeling of permanence that results from coming home every day from the same school to the same home. This description fits all too many families today. But there is hope for some lucky families. That hope is Habitat for Humanity, an organization dedicated to helping families find dignity in home ownership that results from their own hard work, as well as the helping hand from others.

Suzanne establishes her credibility.

Having volunteered for Habitat for Humanity for three years now, I know what kind of satisfaction and happiness these homes can bring to a family.

As Purdue students there is a way for you to be integral in making someone's dream a reality.

Suzanne relates the topic to her audience.

Today, I would like to share with you more about this incredible organization, Habitat for Humanity, their needs and the ways you can get involved.

She previews her main points.

Let's get started by looking at some facts about the organization itself.

She provides a transition.

Habitat has over 3,000 local affiliates or groups in the United States, including over 480 campus chapters, according to the Purdue Habitat Web site. Habitat functions internationally, as well in over 80 countries. Frequently, local Habitat volunteers will team up with volunteers in other areas for blitz projects. These outreach projects are an integral part of the Habitat organization.

This is background information that helps us understand how the organization works.

Habitat's Web site states that families are reviewed and selected based on their need for housing, ability to repay the no-interest mortgage, and the willingness to add at least 250 hours of their own sweat-equity to help build not only their own home, but the home of others. By December 31, Habitat for Humanity of Lafayette will have completed 12 houses during 2005, according to Kate Walker. Habitat's Web site describes the average home as having 1,000 square feet of finished living space with three bedrooms and one bath.

According to Walker, the average local Habitat house costs $44,000. Four thousand dollars of that cost is tithed to building projects in Haiti, which builds 2 to 3 houses there. So funding of a home here actually builds 3 to 4 houses total.

Right now, in Tippecanoe County, Habitat for Humanity has 35 families who are hoping to be matched to a Habitat house, according to Kate Walker, who is the public relations director for the local Habitat for Humanity organization. When responding in an interview, she stated that fourteen of those families have passed the official approval stage and are working on their sweat equity requirement.

Here Suzanne starts to describe the needs of the organization.

In a January 25, 2005, article in the Journal and Courier, it stated that Habitat for Humanity is constantly in need of not only material donations and volunteers to actually help build structures, but especially for volunteers for committees who are charged with fundraising, training and coordinating events.

Transitions to next main point.

As you can see, the organization has great needs, but there are ways we can help.

Here Suzanne starts to provide the satisfaction, or solution, to the needs.

Right here on the Purdue campus, there are three ways that efforts are being made to join with Habitat for Humanity to aid in their mission of eliminating poverty housing.

First, Habitat link is the campus chapter of Habitat for Humanity. A February 26, 2004, article in The Exponent described some of the campus chapter's activities. Every Saturday, 15 to 25 members work on a house in the Lafayette area. They have training sessions, so no prior experience or knowledge is required to help build a home.

The chapter also sponsors Spring Break trips to help build homes in other areas of the country and outside of the U.S. The Exponent article mentioned that 50 members were spending their break on work trips to locations like Colorado, Louisiana, Florida, North Carolina and New York City.

Suzanne continues with her explanation of her solution.

The Purdue chapter also takes part in HabiFest, which is a national effort to raise awareness and educate people about poverty in the area. Students have a contest to build cardboard homes and sleep in them overnight. Fundraising is also a part of HabiFest.

A second link to working with Habitat is the Habitat for Humanity EPICS branch. "EPICS" stands for Engineering Projects in Community Service. The team that is working with Habitat is particularly suited to students majoring in agricultural and biological engineering, building construction and management technology, civil engineering, computer engineering, computer science, construction engineering and management, industrial engineering, management, and mechanical engineering. The EPICS teams are also open to non-engineering majors and their presence is encouraged because non-engineering students may offer a fresh approach to problem solving due to their different perspective. Non-engineering majors may also offer strengths in communication skills and understanding the needs of the client. According to the EPICS Web site, students solve problems including house design and optimization, energy and construction analysis, and providing creative solutions for efficient energy needs. Students take real-life problems and come up with solutions to make the cost of construction and running a home cheaper. Teams are mentored by Purdue faculty, staff, and engineers from local industry in addition to graduate teaching assistants. Currently, according to their Web site, the Habitat team is participating in two national multi-institutional projects and two local projects. A student may participate for up to four years with EPICS and receive one or two academic credits each semester. Individual departments must be consulted to see how the credits may be applied.

A third link to Habitat is that some campus organizations may choose to work on a Habitat house as part of a service project. This approach is more short-term than options one or two. For instance, last year the CFS Multicultural Society for Excellence spent their Spring Break volunteering in Guatemala through the Ambassadors for Children program. They assisted with a Habitat home-building project there, according to the College of Consumer and Family Sciences Web site. Students endured fairly primitive building conditions and worked eight hours a day, with minimal food for meals. Despite the hardships, the students enjoyed the experience and look forward to another similar venture.

Here the visualization step begins. Suzanne asks the audience to envision her plan or solution. She demonstrates the way her audience and the organization will benefit from the plan.

You may be wondering why you might want to join with Habitat in helping to eliminate poverty housing. One reason is the feeling of satisfaction that you will certainly feel in helping others who are less fortunate. You will feel like Brittany Clifton, who went on the Guatemala trip. According to the CFS Web site, Brittany stated, "When we did Habitat, it felt like we were part of the family for the day . . . I would definitely do this again. It felt good to go somewhere and make a difference."

Similarly, in an April 7, 2005, article in the Journal and Courier, Purdue student Stacy Turgeon was quoted as saying that, "Most people who get Habitat homes are working and they're just not making ends meet . . . I like being able to help somebody. They really appreciate it."

Without volunteers like you, the program could not continue. These families would have to live in substandard conditions.

Most recently, on November 7, 2005, Devin Lamb, who is one of the Education and

Awareness Committee chairmen for the Purdue chapter of Habitat, responded to the question of why he feels being in the organization is personally fulfilling. He stated that, ". . . it's awesome to be able to actually see the person you're helping and know that you're making a difference. It can be hard work at times, and coming off a hard day of construction is great as well."

In addition to feeling good about your contribution to those less fortunate, you will gain valuable transferable job skills by being a volunteer. Imagine being able to tell future employers that you have experience working in teams, solving problems, working under stress, communicating with others, working in a diversified workplace and perhaps taking a leadership role. Businesses place a value on community contributions as well as the education you gain in the classroom.

Here Suzanne transitions to the action step.

Now that you know more about the organization, understand their needs and have heard the benefits of being a Habitat volunteer, here is the information you need to actually put the plan into action.

Here Suzanne tells her audience exactly how they can get involved.

To become a member of the Purdue campus chapter of Habitat for Humanity, go to their Web site to download a membership form. The Web site is at:

http://web.ics.purdue.edu/~habitat/join.html

The filled-out form may be turned in at any Habitat meeting listed on the Web site or sent through regular or campus mail to:

Purdue University Habitat for Humanity
Stewart Center, Box #706
128 Memorial Mall
West Lafayette, IN 47907-2034

If you are interested in joining the EPICS branch of Habitat for Humanity and solving the engineering-related issues that Habitat has, go to their Web site at

http://epics.ecn.purdue.edu

You will find a form to fill out showing your interest in the Habitat team. If you have questions not answered by the information on their Web site, you may also visit their office in the

Electrical Engineering Building, room 3484,
or e-mail questions to
epics purdue.edu.

Your volunteer time will enable other families to feel like Ceciley Brown, who has been in her Habitat home less than a year. She was quoted in the Journal and Courier as saying, "I now have someplace to live that's my own . . . I never thought I would. I feel blessed every day." Help deserving families realize their dream of home ownership. Volunteer for Habitat for Humanity.

Clincher or Call to Action—Suzanne ties the clincher back to the attention step, creating a sense of closure for the audience

REFERENCES

Allen, M. (1991). Meta-analysis comparing the persuasiveness of one-sided and two-sided messages. *Western Journal of Speech Communication, 55,* 390–404.

Eagly, A. H., & Chaiken, S. (1993). *The psychology of attitudes.* Orlando, FL: Harcourt.

Festinger, L. (1957). *A theory of cognitive dissonance.* Stanford, CA: Stanford University Press.

Fishbein, M. (1967). A consideration of beliefs, and their role in attitude measurement. In M. Fishbein (ed.), *Readings in attitude theory and measurement* (pp. 257–266). New York: John Wiley.

Fishbein, M., & Ajzen, I. (1975). *Belief, attitude, intention and behavior: An introduction to theory and research.* Reading, MA: Addison-Wesley.

Kim, M. S., & Hunter, J. E. (1993). Attitude-behavior relations: A meta-analysis of attitudinal relevance and topic. *Journal of Communication, 43,* 101–142.

Lucas, S. (2006). *The art of public speaking.* New York: McGraw-Hill.

Miller, G. R. (1972). Persuasion. In C. R. Berger & S. H. Chaffee (Eds.), *Handbook of communication science* (pp. 446–483). Newbury Park, CA: Sage.

O'Keefe, D. J. (2002). *Persuasion: Theory & research.* Thousand Oaks, CA: Sage.

O'Keefe, D. J. (1999). How to handle opposing arguments in persuasive messages: A meta-analytic review of the effects of one-sided and two-sided messages. *Communication Yearbook, 22,* 209–249.

O'Keefe, D. J. (1997). Standpoint explicitness and persuasive effect: A meta-analytic review of the effects of varying conclusion articulation in persuasive messages. *Argumentation and Advocacy, 34,* 1–12.

Perloff, R. M. (2003). *The dynamics of persuasion.* Hillsdale, NJ: Lawrence Erlbaum.

Petty, R. E., & Cacioppo, J. T. (1984). The effects of involvement on responses to argument quantity and quality: Central and peripheral routes to persuasion. *Journal of Personality and Social Psychology, 46,* 69–81.

Sherif, M., & Sherif, C. W. (1967). Attitude as the individual's own categories: The social judgment-involvement approach to attitude and attitude change. In C. W. Sherif & M. Sherif (Eds.), *Attitude ego-involvement, and change* (pp. 105–139). New York: Wiley.

Chapter 10

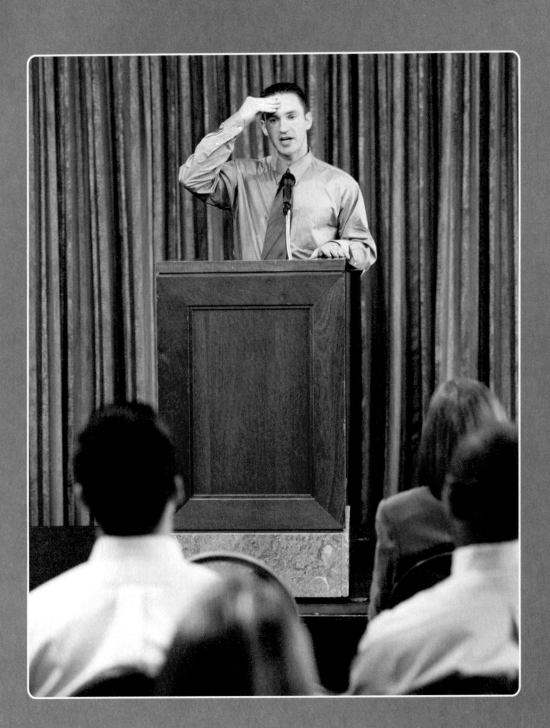

STRATEGIES FOR PERSUASIVE PRESENTATIONS

CHAPTER OBJECTIVES

After reading this chapter, you should be able to:

- Explain the role of ethos, logos, and pathos in presentational speaking.

- Define the differences between initial credibility, derived credibility, and terminal credibility.

- Define reasoning from deduction and explain tips for using it effectively.

- Define reasoning from induction and explain tips for using it effectively.

- Define casual reasoning and explain guidelines for using it effectively.

- Define analogical reasoning and explain guidelines for using it effectively.

- Discuss ethical considerations of using emotional appeals.

*M*att delivered a persuasive presentation on a question of policy to his public speaking class. His speech involved drinking and driving, and his goal was to reinforce the idea that drinking and driving was dangerous, and to create a behavior on the part of his classmates. The behavior he sought to create was utilization of the university's new SAFE RIDE program. This was a service students could use free of charge if they had been consuming alcohol and needed transportation. In his attempt to persuade his audience, Matt showed explicit pictures of drinking and driving crashes and used graphic testimony and narratives to describe victims' experiences.

Matt expected a lively question and answer session. He anticipated multiple questions on the specifics of the program. However, his classmates had little to say during the question-and-answer portion of the presentation. Matt was a little surprised and disappointed.

After leaving class, Matt asked a friend, David, who was also in the class for his reaction to his presentation. David replied that he felt a little numb and upset at the close of the presentation. David felt the pictures had been too graphic and the stories of the victims and their families too intense. The emotions Matt had evoked in the presentation had been too intense and his audience felt uncomfortable. In the end, Matt felt that he didn't achieve his desired result because of the type of appeals he used.

This chapter is designed to help you examine the various types of appeals that you have at your disposal when presenting a persuasive presentation. Often, we look for that magic bullet that will ensure our persuasive attempts are successful. But, there is no magic bullet or easy solution. Persuasion is a process. The strategies discussed in this chapter play a big part in that process. Solid reasoning, effective use of emotion, and credibility can make the difference between an effective persuasive attempt and an ineffective attempt, if you know how to implement them well. Appeals alone aren't magic bullets, but they may be the thing to push your presentation to the next level. This chapter discusses the art of using appeals and some strategies for implementing them successfully.

 ## ETHOS, LOGOS, AND PATHOS

The strategies of reasoning rely on three appeals. According to Greek philosopher Aristotle, in his book the *Rhetoric*, these appeals include: appeals to ethos or credibility, logos or logic, and pathos or emotion. Although Aristotle lived in another time far removed from the society we live in today, these three appeals continue to guide the communication strategies we use in the modern world. We use these three appeals in all types of speaking, but they become even more important when delivering persuasive presentations. In this chapter we will examine each of these three types of appeals.

USING ETHOS IN YOUR PRESENTATION

According to Aristotle, **ethos** refers to the credibility of a speaker. **Credibility** results from the perceptions of audience members about the believability of a speaker. Credibility is made up of two factors: expertise and trustworthiness (O'Keefe, 2002). Speakers are judged as demonstrating **expertise** if they appear experienced, informed, trained, qualified, skilled, and intelligent. According to persuasion researcher Dan O'Keefe, all of these dimensions are concerned with one central question: is the speaker in a position to know the truth or what is right or wrong about a particular topic? If so, we will find them high in expertise.

Trustworthiness is determined by assessing a speaker's honesty, open-mindedness, sense of justice, fairness and unselfishness (Bradley, 1981; Falcione, 1974; O'Keefe, 2002). Ultimately, the audience is asking the question, is the speaker telling the truth as he/she knows it? If the audience believes so, the speaker is deemed trustworthy.

As discussed in other chapters, your credibility is in the eye of your audience. It is the perception your audience has about the credibility you have on a particular topic and it can greatly affect how they react to your presentation. Will they listen attentively or will they take what you have to say with a grain of salt? Your perceived credibility can have profound impacts on how your audience approaches your presentation.

> **TIPS FOR ENHANCING ETHOS**
> ◉ Use strong evidence
> ◉ Establish common ground with the audience
> ◉ Be upfront about goals
> ◉ Use an appropriate delivery style

It is important to keep in mind that credibility can vary from situation to situation and from audience to audience. Credibility is the audience's perception of a speaker and so it will vary greatly depending on the situation. You may have great credibility with your classroom audience as a speaker on nanotechnology. After all, you are an undergraduate engineering student working in the lab of a professor involved in cutting edge research on the topic. If you delivered a similar presentation to an audience made up of professors pursuing lines of research in the area of nanotechnology, your credibility would be questionable.

Similarly, while you may be extremely qualified and competent to deliver a presentation on one topic, you would not be qualified to deliver a presentation on another topic. For example, Brian Williams, a well-respected national news anchor, is well qualified to deliver a presentation to an audience on the media coverage of Iraq. We would be less likely to find Brian Williams competent to deliver a presentation on gracious entertaining; however, we would find Martha Stewart competent to deliver that presentation.

As you have seen, credibility changes from topic to topic and audience to audience, but it also changes during a presentation. There are three types of credibility that help describe the changes to a speaker's credibility during a presentation (McCroskey, 2000). ***Initial credibility*** refers to the credibility a speaker has before he or she begins the presentation. This information may be publicized by posters listing a speaker's credentials. If you are introduced by someone, he or she will usually list your qualifications. You can also explain your own competence in the introduction of your presentation (see Chapter 4). So, before you even begin your presentation, your audience has already formed an attitude about how credible you will be on the topic you will address.

Derived credibility results from the actual messages you present during your presentation. Obviously, what you say or do during the presentation has a great impact on your credibility. While you may have had extremely high initial credibility, you can do things during the actual presentation that erode your credibility. Likewise, you can start a presentation with low initial credibility and, through the use of strong reasoning, effective delivery and strong organization, achieve high credibility in the eyes of your audience.

Terminal credibility refers to the credibility of the speaker at the end of the presentation. So, if you have applied the strategies discussed in this section successfully, you may arrive at the end of your presentation with even more credibility than when you began. Don't underestimate the importance of your credibility. It can have a dramatic effect on the success of a presentation. Terminal credibility is important because it establishes the credibility you have going into future presentations. In other words, the terminal credibility in one presentation affects the initial credibility in your next presentation. So, giving a poor presentation affects your credibility as a whole.

Tips for Enhancing Ethos

How can you establish credibility during your presentation? First and foremost, use strong evidence. You want to use evidence from respected sources (O'Keefe, 2002). Supporting evidence from less than legitimate sources won't do much to bolster your credibility. Analyze your audience and ask yourself, what types of sources will this particular audience respect? Use those sources. You may have to vary supporting material depending on the particular audience you are addressing. You also want to ensure that your supporting evidence is timely. Outdated evidence will limit your ability to achieve your goals.

You cannot underestimate the effect identification and audience involvement will have on a persuasive message.

Second, you want to establish common ground with your audience. As we discussed in Chapter 2, you never want to alienate an audience. If you start off by attacking the position your audience holds, you won't get very far. Begin by showing similarities between you and your audience and then move to areas where you may experience controversy. You want to demonstrate respect for your audience. This enhances liking for you as the speaker and is important in enhancing your character as a speaker.

Third, being upfront about your goals as a speaker goes a long way toward building your trustworthiness. It does nothing for your credibility as a speaker to have a hidden agenda.

Finally, using an appropriate delivery style will also enhance audience perception of your competence. Using fluent vocal delivery is extremely important. Make sure your vocal style is free from any vocal disfluencies. Vocal pauses such as um, uh, etc., cause the credibility of a speaker to diminish (Greene, 1984; Street & Brady, 1982). Wearing appropriate attire can also affect your credibility. Review the guidelines on dressing appropriately in Chapter 11.

USING LOGOS IN YOUR PRESENTATION

Logos refers to logic and appeals to an individual's intelligence. You incorporate logos into your presentations by using arguments or reasoning. We build strong arguments by gathering supporting evidence, organizing solid arguments, and using reasoning to explain how that evidence supports the claims we are making. In order to be effective, you must ask yourself, "How does this piece of evidence support my main point?" "How can I make this connection evident to my audience?" Answering these questions is essentially reasoning.

This chapter will discuss four types of reasoning: deductive reasoning, inductive reasoning, analogical reasoning, and causal reasoning. You will choose the type of reasoning that best fits the evidence you have collected.

Deductive Reasoning

Deductive reasoning or a deductive argument starts with a widely accepted principle and draws a conclusion about a specific case. It moves from the general to the specific and takes the form of the syllogism. All of you have probably heard the famous syllogism:

Major Premise:	All persons are mortal.
Minor Premise:	Socrates is a person.
Conclusion:	Therefore, Socrates is mortal.

Syllogisms, or deductive arguments, consist of three parts: a major premise, a minor premise, and a conclusion. The ***major premise*** is a general statement that is widely accepted. The ***minor premise*** is a specific observation about a case and demonstrates that it fits within the general principle. The ***conclusion*** is a statement that claims your general principle applies to your specific observation or minor premise.

Major Premise:	Artificial sweeteners are unhealthy.
Minor Premise:	Diet soft drinks contain artificial sweeteners.
Conclusion:	Therefore, diet soft drinks are unhealthy.

Tips for Using Deductive Arguments

Deductive arguments are very powerful. If the major and minor premise are true, then the conclusion will naturally follow. Therefore, it is an extremely strong type of argument. In order to ensure your audience will buy your conclusion, you must ensure that your audience accepts your major and minor premises. As a speaker, you have to determine how widely accepted the major and minor premises of your argument are. Will your particular audience accept them? If not, you will have to present evidence to persuade them. Your argument will only be successful if your audience agrees with your major and minor premises. If they fail to accept them, you will not convince your audience.

> *As a speaker, you have to determine how widely accepted the major and minor premises of your argument are.*

Let's examine the deductive argument in the previous example. Will all audiences hold the attitude that artificial sweeteners are unhealthy? Probably not. It would take some persuasion on your part to get your audience to buy your major premise. First, you would want to examine some of the FDA-approved artificial sweeteners. Let's examine one of these: Aspartame. Then you would have to present proof that Aspartame poses potential health threats. You could use the following evidence. According to a 2006 article published in the journal *Environmental Health Perspectives*, Aspartame has been linked to malignant tumors, lymphomas, and leukemias in mice. There are 164 studies examining the health risks of Aspartame that appear in the database Medline. Ninety of these studies were independent studies and 83% of those found Aspartame to be unsafe. Seventy-four of the studies were industry-sponsored studies, meaning that the Aspartame industry funded the studies, and 100% of those studies demonstrated no negative health risks. You would continue to explain what that meant to your audience. You would continue to show examples such as these that link the sweetener to negative health outcomes. Then do the same for each of the other types of artificial sweeteners you decide to address. Hopefully, after presenting all of this evidence, your audience will buy or agree with your major premise.

> **TIPS FOR USING DEDUCTIVE REASONING**
> ◉ Support your major premise
> ◉ Support your minor premise
> ◉ Make the conclusion explicit

Now you need to examine your minor premise. Quickly demonstrate for your audience that the major diet sodas contain these artificial sweeteners. Again, give examples of which sweeteners are in which sodas and in what quantities. If they bought your major premise and your minor premise, they will buy your conclusion as well.

Even though the conclusion will naturally follow in a deductive argument, explicitly state it for your audience (Struckman-Johnson & Struckman-Johnson, 1996; O'Keefe, 2002). Research on persuasive messages has demonstrated again and again that persuasion is more likely when the conclusions of the argument are spelled out for the audience (O'Keefe, 2002).

Inductive Reasoning

Inductive reasoning is the opposite of deductive reasoning. Instead of starting with a widely accepted principle, you start with individual cases and draw a conclusion that applies to all of the cases you examined.

Horse number one has hooves.

Horse number two has hooves.

Horse number three has hooves.

Horse number ten has hooves.

Conclusion: All horses have hooves.

We typically use induction when we cannot examine every case that exists, but we want to make a conclusion about an entire category. For example, while at Purdue you won't have every teaching assistant as an instructor, but you may have experiences with several. Based on your experiences, you might draw a conclusion about all teaching assistants at Purdue. We make decisions based on inductive reasoning all the time. Think about how you choose the courses you take. You ask several people who have taken a course for their assessment. Based on their comments, you draw a conclusion about the course. Then you decide if you will take it or not.

Harris delivered a speech on the healing power of tea. He offered several examples of studies that had been conducted that indicated tea was healthy. He used these examples to support his conclusion that tea is a healthy beverage. This is an example of an inductive argument.

According to a 2002 Dutch study of 4,807 individuals, those who drank 13 ounces or more of tea a day cut their risk of heart attack in half. In another study conducted in the same year in Boston, researchers found that heart patients who drank two or more cups of tea a day were 44% less likely to die over the next four years. Other studies show that tea can lower bad cholesterol. So, as you can see, tea has many health benefits.

Tips for Using Induction

Inductive arguments can be persuasive if you use them well. First, you must make sure you have enough examples of specific cases to draw your conclusion. Drawing a conclusion when your sample size is too small is called a *hasty generalization*. Audiences won't be persuaded by arguments based on small sample sizes. How many samples or examples are enough? That is hard to answer. You must analyze each speaking situation and make that decision as you prepare for different audiences and occasions. Some audiences will be convinced from only a few cases, while others will want a good deal of evidence before buying your conclusion. It just depends on the knowledge and attitudes of a given audience.

TIPS FOR USING INDUCTIVE REASONING
- Provide multiple examples
- Present typical examples
- Qualify your conclusion

Second, you must ensure that the cases you present are typical. If you have cited evidence that seems out of the ordinary, your audience will unlikely be convinced by your argument. If you feel that your cases are atypical, further support your argument by offering some statistics. This will bolster your argument and will probably be more convincing for your audience.

Third, be careful how strong you make your conclusion. Remember, inductive reasoning is based on probability. You will never be able to examine every case in a given category. Therefore, refrain from presenting your conclusion to your audience as if it were a fact. You may want to qualify your argument. It may not be as powerful, but it is truthful and will be more persuasive to your audience.

Analogical Reasoning

Analogical reasoning is reasoning by comparison. You take two similar cases and argue that what is true about one is also true about the other. Analogical reasoning is well-suited for presentations concerning issues of policy. When advocating solutions, it is easy to use analogical arguments. For example, a COM 114 group presentation argued that Purdue needed an updated public transportation system. They described the public transportation system used at the University of Kansas and showed how that system would be a solution to the transportation problems undergraduates face at Purdue. What worked for the University of Kansas would also work for Purdue.

Tips for Using Arguments by Analogy

The key to using analogical reasoning well is to make sure the two things you are comparing are similar in important ways. Are the University of Kansas and Purdue similar in important ways? Are they roughly the same size? Are the transportation needs of the student populations similar? Are they both state-supported universities? Answers to these and other questions are important to examine. If your audience doesn't consider the two things you are comparing similar, then they won't be persuaded by your argument. Making an analogical argument about two issues that are not similar in important ways is called an *invalid analogy*.

> " *The key to using analogical reasoning well is to make sure the two things you are comparing are similar in important ways.* "

Consider the following analogical argument:

> NBC has been selling episodes of sitcoms on iTunes, a popular music downloading site. NBC's programming is receiving increased attention and the downloads are generating large revenues. We should do the same thing with some of the programming on the Boiler Network. This would be a great way to generate revenue for Purdue.

We simply cannot assume that we would generate the same effects from downloads of our local programming or that iTunes would even be interested in disseminating our products. A local station and a national station are unlike in important ways. What works for one will more than likely not work for the other.

Causal Reasoning

Causal reasoning attempts to establish a relationship between two events, such that one of the events caused or led to the other event. We engage in causal reasoning every day. We try to explain what caused the football team to lose its last game, or what caused your roommate to lose his or her job. Although we use causal reasoning every day, it isn't as simple as it seems. Proving that one event caused another is difficult to do. We generally consider two events causally related if the following three conditions are met. First, the cause must precede the event in time. Second, there is an empirical correlation between the events. This simply means that the two events move together. For example, class attendance and course grade move together. As class attendance increases, so does course grade. Third, the relationship between the two events is not found to be the result of some third event (Babbie, 2001).

Imagine that your knee hurts before it rains, and you proclaim that your knee pain causes rain. Criteria one is satisfied: knee pain before rain. Every time your knee hurts it rains. So, with criteria two, these things move or happen together. Criteria three asserts the relationship between the two can't be caused by some outside variable. This example does not meet criteria three. Your knee pain can be explained by the humidity that occurs prior to rain. The humidity associated with the incoming front causes the pain in your knee.

> **CONDITIONS FOR CAUSALITY**
>
> ◉ The cause precedes the event in time
> ◉ There is an empirical correlation between the events
> ◉ The relationship is not caused by a third event

Tips for Using Causal Arguments

While the previous example may seem ridiculous, we often fall prey to this error in reasoning. Just because something occurs before something else doesn't mean the first event caused the second. While this is a necessary condition, it isn't sufficient. In fact, this mistake is so popular there is even a fallacy named for it: ***post hoc, ergo propter hoc*** or "after this, therefore, because of this."

Another key to remember when making causal arguments is that events sometimes have more than one cause. Oversimplifying the relationship between two events may lead your audience to question your reasoning. There is no escaping causal reasoning. We engage in it every day. However, it is important for you to realize that events are rarely so simple. Acknowledging this fact in your presentation will be appreciated by your audience.

We rarely employ one type of argument in a persuasive attempt. Instead we use them in combination. There is even evidence of this within the chapter. Take, for example, the deductive argument presented earlier in this section. The dangers of artificial sweeteners and cessation of diet soda consumption employed a deductive argument as the primary argument. However, the major and minor premises both needed additional support. In the example, induction and causal reasoning were used to support the major premise. In order to be persuasive, you will need to use these arguments in combination.

FALLACIES

Fallacies are errors in reasoning. You want to avoid fallacies in your presentation for two reasons. First, knowingly using fallacious reasoning is unethical and second, it can hurt your credibility as a speaker. As a critical audience member, you want to be aware of fallacies when they are presented to you so. There are many types of fallacies. We have already examined some of them: hasty generalization; post hoc, ergo propter hoc; and invalid analogy. Other popular fallacies with which you should be familiar include red herring, argument ad hominem, straw person, slippery slope, bandwagon, and the false dilemma.

Argument Ad Hominem

Argument ad hominem is Latin meaning "against the person." An *argument ad hominem* occurs when irrelevant personal attacks are made about a person or group to which an individual belongs instead of the argument the person supports. Instead of attacking an argument an individual makes, a speaker will attack the person who made the claim, thereby diverting the attention of the audience from the real issue. Argument ad hominem is a popular fallacy in politics. Politicians often use this to divert attention from the real issue.

> Of course Senator Smith's proposal includes raising taxes. What else can you expect from a bleeding heart liberal.

In this example, the speaker should address Senator Smith's proposal directly rather than call him a name. The focus has shifted from the issue to the character of the individual.

Politicians aren't the only ones who use argument ad hominems. In a recent editorial in the *Journal and Courier,* a citizen wrote "The first thing I would do is pave over illustrious Governor Give Indiana Away Mitch Daniels. . . ." (Journal & Courier, A11). Calling Governor Daniels names isn't going to help her win her argument. However, the writer of this editorial is obviously frustrated and has let her emotions get the best of her. When we become frustrated in an argument and allow our emotions to take over, many of us do resort to attacking someone's character rather than their ideas. If you have a sibling you probably have engaged in this type of fallacy during the heat of an argument!

Are issues of character ever relevant in argumentation? Is it ever ethical and/or effective to bring up an opponent's character? If the character attack is relevant to the issue at hand and it is delivered in a professional and respectful manner, it may be appropriate. Imagine the following situation: Doug, an individual in a fraternity, is running for the office of scholarship chairman. However, Doug has a G.P.A. of 2.1. Does Doug's G.P.A. become relevant? Probably so. How can someone with a low G.P.A. be expected to lead the rest of the house to academic success if he, himself, has been unable to be successful? In this case, as long as his opponent brings this information up with respect, it is relevant. This character issue has a direct relationship to Doug's ability to do his job.

Bandwagon

The **bandwagon** fallacy assumes that because something is popular, it is right, or the best. A speaker may say that everybody else is doing it so you should too—just jump on the bandwagon. Advertisers use this fallacy all of the time. Just because one brand is more popular than another doesn't mean it is better.

Fazad used this fallacy in his presentation when he stated that AMD, the maker of a type of computer chip, had recently been shipping more of its processors to computer manufacturers than was Intel, its competitor. Therefore, he concluded, AMD processors must be better. His conclusion was based on the fact that because they were more popular with computer manufacturers, they must be better. This isn't necessarily so. Maybe they are just less expensive. He needed to use additional evidence besides popularity to support this proposition of value.

You also see the bandwagon fallacy used by politicians. They use polls in a similar way. Just because 72% of the population approves of the job the mayor is doing on developing the riverfront,

Sean Combs' "Vote or Die" campaign with MTV can be considered which type of fallacy?

doesn't mean the approach is correct. In order to evaluate the development plan, it must be examined and compared to other plans around the country. Just because something is popular doesn't make it right or wrong.

Slippery Slope

The *slippery slope* fallacy asserts that some action will inevitably lead to a chain of events that will end in a certain result. A speaker assumes that taking a step will ultimately lead to a second and third, on down the slope to an unwanted outcome. If a speaker claims that taking one step will inevitably lead to some disastrous outcome, then it is a slippery slope.

> If we allow the university to build a new basketball arena, we will be increasing attention on athletics. Students will begin to study less and they won't be as prepared for the job market. The entire reputation of the university will be at risk, and we will go down in the national rankings.

Reducing the university's ranking within public institutions is far removed from building a new basketball arena. It is highly unlikely that building a basketball arena will lead to this series of causal events.

False Dilemma

A *false dilemma*, also known as a false dichotomy, gives the audience a choice between two options when there are many more alternatives. It simplifies the situation when, in reality, the situation is rather complex.

> We either raise tuition or close all computer labs on campus.

Or

> We either create more community parks or juvenile delinquency rates will increase in our community.

We all know that both of these situations aren't that simple. There are a variety of ways to redistribute money on campus so that we can continue to fund the computer labs without raising tuition. Similarly, juvenile delinquency is dependent on a great many other factors than the number of recreation facilities that are available.

Straw Person

The *straw person* fallacy is committed when someone ignores or misrepresents a person's actual position and substitutes a weaker, distorted or misrepresented version of that position, thereby making it easier to refute the opponent's position.

Spotlight on Research

USING FEAR AND GUILT APPEALS EFFECTIVELY

Arousing emotions to achieve your desired effect is complicated. Let's consider a popular emotional appeal, fear appeals. *Fear appeals* are messages that communicate to an audience that they are susceptible to some negative event that will be extremely unpleasant. They are commonly used in health campaigns, and you have seen them in public service announcements. An extremely popular fear appeal was used in the late 1980s and was designed to stop drug usage. It showed an egg with an announcer exclaiming, "This is your brain." The egg is then cracked and dropped into a hot frying pan, and it begins to sizzle and fry. The announcer then proclaims, "And this is your brain on drugs. Any questions?" The thought of our brain sizzling in a pan is a scary picture. The ad definitely arrouses fear.

Kim Witte, a professor and communication researcher, has found that three things things must be present in a fear appeal in order to be persuasive. First, the appeal must arouse fear in the audience. Second, the audience must recognize that they are susceptible to the threat. Third, it must be accompanied by *efficacy*. In other words, the target audience must feel that they are able to perform the recommended response to the threat. She has found fear appeals that provide little detail on how to avoid the threat have little success in terms of persuasive outcomes. For example, simply showing a black, shrunken, and diseased smoker's lung to an audience of smokers does little to stop the audience from smoking. But if you also explain to the audience how they can quit smoking and repair the damage already done to their lungs, you will be more successful in your persuasive goal.

Guilt appeals are often used in our everyday lives as well. Who hasn't tried to guilt their roommate into going out when they really don't want to or guilt your parents into giving you a little extra allowance? There is a good reason why we use guilt to persuade others. It works! However, in a recent meta-analysis, Dan O'Keefe, a persuasion researcher, found an interesting caveat to the guilt appeal. He found that while more explicit guilt appeals do in fact elicit greater feelings of guilt in a target audience than less explicit appeals, they are less likely to result in persuasion. So, in terms of guilt appeals, it is better to be a bit subtle than to hit your audience over the head. Remember these strategies when you are planning your persuasive presentations.

Witte, K., & Allen, M. (2000). A meta-analysis of fear appeals: Implication for effective public health campaigns. *Health Education and Behavior, 27,* 591–615.

O'Keefe, D. J. (2000). Guilt and social influence. In M. E. Roloff (Ed.), *Communication Yearbook 21* (pp. 1–33). Thousand Oaks, CA: Sage.

Anti-gun organizations want to revoke the second amendment allowing citizens the right to bear arms.

In reality most anti-gun organizations don't want to revoke the second amendment. They usually want to increase background checks, waiting periods, and change regulations regarding gun registration.

Red Herring

A **red herring** is a fallacy in which an irrelevant topic is inserted into the discussion to divert attention away from the real issue. The fallacy gets its name from English fox hunts. The farmers, in an effort to keep fox hunters and their hounds from running through their crops, would drag a smoked herring with a strong odor along the edge of their fields. This threw the dogs off of the scent of the fox and kept them from destroying their crops.

The university wants to increase the math requirement in the freshman general education plan. How can we discuss general education requirements when parking is such an issue on this campus?

Politicians are often guilty of the red herring fallacy. In order to avoid controversial issues such as gun control, they will often change the subject so that they will not have to answer a question on a potentially controversial issue.

USING PATHOS IN YOUR PRESENTATION

Appeals to **pathos**, or appeals to emotion, are used in order to generate sadness, fear, elation, guilt, sympathy, or another emotion on the part of your audience. Emotional appeals add heart to your presentation. They can make a presentation more compelling, and they can actually enhance learning and memory (Doerksen & Shimamura, 2001). Emotional appeals are especially important in speeches of policy or value. By arousing emotions in your audience members, they find it easier to identify with your presentation. Some common emotions aroused in presentations include fear, anger, guilt, regret, admiration, sympathy, and pride.

How can you effectively incorporate emotional appeals into your presentations? Emotional appeals can be communicated through language, supporting evidence, and delivery.

Language

The use of emotion can be communicated through words that connotate emotion. By choosing select words packed with emotion, you can

The speaker in this photo is clearly passionate and conveying strong emotion in this presentation. Through the use of gestures and facial expression, the audience feels his passion.

move your audience. Consider the following excerpt from a speech delivered by Kelly, a former COM 114 student:

> In March 1989, oil from an Exxon Valdez tanker **spilled** into the **pristine** Prince William Sound **dumping** 11 million gallons of oil into one of Alaska's most diverse ecosystems. Because it happened in the spring, nature's **time of renewal**, the results were **tragic**. Twenty-eight hundred sea otters, three hundred harbor seals, and nine hundred bald eagles, **the symbol of American freedom**, were killed.

By choosing certain words and phrases, the horror of this tragedy becomes more real for the audience. Had Kelly chosen to deliver the opening of her presentation in the following way, the impact would not have been the same.

> In March 1989, the Exxon Valdez spilled 11 million gallons of oil into Prince William Sound killing thousands of native species inhabiting the area.

The first opening has a much stronger impact on the audience because of the detail and the emotionally charged words that Kelly selected.

Be careful not to overdo it. A few emotionally charged words can go a long way for the audience. Overdoing it can draw the attention of the audience away from the message and onto the words themselves. Therefore, use words that pack emotion carefully.

Supporting Evidence

The use of narratives or extended examples to support your points can have a great emotional impact on an audience. Narratives and extended examples pull audiences into your presentations and naturally grow out of the content of your presentation. The example that follows shows how Abigail involved her audience emotionally in her presentation.

Monica Jasmin was six months pregnant with her second son, Luke. She was being very careful about the food she was eating. She avoided caffeine and stayed away from unpasteurized cheeses. She thought she was eating nutritiously when she chose a turkey sandwich from a deli tray at her office. However, the turkey sandwich that Monica ate was infested with Listeria Monocytogenes, a bacterium that can cause the disease Listeriosis. On December 13th, she developed a fever and severe muscle pain. Her husband Tim rushed her to the hospital, but it was too late. At 6:36 a.m. she lost their baby, Luke.

By using this narrative, Abigail is able to arouse an emotional response in her audience. This story puts a face on a little known but potentially devastating disease that can occur anytime to anyone. By making us relate more to the topic, we are more involved and motivated to process her presentation on food-borne illness. Without this vivid example, her speech would not have had the impact she was hoping for.

Delivery

Emotion can also be communicated through the delivery of your presentation. By incorporating pauses, facial expressions, and vocal variety into your presentation, you can also move your audience. Speak from your heart and your audience will feel your message. By demonstrating conviction and honesty, the language choices and narratives you have chosen will come alive for your audience. Remember, if you don't speak with conviction, your emotional appeals are likely to fall flat.

Visual Aids

Sometimes the adage "a picture is worth a thousand words" is true. Imagine that you are trying to persuade your classmates to donate time or resources to the local humane society. A description of the homeless animals in our community is not

> **TIPS FOR ENHANCING PATHOS**
> - Balance emotional appeals with appeals to logic
> - Use emotionally charged words carefully
> - Use vivid narratives rich in detail
> - Use visual aids
> - Use vocal variety

nearly as compelling as the pictures of these animals. Trying to describe how matted, dirty, and thin Max, a lovable mix breed, was at the time of his rescue wouldn't do his situation justice. Only a picture of Max could adequately communicate his condition when found by the local shelter.

Although pictures can be powerful tools of persuasion, make sure they aren't too graphic for your audience. Gruesome pictures of animal cruelty or human suffering may be too much for an audience to handle. Matt, in the opening example, erred on using visual aids that were too graphic for his audience. Instead of focusing on his message,

> *You should refrain from using emotional appeals when addressing questions of fact.*

they tuned out. Choose pictures that convey your point but won't overwhelm your audience.

Enhancing the Use of Pathos

Serious debate concerning the ethics of emotional appeals has ensued for many years. Some scholars advocate never using emotional appeals at all. They argue that emotional appeals have led to horrible human suffering. After all, Hitler used emotional appeals to promote hatred.

As long as emotional appeals are balanced with appeals to logic, it is perfectly acceptable to use them. Make sure that they are appropriate to the topic you are addressing. However, you will be unlikely to move an audience member to action without involving their emotions. Just remember, all persuasive speeches should be built on evidence and sound reasoning. Emotional appeals should never be used in place of logic and good evidence.

SPEAKER TIP:

Amy Stoehr

Executive Vice President
STAR POWER® Systems, Inc.

Tell stories. People relate to personal experience.

CONCLUSION

Effective reasoning will have a strong impact on the success of your presentation. It is important that you learn how to use appeals to pathos, logos, and ethos well. Taking advantage of credibility by working on your competence and character will cause an audience to view your presentation more favorably. Credibility isn't enough. You must also appeal to the intellect of your audience by using logos or logic. Examine your evidence closely and use the type of reasoning (inductive, deductive, causal or analogical) that is most effective for your type of supporting material. Remember to avoid fallacies as you construct your arguments. They can be devastating to your presentation. Finally, don't forget the impact of pathos, or the emotional appeal. It can be quite compelling when combined with the other types of reasoning. However, your use of this appeal should be guided by good ethics.

KEY TERMS

Analogical reasoning	Expertise	Major premise
Argument ad hominem	Fallacy	Minor premise
Bandwagon	False dilemma	Pathos
Causal reasoning	Fear appeals	Post hoc, ergo propter hoc
Conclusion	Guilt appeals	Red herring
Credibility	Hasty generalization	Slippery slope
Deductive reasoning	Inductive reasoning	Straw person
Derived credibility	Initial credibility	Syllogism
Efficacy	Invalid analogy	Terminal credibility
Ethos	Logos	Trustworthiness

EXERCISES

1. Peruse the "Letters to the Editor" in the *Exponent, Journal & Courier*, or other newspaper and look for any fallacies in reasoning. Identify the fallacy. What was the effect of the fallacy on the writer's argument?

2. Advertisements are another common outlet for fallacious reasoning. For example, for many years Trident chewing gum promoted their brand by telling consumers that "4 out of 5 dentists

agree" that Trident was the best brand in the chewing gum category. Examine the advertisements in a popular magazine or look through the archives of classic print advertisements on Adflip (http://www.adflip.com). Identify any examples of fallacies you see. Why do you think advertisers continue to use fallacies in their appeals?

REFERENCES

Aristotle. *Rhetoric*. (W. R. Roberts, Trans.). New York: Modern Library.

Babbie, E. (2001). The practice of social research. Belmont, CA: Wadsworth.

Bradley, P. H. (1981). The folk-linguistics of women's speech: An empirical examination. *Communication Monographs, 48*, 73–90.

Falcione, R. L. (1974). The factor structure of source credibility scales for immediate superiors in the organizational context. *Central States Speech Journal, 25*, 63–66.

Doerksen, S. & Shimamura, A. P. (2001). Source memory enhancement for emotional words. *Emotion, 1*, 5–11.

Greene, J. (1984). Speech preparation processes and verbal fluency. *Human Communication Research, 11*, 61–84.

McCroskey, J. C. (2000). An introduction to rhetorical communication. Boston, MA: Allyn & Bacon.

O'Keefe, D. J. (2000). Guilt and social influence. In M. E. Roloff (Ed.), *Communication Yearbook 21* (pp. 1–33). Thousand Oaks, CA: Sage.

O'Keefe, D. J. (2002). Persuasion: Theory and research. Thousand Oaks, CA: Sage.

Road improvement: What roads need improved and why? (2007, April 1). *Journal & Courier*, A11.

Street, R. L., Jr., & Brady, R. M. (1982). Speech rate acceptance ranges as a function of evaluative domain, listener speech rate and communication context. *Communication Monographs, 49*, 290–308.

Struckman-Johnson, D., & Struckman-Johnson, C. (1996). Can you say condom? It makes a difference in fear-arousing AIDS prevention public service announcements. *Journal of Applied Social Psychology, 26*, 1068–1083.

Witte, K., & Allen, M. (2000). A meta-analysis of fear appeals: Implication for effective public health campaigns. *Health Education and Behavior, 27*, 591–615.

Chapter 11

DELIVERING THE PRESENTATION

CHAPTER OBJECTIVES

After reading this chapter, you should be able to:

- Explain the importance of good delivery to a successful presentation.

- Explain the characteristics of good delivery.

- Identify the four methods of delivery.

- Explain the guidelines of successful impromptu speaking.

- Explain the elements of vocal delivery that are vital to successful presentations.

- Discuss the aspects of physical delivery and their importance to presentational speaking.

$\mathcal{Z}$oe, a former student, prepared thoroughly for her presentation. She found an interesting topic, conducted excellent research, did a thorough and accurate audience analysis, and used an organizational style tailored to the challenges her topic presented. In preparing for the presentation, Zoe could not have been more thorough. She volunteered to go first and couldn't wait to share her information with her peers. Her presentation went fine. She presented a well-researched and well-organized speech. However, after the presentation was over, I could see that she was extremely disappointed. I asked her what was wrong. She told me that although she felt good about the mechanics of her presentation, she didn't feel her audience paid attention or got excited about the possibilities of her proposal. I had to agree with Zoe. The class wasn't moved by the presentation as she had expected.

What went wrong? Although Zoe had excellent examples, flawless transitions, and moving testimony and arguments, she never connected with her audience. She stayed glued behind her notes and the lectern. She made little eye contact with her audience and was therefore unable to adapt to audience feedback.

What Zoe had failed to realize is that presentations contain two components: the verbal message and the nonverbal message. She had prepared thoroughly for the verbal portion of her presentation but had failed to focus on the nonverbal aspects. Simply put, Zoe had failed to reach her goal because of poor delivery.

 ## THE IMPORTANCE OF GOOD DELIVERY

As Zoe learned, it really doesn't matter how well crafted a presentation is; if the delivery is flat, the presentation will not achieve its potential. As you have been reading, a good presentation relies on solid content, effective organization, and convincing delivery. Good delivery provides three important elements to a presentation: it sets the tone for the presentation, makes the presentation more compelling, and helps illustrate the message for the audience (Ekman, 1969).

After participating as an audience member in a few presentations, it becomes easy to see why good delivery is important to a presentation. But students often worry about how to incorporate effective delivery techniques into their actual presentations. By the end of this chapter, which examines the characteristics of effective delivery, guidelines for delivering a speech, and ways to optimize your vocal and physical delivery, this will be clear.

CHARACTERISTICS OF EFFECTIVE DELIVERY

EFFECTIVE DELIVERY IS CONVERSATIONAL

Although presentations are more formal than conversations, your presentation should maintain a conversational style. You want each audience member to feel that you are speaking directly to him or her, and not to a group of people. By establishing and maintaining eye contact and responding to audience feedback (see Chapter 1), you will be better able to connect with each member of the audience.

> *Your presentation should maintain a conversational style.*

Another important feature of conversational style is expressiveness. Think about how you express your thoughts and emotions in conversations with your friends. What kinds of things do you do with your voice and face? Do you raise your eyebrows or smile? Whatever it is that you use to express yourself in everyday conversation, you should also use with an audience. Use vocal variety, facial expressions, and an upright posture that indicates you are approachable and open. We will address each of these components later in the chapter and focus on skills that will help you develop a conversational style.

EFFECTIVE DELIVERY IS NATURAL

One of the most important aspects of delivery is to be natural. Any vocal or nonverbal feature that distracts from the message should be avoided. Think about your natural conversational style. You want to be consistent with that style. If you use a lot of gestures when you speak, use them in your presentations as well. If you are a person who uses few, if any, gestures, don't add them to your presentation; it won't seem natural for you or the audience, and the presentation may seem forced. You want your delivery to be effective and engaging but almost go unnoticed. Natural delivery does not detract from the message or presentation; it enhances it.

> *Natural delivery does not detract from the message or presentation; it enhances it.*

EFFECTIVE DELIVERY IS VARIED

One of the most important aspects of effective delivery is that it is varied. It becomes very monotonous to listen to a speaker whose voice does not change in volume or pitch. Sometimes speakers develop a pattern of varied delivery that becomes predictable to the audience. For example, when they finish a final point, they will move to the other side of the room. Although they are making changes and varying their delivery, it is too predictable. We want the delivery to take the audience by surprise; anything less becomes monotonous.

EFFECTIVE DELIVERY ENHANCES THE MESSAGE

Good delivery enhances and adds impact to the message. As part of this process, delivery should help the audience interpret the message. Increased volume can emphasize an important point; a pause helps indicate that extra attention should be paid to an aspect in the presentation.

Unfortunately, in too many speeches, delivery detracts from the message. A speaker who speaks too softly distracts from the message, forcing audience members to strain to hear them. Poor pronunciation and the use of slang words can also detract from the message. A presenter who paces from one end of the room to the other makes it very difficult for an audience to focus on the important elements of the lecture.

 METHODS OF DELIVERY

To better understand elements of effective delivery, it is important to understand the different methods that are available: impromptu, manuscript, memorized, and extemporaneous. Each one of these methods has strengths and weaknesses. It is important that you analyze your situation and pick the method best suited for your situation.

IMPROMPTU

The impromptu delivery method is probably the most common type of method used in presentational speaking. **_Impromptu speaking_** is characterized by little or no time for advanced preparation. We often call this type of speaking "off the cuff." Imagine that you are at a staff meeting and your boss asks you to report on developments in your division. Obviously, you had no advanced warning that you were going to be asked to deliver this information, but now you are on the spot and must deliver a message that is both organized and effective, without having time for the usual preparation. This is impromptu speaking, and we all experience it on a fairly regular basis.

If you continue to use the strategies discussed in this book, impromptu speaking isn't any more challenging than any other type of speaking. Here are some guidelines that will help you organize and feel more confident with the impromptu method of delivery.

Guidelines for Impromptu Speaking

Step One: **Prepare to Speak**

You don't have to start speaking the minute you have been asked to. Take a deep breath, rise from your chair, and walk to the front of the room to the lectern. Use this time to gather and organize your thoughts.

Step Two: **Determine your purpose**

Try to develop one point or two points as you walk to the lectern to begin speaking. Think about what point or points you want to make. Because you will have a very limited amount of time in which to prepare and speak, focus on one issue that you know well and can adequately address. Avoid complex issues or ideas about which you have limited knowledge.

Step Three: **Support your purpose**

Support your purpose or points with examples, narratives, or other supporting evidence. Regardless of the type of evidence you choose, you want to provide specific details for your audience so that you justify your position or purpose.

Step Four: **Prepare the introduction**

Develop an introduction. A brief sentence will suffice in an impromptu presentation. You might refer to the event at which you are speaking or to another comment that has recently been made.

Step Five: **Prepare the conclusion**

Finally, conclude the presentation. One of the most common mistakes in this method of delivery is that the conclusion often rambles. Follow the guidelines in Chapter 4 for an effective ending (be brief, clear, and memorable). You want to come to a definite stop. Simply restate your point or points and end with a memorable thought or a call to action.

Here are some additional considerations that will help you prepare for impromptu presentations:

◇ **Don't rush**
   Take your time before you start to speak. Make sure your thoughts are clearly laid out in your mind before you begin speaking. Also, speak slowly and don't rush through the presentation.

◇ **Don't apologize**
   Start your presentation with your introduction. Avoid statements such as, "You'll have to forgive me; I had little time to prepare today." Your audience will know this and they will not be expecting a masterpiece.

◇ **Focus on the topic**
   Keep the focus of your presentation on the topic at hand. Remember your purpose and don't stray from it. It is also important that you avoid any negative cognitions. Keep your mind on your subject matter and keep negative thoughts at bay.

◇ **Be brief**
   Remember, this is a brief presentation. Try to stay focused and avoid rambling. You don't have to say everything that you know about a particular topic. Choose your purpose, state your point or points, provide support, and then conclude.

◇ **Foresee speaking situations**
   If at all possible, try to anticipate those situations in which you may be called on to speak. From experience, you may know that you will have to report on your division's progress at certain staff meetings. Plan in advance what you would like to say if the situation presents itself.

Impromptu speaking has many advantages. It allows for natural delivery that aids in your ability to connect with your audience. You are free from notes and can focus on presenting your message in a conversational manner. It also affords you the ability to adapt easily to your audience's needs.

Impromptu speaking does have drawbacks, however. Individuals often feel very anxious in these situations. Additionally, many times these presentations are less than optimally organized. While these drawbacks may make impromptu speaking seem a bit daunting, following the strategies outlined in this chapter will help you be successful. With a little practice, anyone can be a good impromptu speaker.

MANUSCRIPT

The *manuscript* method requires that you write out your speech word-for-word and deliver the presentation by reading directly from the actual manuscript.

Manuscript speaking is important when the exact wording of the presentation is paramount. For example, speeches of the president of the United States are written by professional speech-writers to address particular goals in particular situations. The president delivered one such speech to console the American people after the events of September 11, 2001. These speechwriters spend a great deal of time choosing the right phrases and words that will evoke specific feelings and emotions in a particular audience. Therefore, the exact wording is extremely important.

> ❝ *Manuscript speaking is important when the exact wording of the presentation is paramount.* ❞

This type of delivery is the best method of choice when the stakes are high. A misspoken phrase can have significant ramifications for the president and could even affect national policy or security. Rarely, if ever, will you give a speech of this magnitude, but there may be times when exact phrasing may be important: at a press conference when your words may be quoted by the press, or even when delivering a eulogy. Whenever exact wording is paramount, consider using the manuscript method; this is its primary advantage.

One drawback to manuscript speaking is that it is a difficult style to deliver well. As a presenter, you want to connect with your audience. In order for this to happen, you must maintain good eye contact and vocal variety. These are hard to maintain when reading from a document. It takes many years of practice to deliver this style of speaking effectively. In addition, manuscript speaking does not allow the presenter the flexibility of adapting the presentation to the needs of his or her audience, which is very important to presentational speaking.

MEMORIZED

Another style of delivery is to memorize the text of the speech and then simply recite it to your audience. As in the manuscript speech, the *memorized* method requires that the text of the presentation is written out word-for-word and the speech is then delivered from memory. This type of style has many limitations. I have seen numerous speakers who adopted this style lose their place in their speeches and become flustered. Delivery in memorized presentations also seems very stiff, and an audience can usually tell when a speech is memorized. It lacks the vocal and physical variety normally found in other methods of delivery, such as the impromptu and extemporaneous methods. Much like the manuscript style, the memorized presentation limits your ability to adapt and, therefore, connect with your audience. This connection is something that is important to audiences, so you should consider this constraint when choosing your method of delivery.

Sometimes your instructor will recommend that you memorize certain elements of your presentation. For example, many instructors recommend memorizing the attention getter and the clincher. This ensures that you are able to make adequate eye contact at these critical points in the presentation. They may also recommend that you memorize some quotations or pieces of evidence.

Unless you are delivering a very short presentation, such as a toast at a wedding or an introduction for a speaker, the memorized style is probably not your best choice. The pitfalls that accompany this type of presentation outweigh most of the benefits.

EXTEMPORANEOUS

The *extemporaneous* presentation is a prepared and practiced method of delivery. However, unlike manuscript and memorized methods, the speech is not written out word-for-word. You simply outline the main ideas of your presentation and use these as a memory aid as you deliver the presentation. Each time that the presentation is delivered, it is a bit different because you choose the exact wording of the presentation at the time you deliver the material. By allowing the flexibility to choose the right words for the right situation, extemporaneous delivery allows the presenter to adapt to the audience. For example, imagine delivering a presentation to some colleagues within your organization. From their feedback you notice they are not following some of the supporting material you have provided. The extemporaneous style allows you to go over this section of the presentation again, in a different way, in hopes of reaching those individuals in your audience.

> " *You choose the exact wording of the presentation at the time you deliver the material.* "

In addition to providing the flexibility to adapt to your audience, the extemporaneous presentation also allows for more dynamic delivery. Because you are not tied to your notes or relying on your memory, you have the flexibility to maintain eye contact and other delivery features that will make the presentation more interesting for your audience. Extemporaneous speaking is the preferred speaking style in today's organizations, and its popularity is the reason it is stressed in this course.

In the remaining sections of this chapter, we are going to examine aspects of vocal and physical delivery as well as give you some pointers on how to practice for your presentation.

VOCAL DELIVERY

Sometimes speakers underestimate the power of *vocal delivery*. Like Zoe, they work very hard on researching, organizing, and practicing the speech, but they forget that their vocal delivery can enhance meaning and add impact to the presentation. Vocal characteristics such as volume, rate, pauses, pitch, enunciation, and pronunciation are all aspects of what we call *paralanguage,* or the nonverbal aspects of vocal delivery. These enhance the verbal message, and, therefore, help illustrate the message for the audience. Practice using these skills to increase your effectiveness as a speaker.

VOCAL VARIETY

The most important aspect of vocal delivery is vocal variety. *Vocal variety* is modifying the volume, rate, pitch, and use of pauses in a presentation. As a speaker, you want to emphasize vocal variety to add impact to your presentation. In the section below we discuss each of these issues, along with other elements of vocal delivery. The key to remember is to vary the use of all of these components.

Volume

Volume is the loudness of a speaker's voice and one of the most important aspects in terms of intelligibility. In some speaking situations, you will use an electronic device, such as a microphone, that will enhance your own voice and enable the audience to hear you no matter how softly you speak. However, many presentations you make will be delivered without the aid of electronics. Therefore, it is important for you to get a feel for how loudly to speak. If you speak a little louder than you think is necessary, you are probably speaking at the right level. Look around the room once you begin your presentation. Does the audience seem to be straining to hear you? Do the people sitting in the back of the room seem to be leaning forward in their chairs? If so, raise your volume. Most of the time speakers err on the side of speaking too softly rather than too loudly. However, some of us do have rather strong and booming voices. Check audience feedback to make sure people are comfortable with the level you are speaking at. If they seem to be straining forward in their seats, you are probably speaking too softly. If they seem uncomfortable and are leaning back, you might lower your voice. When you practice, friends and family members can give you feedback on how effective your volume level is. Try to remember, however, that each speaking situation is unique. The size of the audience, along with the acoustics of the room, will make a difference in the volume you need to project. Attuning to audience feedback is probably the safest way to assure that you are speaking at a volume that is effective.

Rate

Rate is the speed at which we speak. The typical American speaks about 150 words per minute. This range varies greatly throughout the U.S. People in the South generally speak more slowly than people on the East Coast. Although we can process language much faster than this, this seems to be the rate most of us are used to and comfortable with in presentational situations. Therefore, you want to strive to fall somewhere around this figure. If you speak too fast, audience members may have a hard time following you. If you speak too slowly, audience members may find themselves wanting to finish your words and phrases for you rather than focusing on your message. Again, look for audience feedback; if members of the audience seem to be straining to hear you, you may be speaking too quickly.

Pitch

The *pitch* refers to the placement of your voice on the musical scale. Some of us have very low-pitched voices and some have rather high-pitched voices. The important aspect of pitch is that you vary the pitch of your voice. Otherwise, your speech will become very monotonous for your audience. You also want to be careful that you do not fall into a pattern of using pitch in the same way over and over again. For example, some women's voices rise in pitch at the end of a statement, turning every statement into a question. This can be very irritating for an audience.

One good way to examine the range of your natural pitch is to tape record yourself speaking. By listening to yourself, you can get a good idea of your vocal habits and the natural characteristics of your speaking voice. From this examination, you will gain a much better idea of how to vary the pitch of your speaking voice.

Pauses

Pauses are brief silences between words, phrases or sentences. Pauses are another tool you have to add dramatic impact to your delivery. After delivering an important point, pause for a second and let the audience think about what you have just said. The planned use of incorporating pauses into a presentation can have a big impact on its effectiveness.

Consider the impact of a statistic. Simply stating, "According to Ascribe, a public interest newswire, 57 million pounds of ground beef, poultry, and deli meats were recalled in 2003. Seventy-six million people reported being victims of food-borne illness during this time as well." These are powerful statistics, so let the audience absorb them. Pause between the two sentences and at the completion of the quote so that the audience can really think about the power of these numbers. Often, speakers rattle through their statistics too quickly, thereby limiting their effectiveness.

Use pauses to highlight important material and to add impact to certain aspects of your message. You will be surprised how much they can add to a presentation.

Vocal Nonfluencies

Sometimes, we are uncomfortable with silences and so we fill them with vocal nonfluencies or vocal fillers. *Vocal fillers* or *vocal nonfluencies* are vocalized pauses ("uh") or sounds ("um") that fill breaks or pauses between meaningful words or sentences. They are used when a speaker is trying to decide what to say next. These usually occur in the middle of a sentence or thought. We use them to fill in that "dead time" while we are mentally composing what comes next.

Some common vocal fillers are "um," "like," "you know," and "you know what I mean?" Vocal fillers can be extremely distracting, taking away focus from the intended message. While a few vocal fillers are acceptable, overuse can have a negative impact on the presentation. In fact, several investigations have found that as vocal nonfluencies increase, perceptions of speaker credibility decrease (Burgoon, Birk, & Pfau, 1990; Engstrom, 1994). With practice, you can learn to limit your use of vocal fillers (Greene, 1984).

> " *While a few vocal fillers are acceptable, overuse can have a negative impact on the presentation.* "

ENUNCIATION

Enunciation is the act of articulating words clearly and precisely. Enunciation is yet another important aspect of good vocal delivery. You want to make sure that you deliver words clearly and distinctly so that the audience understands you. Many times in casual conversation, we cut off the endings or beginnings of words. This is very common. We often say 'cause instead of because, goin' instead of going. Although this is acceptable in casual conversation, in a formal presentation it may cause an audience to question your competence and credibility.

PRONUNCIATION

Pronunciation is the articulation of a word in accordance with the accepted standards of the language. Mispronunciation of a word during your speech can ruin your credibility. Why should an audience consider you an expert in the field if you are mispronouncing key words related to your topic? It becomes imperative that you are certain of the pronunciation of unfamiliar or difficult words. If you are unsure, consult a dictionary.

It is easy to mispronounce even common words. Again, while acceptable in casual conversation, mispronunciation of everyday words is unacceptable in front of an audience. This type of mistake will not only call your competence into question but can also confuse your audience. For example, many people say "affect" when they

COMMONLY MISPRONOUNCED WORDS

Word	Correct Pronunciation	Incorrect Pronunciation
Across	a-CROSS	a-CROST
Athlete	ATH-leet	ATH-a-leet
Comfortable	COM-fort-a-ble	COMF-ta-ble
Espresso	Ess-PRESS-oh	ex-Press-oh
February	FEB-roo-air-y	Feb-yoo-air-y
Library	LIBE-rare-ee	LIB-air-ee
Nuclear	NUKE-lee-ar	NUKE-yoo-lar
Probably	PRAH-bab-ly	PRAH-bal-ly
Supposedly	Sup-POSE-ed-ly	Sup-POSE-ab-ly
Toward	TOW-ward	TOR-ward

mean "effect." This difference in words can muddle an important point for an audience. The table on the previous page provides the proper pronunciation of many commonly used words.

PHYSICAL DELIVERY

Another aspect of your presentation is the ***physical delivery***, or how you present your body. How you carry yourself, gesture, move, and make eye contact are all essential features of the presentation. Let's examine each of these so that you can incorporate them effectively into your presentation.

GESTURES

Humans have extremely expressive hands, and they are used quite often in communication (Anderson, 1999). Although we commonly use our hands in one-on-one interactions, people never seem to know what to do with their hands during a presentation. The use of ***gestures*** is one of those areas that cause speakers much concern. Often, speakers put their hands in their pockets and start playing with their change. Other times, speakers will tuck their hair behind their ears again and again. Sometimes speakers clinch their hands behind their backs. Not only are these gestures ineffective, they also distract from the message. Remember, one of the goals of delivery is to enhance the verbal message. If your gestures detract from rather than complement the message, they will be ineffective.

This speaker uses illustrators to enhance the meaning of her presentation.

In order to use gestures effectively in presentations, you need to understand that there are three different types of gestures: adaptors, emblems, and illustrators (Ekman & Friesen, 1969).

Adaptors are non-verbal behaviors that reveal things about our internal state, and they tend to provide comfort when we are in stressful situations. As previously mentioned, many speakers tend to tuck their hair behind their ear again and again during a presentation. This tucking behavior is an adaptor and communicates to the audience that the speaker is anxious or unsure of themselves. Other examples of adaptors include constantly moving your feet and crossing your arms. Adaptors should be avoided in presentations. They can affect your credibility because they communicate apprehension. Often, however, we are unaware of our use of adaptors. It is important that you watch yourself on video to determine if you are engaging in this type of gesture. You can also practice in front of an audience and ask them to watch for any sign of adaptors.

Emblems are gestures that can be directly translated into verbal language. Examples include the o.k. sign, the thumbs up sign, and the peace sign. They are unique to a given culture. So, if you do use an emblem in your presentation, you need to make sure that it is universally understood by your audience.

Illustrators are the most common type of gesture, and they are hand or arm gestures that accompany and enhance the verbal message you are delivering. Unlike emblems, they cannot be substituted for words. They may include movements that emphasize words, movements that demonstrate size (e.g. "about this big"), or even emphasize relationships (Anderson, 1999). For example, Peter raised one hand and lowered the other as he said to his audience, "As education levels rise, the number of televisions in the home declines." His gesture simply illustrated his message for his audience.

In order to illustrate or complement your verbal message, your gestures must appear natural. If you are a person who uses few gestures in natural conversation, then use few in your presentations. Gestures can add a great deal of impact to the presentation, if used appropriately. As you become an accomplished speaker, you will develop a style that works for you. One guideline to follow is this: if the gesture distracts from the message, do not use it.

MOVEMENT

Common questions beginning students ask in this course are, "Where do I stand?" "Should I walk around or stand still?" "Should I use the podium or not?" Your instructor will provide guidelines for using the podium or lectern in your classroom. Outside of the classroom, it depends on the situation and the type of presentation.

Regardless of the speaking situation, there are a few guidelines that apply. Much like gestures, *movement* can add a good deal of impact to your presentation. However, it can also be very distracting. You must move with purpose to be effective. Many times novice speakers start to pace in front of their audience. You have probably seen professors use this same strategy. They walk from one side of the room to the other with no purpose. It is very distracting. We start concentrating on when they will cross the room rather than the verbal message itself.

Movement during your presentation can be very effective if you do it with purpose. Move to add impact to a particular or compelling point within the presentation. If you are standing behind a lectern, you might walk to the side of it to make an important point. You can also move during transitions to signal to the audience that you are moving from one point to another. No matter when you decide to move, it must be done with purpose.

EYE CONTACT

Eye contact is probably the most important component of physical delivery. It allows us to connect with our audience. Eye contact ensures that our presentation remains conversational and that members of the audience feel that we are addressing each of them individually.

Eye contact with an entire audience can be a bit uncomfortable at first. It may seem a bit strange to focus on members of the audience by looking directly at them. Therefore, many speakers avoid eye contact. Other speakers tend to favor one side of the room over the other. You may notice this phenomenon with some of your professors. They lecture to only one side of the room. If you are lucky enough to be sitting on their preferred side of the classroom or lecture hall, you feel that you have connected with them. If you are sitting on the side that received little or no eye contact, however, you will feel disconnected from the speaker. Favoring one side of the room is a very common mistake. If

Look directly at your audience and not above them to ensure good eye contact.

you think you are guilty of this common nonverbal delivery mistake, have friends watch your practice session and give you feedback, or videotape yourself to see. In American culture, presenters who do not maintain eye contact with the audience are perceived as less trustworthy, competent, and concerned than those who maintain adequate eye contact. Therefore, when addressing your audience, it is important that you develop and implement this delivery strategy effectively.

You also want to make sure that your eye contact is effective. You need to look directly at audience members. A popular myth about presentational speaking is that a speaker should look over the heads of the audience to a spot on the wall. This will not be effective and your audience will not perceive that you have made adequate eye contact. You must look directly into the faces of your audience members.

You cannot overestimate the importance of eye contact. Not only is it a tool for connecting with your audience, it also allows you to get feedback from your audience. Are they interested? Do they seem confused? With effective eye contact, you can gauge audience feedback and make necessary adaptations as the presentation progresses.

FACIAL EXPRESSION

Your *facial expressions* during your presentation are a very important source of emotional information (Anderson, 1999). As this text has mentioned again and again, you have to identify and connect with your audience in order to reach them. Your facial expressions are a valuable tool in this process. Communicate through your facial expressions (e.g. smiling, squinting, scowling) the emotions you want your audience to feel.

Too many times speakers stand at the podium like wooden statues and stare blankly out into the audience. This is hardly going to influence your audience or engage them. You want to motivate them to listen and get excited about your ideas. One key way to do so is through facial expressiveness (Towler & Dipboye, 2001). Expressiveness can actually motivate an audience. Don't restrict yourself in front of your audience—it is a good thing to show a little emotion through facial expressions.

APPEARANCE

A common question students always ask is, "What should I wear?" There is no simple answer. Some research indicates that a professional *appearance* adds to your credibility (Morris, Gorham, Cohen, & Huffman, 1996). However, simply putting on a suit regardless of the speaking situation is not a sure-fire way to increase your credibility. In fact, in some situations, this type of attire may actually hurt you. For example, suppose that you have been hired by the county outreach program to provide lectures to area farmers on new developments in pesticides. Showing up to one of these sessions dressed in a suit may hurt your credibility with this particular audience. Farmers will be dressed in work clothes and in order to feel that you have credibility, they need to be able to relate to you and feel that you are similar to them. Appearance is an important part of this process.

> " *A good guideline is to dress slightly better than you anticipate your audience to be dressed.* "

You will want to dress professionally for the particular audience that you are addressing. What is professional attire for an accountant is not the same for a computer programmer. Research indicates that being radically over- or underdressed for an occasion can lead to negative perceptions toward the speaker on behalf of the audience (Roach, 1997). Thus, a good guideline is to dress slightly better than you anticipate your audience to be dressed.

Much like all the other aspects of nonverbal delivery, it is important that your appearance does not distract from your message. You want to present a comprehensive picture of competence. A professional appearance that takes into account the context can help you achieve this goal.

SPEAKING WITH A TRANSLATOR

One speaking situation that can really impact delivery is speaking with a translator. Speaking with a translator is a difficult task to perform well. However, in our global world, more and more of us are being faced with complex speaking situations such as this. Many of you will work for companies with global offices and interact with colleagues who speak different languages. It is not uncommon to make a presentation to an entire audience who speaks another language than you do. Therefore, it is important that you learn some tips for facing this type of speaking situation.

There are primarily two ways in which translation can work. The most formal method is called ***simultaneous translation***. It requires audience members to wear earphones, and your presentation will be presented in another language as you speak. Many times, you will need to prepare a manuscript speech if this method of translation is used. The second way is more interactive. It is called ***delayed translation***, and it allows you to speak and then wait while your presentation is presented in small pieces for your audience. This method allows the translator to ask questions of clarification as you deliver your material and also allows the audience to listen to both you and the translator.

The best situation is to know your translator in advance and to have an established relationship with them. It is also best if they are an expert in your topic area. So the best possible situation would be for you to present your presentation while your business colleague performed the delayed translation. Your colleague would know you and your conversational style, as well as be familiar with the content area. This would be the easiest situation to face, as it reduces the chance for confusion and misunderstanding as you make your presentation.

Even if you don't know your translator in advance of the presentation, ask for a meeting to get to know them. Practice your presentation with the translator and give them an opportunity to ask questions and clarify any confusion that may arise. Avoid meeting your translator for the first time at the presentation.

During the practice session, it is important to determine a couple of things. First, how fast can you talk? Will the translator be able to keep up with you? Work this out in advance. It will probably require you to speak a little more slowly than you usually do. Second, don't get carried away. It is easier for a translator to deliver your ideas more accurately if you break them down into small ideas. Always complete an idea before you stop to wait for the translation. Third, it is more important then ever that you use transitions, especially sign posts, to help the translator stay up with your material and organize it for the audience.

One odd artifact of the delayed translation process is what do you do when the translator is speaking? After all, you are still out there front and center. The most important thing is for you to stay engaged. Don't look down at your notes. Continue to watch the translator and look interested. Try to refrain from distracting nonverbal behaviors during this time as well.

While you might think that speaking with a translator is a rare situation, it is becoming more and more common. During this past year, I presented with a translator on three different occasions. Be prepared. There is nothing worse than having a presentation flop because you or your translator were not prepared for the challenge.

 ## PRACTICING THE PRESENTATION

As in the example at the beginning of the chapter, you can plan, organize, and research an incredible presentation, but if your delivery is flat, all that planning will have been in vain. You simply have to practice your speech in order for it all to come together. Menzel and Carrell (1994) emphasize that more preparation leads to more effective speeches. In order for you to have enough time to rehearse thoroughly, you should complete your full-sentence outline or preparation outline three days before you plan to deliver your presentation.

Here are some step-by-step guidelines to help you with your practice sessions.

Step 1: **Practice aloud with your preparation or full-sentence outline.** Check the outline for the following items: Is it too long or too short? Is it organized appropriately? Do you have adequate support for each idea? Once you have answered these questions and fixed any deficiencies, it is time to write the speaking outline (check the guidelines in Chapter 7).

Step 2: **Practice delivering your speech from your speaking outline.** Rehearse the presentation several times until you are comfortable with the outline you have prepared. Go through the speech from beginning to end. Make sure you rehearse all aspects of the presentation. If you tell a narrative as the attention getter, make sure you practice the entire narrative. If you are using visual aids, they should be completed at this point and incorporated into the practice sessions. Remember, you should not be memorizing the speech, but becoming comfortable with the ideas of the presentation.

Step 3: **Add delivery cues.** Once the verbal message seems solid, start adding some of the aspects of delivery that

SPEAKER TIP:

Rusty Rueff
CEO of SNOCAP,
a digital music start-up

Describes how he prepares and practices for a presentation. "For large speaking engagements that I know about in advance, it can take months of preparation. Regardless of the presentation type, I always spend time practicing. It's important."

Spotlight on Research

PRACTICE IMPACTS PERFORMANCE

Over one hundred students enrolled in a public speaking course were videotaped delivering speeches. The students also filled out questionnaires regarding preparation time, speaking experience, and other variables, such as GPA. Researchers then rated the effectiveness of the students' delivery. As it turns out, speeches with the best delivery were given by students who had practiced in front of a live audience. Practice with an audience was a better predictor of effective delivery than speaking experience or student GPA.

As you can see, practicing in front of a live audience can have a big impact on your overall delivery. Find a couple of friends or family members to act as your audience. Run through the presentation in front of them several times. Practice is essential to good speaking, so don't underestimate it.

Menzel, K. E., & Carrell, L. J. (1994). The relationship between preparation and performance in public speaking. *Communication Education, 43,* 17–26.

will add impact to your presentation. Don't forget to mark delivery cues on your speaking outline so that you will be sure to incorporate them into your presentation. You might also try videotaping yourself or speaking into a tape recorder. All of these methods will help you get a good idea of what the speech will sound like to other people. However, the best way to determine how your presentation will be received is to present it to others. Ask your friends and family to act as audience members and to provide feedback. This will help you tweak those last-minute details.

Step 4:   **Put it all together.** Try to replicate the actual speaking situation as closely as possible. If you are giving a classroom presentation, see if you can get access to your classroom and practice there. If you are giving a presentation to your organization, try to gain access to the conference room and have a quick run-through. Practicing in the actual circumstances where you will be delivering the presentation is an excellent way to ensure that you are prepared.

The most important aspect of preparing for your presentation is to start early. If you don't leave yourself enough time to work through all of the little details of your presentation, your audience will know it. Lack of preparation time can also affect your confidence. So give yourself plenty of time to rehearse for your presentation.

CONCLUSION

The verbal content of your presentation is only one aspect of the message you are trying to convey to your audience. You simply cannot overestimate the impact that the nonverbal aspects of communication can have on your presentation. It is important that you pay close attention to both your vocal delivery (volume, rate, pitch, pauses, enunciation, and pronunciation) and physical delivery (gestures, movement, eye contact, appearance). In order to put all of the aspects of your presentation together, you must leave yourself plenty of time to rehearse it. Guidelines for practicing your presentation include delivering your speech from the speaking outline, adding vocal and physical delivery cues, and practicing in circumstances similar to those of the actual presentation. In general, you should strive to take the delivery of your message as seriously as you do the construction of the presentation.

KEY TERMS

Adaptors	Illustrators	Pronunciation
Appearance	Impromptu speaking	Rate
Delayed translation	Manuscript delivery	Simultaneous translation
Emblems	Memorized delivery	Vocal delivery
Enunciation	Movement	Vocal fillers
Extemporaneous delivery	Paralanguage	Vocal nonfluencies
Eye contact	Pauses	Vocal variety
Facial Expression	Physical delivery	Volume
Gestures	Pitch	

EXERCISES

1. Critique your delivery of a speech for this class. While viewing the taped speech, evaluate your performance on the vocal delivery and physical delivery techniques discussed in this chapter. Set goals for improvement for your next speech.

2. View one of the student videos posted to your Web site. Evaluate the delivery demonstrated on this tape. What recommendations would you make to this student for improvement?

3. Invite your roommates, family or friends to listen to a trial run of a presentation for this course. Ask them to provide feedback on your overall delivery techniques, or ask them to evaluate specific areas, such as vocal fillers or vocal variety.

REFERENCES

Anderson, P. A. (1999). Noverbal Communication, Forms and Functions. Mountain View, CA: Mayfield Publishing Company.

Burgoon, J. K., Birk, T., & Pfau, M. (1990). Nonverbal behaviors, persuasion, and credibility. *Human Communication Research, 17,* 140–169.

Ekman, P., & Friesen, W. (1969). The repertoire of nonverbal behavior: Categories, origins, usage, and coding. *Semiotica, 1,* 49–98.

Engstrom, E. (1994). Effects of nonfluencies on speaker's credibility in newscast settings. *Perceptual and Motor Skills, 78,* 739–743.

Greene, J. O. (1984). Speech preparation processes and verbal fluency. *Human Communication Research, 11,* 61–84.

Menzel, K. E., & Carrell, L. J. (1994). The relationship between preparation and performance in public speaking. *Communication Education, 43,* 17–26.

Morris, T. L., Gorham, J., Cohen, S. H., & Huffman, D. (1996). Fashion in the classroom: effects of attire on student perceptions of instructors in college classes. *Communication Education, 45,* 135–148.

Roach, K. D. (1997). Effects of graduate teaching assistant attire on student learning, misbehaviors, and ratings of instruction. *Communication Quarterly, 45* (3), 125–141.

Towler, A. J. & Dipboye, R. L. (2001). Effects of trainer expressiveness, organization and trainee goal orientation on training outcomes. *Journal of Applied Psychology, 86,* 664-673.

Chapter 12

PRESENTATION AIDS

CHAPTER OBJECTIVES

After reading this chapter, you should be able to:

- Explain the major advantages of using visual aids in a speech.

- Understand how to use a numerical chart effectively.

- Understand how to display presentation aids effectively.

- Understand guidelines for creating effective multimedia presentations.

- Understand the guidelines for presenting with presentation aids.

*B*ecause of the pervasiveness of computers, it is rare to see presentations in a professional context that do not make some use of presentation aids. In fact, most people think that they have to have some sort of presentation aid, such as a slick set of PowerPoint slides, or their presentation will be perceived as ineffective. Because computers make the creation of aids very easy, however, most people do not spend the time necessary to make good decisions about how to integrate them into their presentations.

Presentation aid is defined as any item used to enhance the presentation itself. Examples of presentation aids include: physical objects, charts, graphs, maps, models, diagrams, audio-video material, photographs, etc. Aids can also be presented through a variety of mediums, such as overhead projectors, computers, and televisions. Regardless of the presentation aid's medium or type of content, the key to using them is that they must enhance understanding. Presentation aids cease to aid presentations when they detract from the presentation itself. It is very easy to use presentation aids inappropriately. This chapter will help you understand the different types of common presentation aids and how to integrate them successfully into presentations.

FUNCTIONS OF PRESENTATION AIDS

Presentation aids can function in a variety of ways. When used properly, presentation aids can have significant impact on the presentation and the speaker.

Esztergom Basilica in Hungary
Example of Neoclassical architecture.

INCREASE CLARITY AND RETENTION

Presentation aids are used to enhance audience understanding. They can achieve this goal in three specific ways. First, they can clarify complex information. Large amounts of statistics and numerical information are difficult for an audience to process. By providing this information in a more concise manner, for example within a chart, the audience's ability to process the information and understand your material is greatly enhanced. Second, presentation aids help to illustrate abstract information. How could an audience be expected to understand the differences between Neoclassical and Gothic architecture if they didn't see examples of these types of styles? The two photos featured on pages 288 & 289 clearly show the differences between these two styles. It would be hard to imagine

> **"** *Second, presentation aids help to illustrate abstract information.* **"**

Façade of Duomo in Florence, Italy
Example of Gothic architecture.

explaining these different styles to an audience with words alone. The pictures are necessary in explaining your point to your audience.

Finally, presentation aids actually improve the memorability of the information in the presentation. Studies have shown that audiences will retain only 20% of what they hear. However, when an audience hears and sees the information a speaker presents, that number jumps to 50% (Pike, 1992).

INCREASE PRESENTATION EFFECTIVENESS

Presentations that incorporate aids have also been shown to be more effective (Christe & Collyer, 2005). Visual aids can actually increase the persuasiveness of a presentation. A study conducted by the University of Minnesota's School of Management and the 3M Corporation found that the use of visual aids can increase the persuasiveness of a presentation by up to 40% (Vogel, Dickson, & Lehman, 1986).

INCREASE SPEAKER EFFECTIVENESS

Using presentation aids can actually affect the audience's perceptions of the speaker. Research has indicated that an average speaker who uses presentation aids will be perceived by the audience as better prepared, more credible, more professional and more dynamic than an average speaker who does not use presentation aids. Research has also indicated that communication apprehension is decreased for those speakers who use presentation aids (Ayres, 1991). The speaker can relax because the focus of the audience is directed toward the visual aid.

> *Using presentation aids can actually affect the audience's perceptions of the speaker.*

TYPES OF PRESENTATION AIDS

NUMERICAL CHARTS

Charts play a critical role in many presentations. Often, much of the information we need to illustrate is numerical in nature. Numerical data, especially tabular data, is very difficult to communicate verbally. "The primary purpose of any chart is to demonstrate relationships more quickly and more clearly than is possible using a tabular form" (Zelazny, 2001, p. 3).

This makes charts perfect choices for oral presentations during which audiences are limited in their ability to study complex sets of information. We are usually interested in displaying relative differences among numbers rather than the details of the specific numbers themselves. This is where charts can become very helpful.

Charts graphically illustrate complex information so the meaning of the numbers is clearer to the audience. In the context of an oral presentation, it is difficult for an audience member to carefully study a large table of rows and numbers. Not only is tabular information difficult to see, it is time consuming to process. To illustrate this, compare the following two ways of presenting the same information. The first figure represents the

> *" Charts graphically illustrate complex information so the meaning of the numbers is clearer to the audience. "*

How Do People Get to Web Sites		
	Year	
	2002	**2003**
Direct Navigation	50.12%	65.48%
Web Links	42.60%	21.04%
Search Engines	7.18%	13.46%

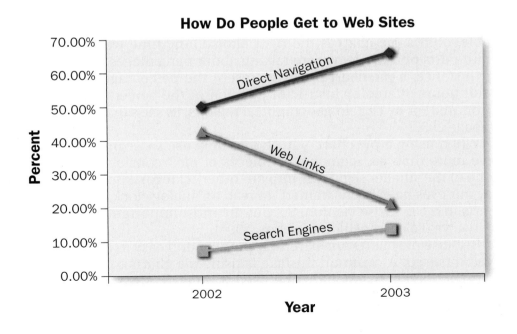

This line chart demonstrates at a glance the trends in navigating Web sites.

data in tabular form, while the second represents the same information in a chart. Though both are useful, the chart is easier to understand. In fact, you do not need to even know the exact numbers to see the general pattern of behavior. According to both the table and the chart, more users prefer to go directly to sites than to browse to them or search for them. Also, people are browsing to sites less over time. The exact numbers do not matter as much as the point they make.

The key to using charts effectively is to know what type of chart to use based on the type of information you are trying to communicate. In this section we will cover three types of numerical charts: pie, bar, and line/column. All of these charts allow you to make different types of comparisons between and among numbers. Depending on the types of comparisons you need to make, you need to use different types of charts. Pie charts allow you to make comparisons between the relative sizes of different parts of a larger whole. Bar charts allow you to compare how different things rank in size. Line and column charts allow you to make comparisons of data over time, or to make comparisons about the frequency at which certain items are distributed. Though there are many additional types of charts, these are very popular and mastery of these will allow you to communicate many different types of numerical data clearly and succinctly. The following sections describe each type of numerical chart in more detail and provide tips on using them more effectively.

Pie Charts

Pie charts are one of the most popular types of charts. They are used when you are comparing parts of a whole. If you are interested in showing how different parts of something go together to make up a whole, then a pie chart is the right choice. Any time we are talking about parts of a whole, we are talking about percentages of the total. For instance, a pie chart might represent the percentage of student credit hours offered by instructor position or the percentage of sales accounted for by certain geographical regions, as seen in the example on page 293.

When using a pie chart, you should only use six segments. If you have more than six segments or "pieces of pie," consider collapsing some of the smaller segments into an "other" category. Because of the way our eyes have been "trained" to read an analog clock, we read pie charts in a clockwise fashion. So, put the most important segment at the twelve o'clock position (Zelazny, 2001).

Because pie charts are extremely popular and easy to use, they are often misused. A common mistake is using pie charts to make comparisons. Pie charts shouldn't be used to make comparisons across years, divisions, etc. They are not well-suited for examining trends. They simply take a snapshot in time. For example, if we wanted to examine percentage of majors in the School of Liberal Arts for 2005, a

Sales by Division

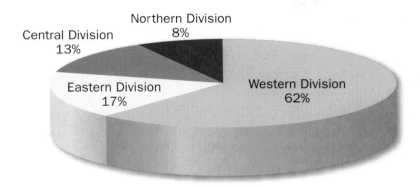

**Percentage of Student Credit Hours
by Instructor Position**

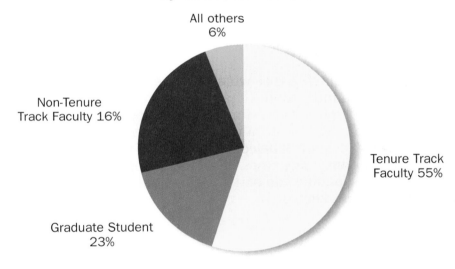

pie chart would be the answer. However, if we wanted to compare percentages of majors in liberal arts in 2004 with those in 2005, then a column chart would be a better choice.

Bar Charts

Bar charts are extremely helpful when making comparisons among different types of items. These types of charts allow for easy visual ranking across items in a category. Like the pie chart, the bar chart is a snapshot in time. For instance, if I wanted to compare sales calls made by various salespersons in my division, I might use a bar chart like the following. In this example, it would be easy for your audience

Sales Calls by Employee

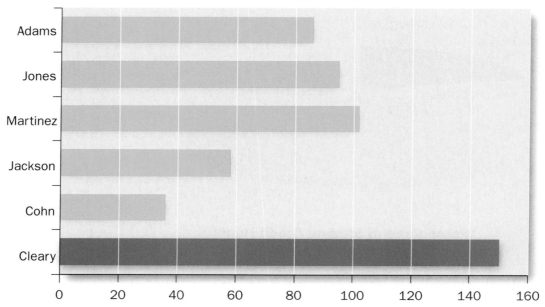

to recognize at a quick glance which salesperson had made the most calls in the last month.

When using bar charts, it is important to keep in mind that the vertical dimension is not a scale; it is not used for measuring—just labeling. In our example, it is labeled with names of salespersons, but this could easily be company names, industries, geographical regions, etc. The space that separates the bars should be smaller than the width of your bars (Zelazny, 2001).

Line/Column Charts

Line charts and *column charts* are most appropriate when one is comparing changes over time in a set of data. They are not well-suited for snapshots, but examine trends. If the chart has few data points, under six or seven, a column chart is usually preferred. Column charts are better suited for data that occurs within a set time period. So, if you want to trace changes over several years, each column would represent one year. Like the bar chart, the space between columns should be smaller than the columns themselves (Zelazny, 2001). There is an example of a column chart on page 295.

> Bar charts are extremely helpful when making comparisons among different types of items.

In a chart with many data points, line charts usually work best. They are most effective for data that has no set beginning and ending date (Zelazny, 2001). When using line charts, make the line bolder than the base line. This will ensure that your chart stands out and can be easily read. The "How Do People Get to Web Sites" on page 291 is a good example of a line chart, as is the chart on life expectancies presented below.

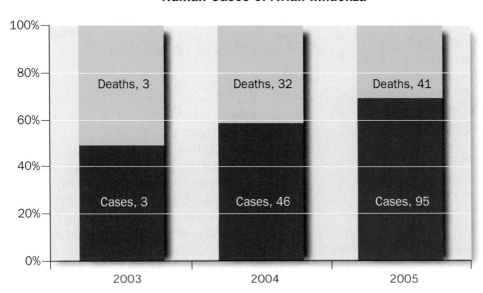

Human Cases of Avian Influenza

Stacked bar charts can display multiple types of information very succinctly. In this example, the numbers illustrate that while more people are contracting Avian flu over time, the percentages show that a smaller percentage of people are actually dying of the flu. This chart lets you demonstrate both of these in one chart rather than two.

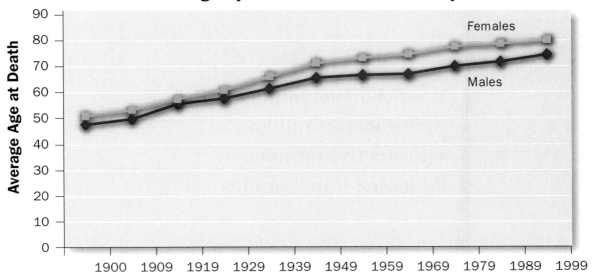

Longevity Trends Over the Last Century

This line chart has many data points. However, this type of chart is well-equipped for displaying the data in a manner that is easy to interpret for your audience.

TIPS ON USING NUMERICAL CHARTS

◎ Visually try to signify the most important numerical information by ranking (highest to lowest or lowest to highest) the information in the chart, or otherwise visually distinguishing important information

◎ Use high contrast colors

◎ Keep the number of segments in a pie chart at six or fewer. If you need more segments, you can often combine many smaller components into an "others" category

◎ Avoid creating a separate legend. Instead, put the labels in the appropriate positions in the chart

◎ Avoid using special effects, such as tilting to show perspective. This interferes with the ability to see proportions accurately

There are three easy steps in choosing the right chart type. First, you must determine what you want to convey to your audience. What is the specific point you are trying to convey? Once you have identified this, ask yourself what type of comparison does your goal imply? Is it a component comparison, an item comparison, or a time series comparison? Finally, the answer to this question will lead you to choose the correct chart type.

Text Charts

Text charts list key ideas or phrases under a heading. Usually, this is the type of chart you see on text PowerPoint slides. They often use bullets and list items such as goals, function, guidelines, etc. Often, people misuse text charts by listing too much information on the slide. Read the guidelines in the section on using presentation software effectively for more advice on using text charts well. An example of a text chart appears below from a presentation on family types.

This is a PowerPoint slide from a speech on family types and is a good example of a text chart. Notice how the slide is easy to read and free from clutter.

Family Typologies

- Consensual families
- Pluralistic families
- Protective families
- Laissez-faire families

MAPS

Maps organize information spatially. So, if you have arranged your main points in a spatial pattern, chances are you will need to use a map as a presentation aid. They are particularly helpful when you are trying to discuss geographically-oriented topics. They are also useful anytime you want to break information down by regions. Perhaps you are delivering a presentation on a recent flu outbreak and you want to demonstrate how it has spread across a particular state. Maps can also be used to provide directions within a speech.

❝ Make sure your maps are easy to read like the one in this example. ❞

The map in this example shows the Ho Chi Minh Trail very clearly. Clarity is a key issue here. Maps often provide too much detail and make it hard for an audience to see the actual idea you are trying to communicate. Make sure your maps are easy to read like the one in this example.

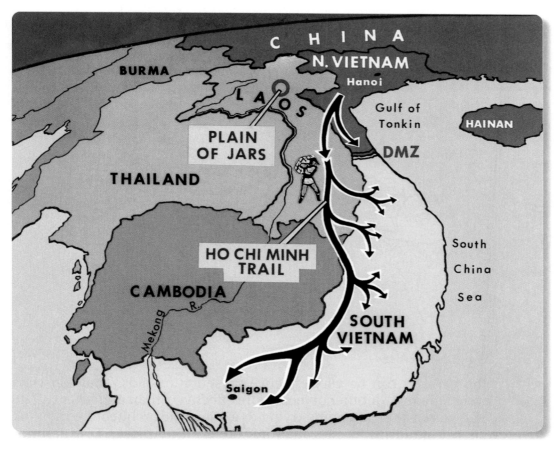

This is a map of the Ho Chi Minh Trail. Notice how the trail is clearly marked and visually easy to distinguish for the audience.

DIAGRAMS

A *diagram* is a simple illustration that demonstrates the key ideas and how they relate to each other. Many times we are trying to communicate the steps in a process. Diagrams are helpful in this endeavor. A student in COM 114 recently presented a speech on how banks process checks. He used a diagram to illustrate the steps in that process. Additional examples of diagrams can include flow charts and organizational charts.

The following diagram illustrates the emergency exits on a commercial airline. This type of diagram drastically increases a person's ability to understand exactly where the exits are located. As you will notice, the diagram highlights the exits in a contrasting color so that they are easily apparent to the audience.

Aviation safety diagram identifying emergency exits. The diagram uses color strategically and refrains from presenting irrelevant details.

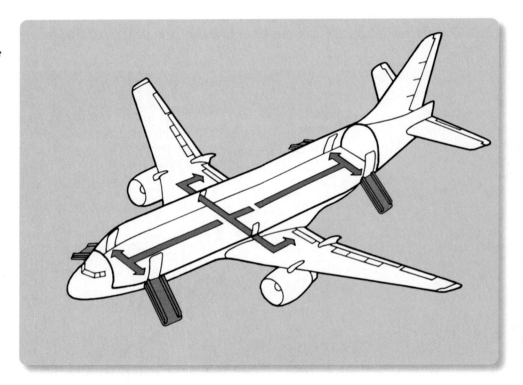

PHOTOGRAPHS

Photographs can be very effective presentation aids. They illustrate events, people, or other objects more effectively than a speaker can do with words alone. Imagine trying to explain the architecture of Frank Lloyd Wright without showing some of his masterpieces. Oral descriptions cannot do his work justice. Unless an audience can see these

*Example of Frank
Lloyd Wright's
architecture.*

beautiful works of art, they will not understand his genius. The picture above shows his design of the Guggenheim Museum in New York. A mere description could not do this piece of art justice. Your audience has to see it to appreciate it.

Photos are easy to locate. They are all over the Internet. If you are going to use photographs, make sure they are very large and easy to see. The best way to do this is to scan them into a computer and print them out on transparencies, or include them in a PowerPoint presentation. If you don't have access to a scanner, a copy shop can copy a photo onto a transparency for you. Your audience would have to be very close to you to see an actual photograph of any size. To achieve maximum impact, take this extra step to ensure all audience members can see your aid. If you do use a photo from the Internet, make sure you cite the source from which it was retrieved. Like all material that you use for your presentations, you must give proper credit when you use someone else's information.

AUDIO/VIDEO

Audio and/or video can help bring presentations alive in ways that make your presentations very memorable. Some types of information benefit from audio/video information. We live in such a media saturated world that not including audio/video information often seems like an oversight for many audiences. Because audio/video information is so compelling, many people prefer getting news and entertainment from television than from reading newspapers or other sources of print information. Whether or not this is a good thing is something that is often debated, but the point is that you can often use this source of information to succinctly make points that are difficult to make with words. The primary difficulty with audio and video is that they entail using additional equipment, such as VCR's. If you have to use this type of equipment, you should be sure that your tapes are queued to the right spot prior to your presentation. You should also avoid trying to fast-forward or rewind to locate material during the presentation. The ideal solution is to capture this information digitally and play it using presentation software. This way you can completely control what your audience sees and hears. There are additional guidelines for using audiovisual equipment in Chapter 4.

 CREATING MULTIMEDIA PRESENTATIONS

Most professional presentations today make use of what is called "presentation software" that utilizes computers and display devices, such as liquid crystal display (LCD) projectors. The most common software on the market today that creates these types of presentations is Microsoft PowerPoint, though other packages offer similar functionality. This type of software lets you create "slides" that can contain text, images, audio, video, and animations to help guide users through your presentation. Some studies have found that audiences prefer PowerPoint slides over flip charts and transparencies (Austin-Wells, Zimmerman, & McDougall, 2003).

Presentation software is relatively easy to learn, and all of you have probably seen many presentations that use this type of multimedia. Some of you may have even used this type of software before. In fact, if anything, presentation software is overused, or used ineffectively, because it is so pervasive and easy to use (Tufte, 2006). The following sections will help you identify when and why you should use this type of tool, and when you should not.

ADVANTAGES TO USING PRESENTATION SOFTWARE

There are several reasons to use presentation software. First, because presentation software provides you with visual information to support your presentation, you provide audiences with another exposure to your material that helps them retain important information. Second, presentation software breaks up the monotony of your presentation and adds visual interest to your information. Third, by using this type of software, you can integrate different types of information into one standard format that you can easily manipulate during your presentation. For instance, if you need to use charts, sounds, and text to display different types of supporting information, you can do so entirely within a single set of slides, minimizing the need for multiple pieces of equipment. Last, presentation software often provides tools for creating speaking notes, outlines, and other types of materials, such as handouts or transparencies.

USING PRESENTATION SOFTWARE EFFECTIVELY

Many people do not use PowerPoint and other tools to maximum advantage. One common mistake people make is to include way too much information on one slide. They often use PowerPoint as a way to outline the whole presentation and then show that outline on their slides as they go. In this type of presentation, every point and sub-point in the presentation gets represented on slides, and the speaker simply advances through all of these points as they move through the presentation. This creates a boring, text-heavy, and largely useless set of slides that do more to detract attention away from the speaker than anything else. When used this way, there are normally a very large number of slides, and this causes problems for speakers because they always have to keep up with exactly where they are in the presentation and make sure the right slide, or part of a slide, is showing. Many of you have probably seen presentations where speakers had so many slides they end up playing catch-up with their slides because they forgot to advance them often enough as they were speaking. You don't want to be in this type of situation yourself. The following guidelines will help you create more effective PowerPoint presentations.

Keep Them Simple

Keep the number of slides to a minimum. Only put genuinely useful information that actually supports your points on slides. In a 10-minute presentation, you should have no more than 4 or 5 slides. If you have more than that, you complicate what you have to keep up with during the presentation (working the slides instead of focusing on the audience) and are constantly shifting audience attention away from you. If an audience is continually wondering what the next slide will be, then they are not focusing on your message.

> " *In a 10-minute presentation, you should have no more than 4 or 5 slides.* "

Use Only When Needed

Only show slides when you are specifically addressing them. This keeps the presentation focused on you rather than your presentation aid. PowerPoint lets you "blank" the screen with a simple keyboard command when you are not using the slide. People do not use this feature enough.

Use Effective Design Principles

When preparing your presentation slides, use high-contrasting colors, large font sizes, and consistent typefaces. Nothing is worse than a PowerPoint presentation with so much small text that the audience cannot read it easily. You should not have more than four to six words per line of text. Also, people find it easier to see large bright text (yellows and whites) on dark backgrounds (black and blues), than dark text on light backgrounds when it is projected onto a screen. The reverse is true for printed material. Finally, try to keep the number of fonts you use to a minimum. Choose one or two, and use them consistently across all slides.

> " *Keep the special effects, such as slide transitions, sound effects and animations, to a minimum.* "

Avoid Special Effects

Keep the special effects, such as slide transitions, sound effects and animations, to a minimum. Many amateur PowerPoint users load their presentations with so many prebuilt special effects that their presentations become goofy and annoying. These features should always be used very sparingly. Other than the occasional subtle slide transition, these features do more harm than good, and should be avoided.

Avoid Standing in the Shadows

Remember, you are the presentation, not your PowerPoint slides. If the slides could speak for themselves, you could simply put your PowerPoint presentation up on the Web and allow your audience to read it for themselves. Because you are the focus of the presentation, avoid standing off to the side of the screen in the shadows. Because the lights are dimmed, the area to the side of the screen is usually very dark. It becomes easy for you, the presenter, to get lost. Don't let that happen. Make sure the room is well lit before you begin your presentation so that the audience can see you. This way they can identify you before you dim the

> " *Never forget, you are the presentation, not the presentation aids.* "

lights. Make sure that you continue to connect with the audience even though the room is dark. Stay in the most well-lit area in front. If the presentation contains a question and answer session, turn up the lights for that segment. Never forget, you are the presentation, not the presentation aids.

TIPS FOR DESIGNING PRESENTATION AIDS

PREPARE PRESENTATION AIDS CAREFULLY

Your presentation aids are a part of the overall effect of the presentation and deserve as much attention as all of the other parts of the planning process. Spend time carefully proofreading your presentation aids. Check spelling and grammar closely. Nothing can ruin your credibility more quickly than a typo. Create your presentation aids in advance so that you have ample time to catch mistakes. Get a friend to read over them for you. Another trick that may be helpful is to read visual aids backwards. Sometimes, we just can't find those mistakes because we know what should be there and we see what we expect to see. Reading them backwards can help catch some of those small oversights like double words or missing articles. You can never check too closely.

CHOOSE FONTS CAREFULLY

There are basically two types of fonts: serif and sans serif. Serif typefaces have curls at the ends of the letters. Sans serif fonts do not have these curls and are plain at the ends of the letters. When selecting fonts for projection, such as with a transparency or PowerPoint slide,

Sans Serif Font	Serif Fonts
Arial	Century Schoolbook
Century Gothic	Times New Roman
Verdana	Garamond
Tahoma	Palatino

choose sans serif fonts. They can be read more easily by your audience members.

Regardless of which font you decide to select, stick to just one. You can use features such as bold, color and size to add impact. Font size should stay between 18 and 24. Anything larger than 24 points is overwhelming. However, audiences have trouble reading fonts smaller than 18.

USE COLOR

Color can be a very effective tool in a presentation. According to research, color can increase motivation and participation of an audience by up to 80 percent (Zelazny, 2001). Color also enhances learning and improves retention by more than 75 percent (InFocus, 2004). Color advertisements outsell black and white advertisements by 88 percent (Green, 1984). This gives you some idea how important color can be.

> *Color can increase motivation and participation of an audience by up to 80 percent.*

While color can have a dramatic impact on a presentation, it is still important to use it with caution. Certain color combinations are not advisable due to deficiencies in color perception (color blindness)—red/green, brown/green, blue/black and blue/purple. These color combinations should always be avoided (Mucciolo & Mucciolo, 1994).

As with any other element, color can be overdone. Be careful about overwhelming the audience with too much color. Color should be used to highlight certain key aspects that you want to draw attention to.

KEEP THEM SIMPLE

Avoid putting too much information on a presentation aid. Each aid should contain only one idea or illustrate only one concept. If you need to use two different charts that have no relationship to each other, use separate presentation aids. Often times, students will put three different presentation aids on one transparency. Don't fall into this trap. This only confuses your audience. They will wonder why these three unrelated pictures are on the same transparency rather than focusing on your message.

When using text on a presentation aid, use only six lines of text per aid. Each line should be limited to six or seven words. This will keep your visual from overwhelming the audience.

TIPS FOR USING PRESENTATION AIDS

Using presentation aids takes practice. They take time to prepare properly. However, if you invest time in creating them, and make good choices about what to use, then your presentation will benefit from their inclusion. The following tips will help make sure your use of presentation aids is as effective as possible.

AVOID USING THE CHALKBOARD

By preparing your aids beforehand, the need for you to use items like a chalkboard to illustrate points is eliminated. Chalkboards or other tools for rapidly displaying information have their place, especially in regards to answering questions from the audience. However, they are not appropriate presentation aids. It is hard to write neatly when time is an issue. Turning one's back to the audience so that you can draw on the board will only interfere with your ability to connect to the audience. Even if you were able to prepare the drawing on the chalkboard ahead of time, it would lack the professionalism you are trying to achieve.

PRACTICE, PRACTICE, PRACTICE

Use your presentation aids during practice sessions for your presentation. You should know exactly when to show them, and when you should remove them from view. This is easy if you keep your aids to a minimum. Having many presentation aids complicates your presentation and can be a source of confusion for you during the presentation.

> *"You should have a backup plan in case of technical difficulties. You should construct your presentation so that if the technology doesn't work, you can still go on."*

HAVE A BACKUP PLAN

Presentation aids that use technology are always prone to possible failure. You should have a backup plan in case of technical difficulties. You should construct your presentation so that if the technology doesn't work, you can still go on. Also, you can always bring an alternative version of your presentation aid. For instance, if you hope to use a computer to project PowerPoint slides, you might bring a backup set of transparencies to use as an alternative. If worse comes to worse, be prepared to deliver the presentation without them. As a speaker, you should always be prepared for this possibility.

STAY FOCUSED ON YOUR AUDIENCE

Many novice speakers get so caught up in making sure their presentation aid is working correctly that they end up speaking to their aid rather than to the audience. This is very common in PowerPoint presentations. By keeping your presentation aids simple, and practicing, you can use your aids successfully and still focus on your audience.

AVOID PASSING OUT PRESENTATION AIDS

Handouts are very tempting to create, and it is OK to use them. However, the mistake comes when you pass them out before, or worse, during your presentation. All this serves to do is distract your audience away from what you are saying. If at all possible, provide handouts at the end of your presentation if you want your audience to have something to refer to later. Also, avoid passing objects around. This causes even more confusion because people are seeing your objects at different times. Handouts and objects that are passed out usually cause more harm than good.

DISPLAY PRESENTATION AIDS ONLY WHEN EXPLAINING THEM

Presentation aids are designed to attract the attention of our audience, and that is exactly what they do. If you display an aid when you are not discussing it, some members of the audience will focus on the aid rather than the message you are delivering. So a good rule to follow is this—present the aid only when you are discussing it. After you have completed your explanation, remove the presentation aid. If it is a transparency, turn off the overhead projector; if it is a PowerPoint slide, black the screen.

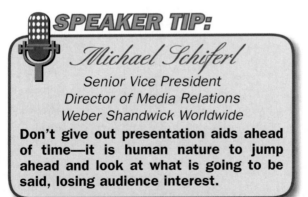

SPEAKER TIP:

Michael Schiferl

Senior Vice President
Director of Media Relations
Weber Shandwick Worldwide

Don't give out presentation aids ahead of time—it is human nature to jump ahead and look at what is going to be said, losing audience interest.

EXPLAIN YOUR PRESENTATION AIDS

No matter how professional and clear your visual aids are, they cannot speak for themselves. You need to explain them to your audience. The audience doesn't know what to look for when examining your presentation aid. What is important about the presentation aid? Point that out to the audience. Even though it may be tempting, don't rush through the explanation of your presentation aid. You selected this material for a reason. Take the time to give your audience a thorough explanation.

Conclusion

Using presentation aids can significantly aid an audience in understanding your message, if they are used effectively. Certain types of information, such as numerical information, can drastically benefit from the use of presentation aids. The key is to make sure that whatever you use actually adds meaning to your message. Gratuitous or ill-prepared visual aids will detract from your message, not enhance it.

Key Terms

Bar charts

Charts

Diagrams

Line/Column charts

Pie charts

Presentation aid

Exercises

1. Charts are one of the most effective visual aids you can use in a presentation to display numeric information. One of the most efficient ways to create a chart for a presentation is to use Microsoft Excel's chart wizard. If you are unfamiliar with Excel, you can visit this site, http://www.utexas.edu/its/training/handouts/excelchart/, for an easy-to-use handout on creating charts in Excel. Excel charts can be copied onto an overhead or pasted onto a PowerPoint slide for display during a presentation.

2. PowerPoint is the most common presentation software used by professionals to create visual aids. If you are unfamiliar with PowerPoint, you can visit this site, http://www.utexas.edu/its/training/handouts/UTOPIA_PowerpointGS/, for an easy-to-follow handout on how to create PowerPoint slides.

3. Watch a portion of a "how-to" type television show (cooking, gardening, home improvement), an infomercial or a segment of a home-shopping network show. Notice how the speaker uses visual aids to communicate the message. Note how the visual aids enhance clarity, interest and retainability of the speaker's message.

REFERENCES

Austin-Wells, V., Zimmerman, T., & McDougall, G. J. (2003). An optimal delivery format for presentations targeting older adults. *Educational Gerontology, 29*, 493–501.

Ayres, J. (1991). Using visual aids to reduce speech anxiety. *Communication Research Reports, 72*, 73–79.

Christe, B., & Collyer, J. (2005). Audiences' judgments of speakers who use multimedia as a presentation aid: A contribution to training and assessment. *British Journal of Educational Technology, 36*, 477–499.

Green, R. E. (1984). The persuasive properties of color. Marketing Communications, October.

InFocus Corporation (2004). Using Fonts Effectively in Your Multimedia Presentation. Retrieved April 10, 2004, from http://www.presentersuniversity.com/coursesarchives fonts.php.

Mucciolo, T., & Mucciolo, R. (1994). Purpose movement color: A strategy for effective presentations. New York: MediaNet, Inc.

Pike, R. W. (1992). Creative training techniques handbook. Lakewood Books: Minneapolis, MN.

3M Corporation (1995). The Power of Color in Presentations. Retrieved April 10, 2004, from http://www.3m.com/mettinnetwork/readingroom/meetingguide_power_color.html

Tufte, E. R. (2006). The cognitive style of PowerPoint: Pitching out corrupts within. Cheshire, CT: Graphics Press LLC.

Vogel, R. D., Dickson, G. W., Lehman, J. A. (1986). Persuasion and the role of visual support: The UM/3M Study (Minneapolis: University of Minnesota School of Management).

Zelazny, G. (2001). Say it with charts (4th ed.). New York: McGraw-Hill.

Chapter 13

310

PRESENTING AS A GROUP

CHAPTER OBJECTIVES

After reading this chapter, students should be able to:

- Structure an effective group presentation.

- Understand the importance of practicing as a group.

- Conduct effective Q&A sessions.

*I*n a 2005 episode of the NBC reality series "The Apprentice," one of the teams, Net Worth, lost a challenge due to a disorganized group presentation. Although their product line—a tech-friendly clothing line designed for clothing manufacturer American Eagle— was as good as the competition's, their ability to present ideas as a team and persuade the executives of American Eagle to implement their product line was deficient. So, ultimately, they were unable to sell their ideas to the client. In this situation, the executives from American Eagle said, "The poor presentation and the lack of research supporting their claims cost them the challenge."

Net Worth isn't alone. Too many times lack of group coordination before and during the presentation can have profound implications for the group. It may weaken your credibility, the credibility of the organization, or even cost you and your firm an account. Making sure that you know how to organize and present as a group is extremely important in today's business world. It is even an important skill in many of the courses you take during your college career. Think of all the courses in which a group presentation is required. Utilizing the steps and strategies outlined here will help ensure that you are successful in your future career and in your current academic career.

PREPARING AND DELIVERING THE GROUP PRESENTATION

Much of the presentation process is identical, whether you are preparing an individual presentation or a group presentation. Good group and individual presentations share many commonalities: there must be a clear goal, thorough audience analysis, adequate research to support your claims and clear organizational structure. The difference is that these activities must be coordinated throughout the group, which does present some unique challenges. There is also added difficulty in just how you make a uniform presentation when you have several speakers rather than just one. The following guidelines will help you overcome some of the challenges associated with coordinating and delivering effective group presentations. The guidelines are presented in two ways. First, each section presents the fundamentals that apply to a particular concept regardless of speaking context. Secondly, when appropriate, the concepts are applied to your actual group project in this course so that you can see how to incorporate them more effectively.

THE PREPARATION STAGE

CHOOSE A LEADER OR POINT PERSON

All group presentations and group projects will go more smoothly if one person acts as the liaison between the client and the other group members. This individual is responsible for knowing who is doing what and making sure the group has the resources it needs to accomplish the task at hand. The leader is also responsible for coordinating group meeting times, sharing contact information, and establishing group practice sessions. In short, the group leader is not an autocratic dictator demanding that his or her ideas and goals are carried out; rather, this individual makes sure the group stays on task and works to make sure that information is exchanged by all group members. The leader really serves as a group organizer or project manager.

In your group project for this class, the group leader will make sure all team members have exchanged phone numbers and e-mail addresses. The leader will also be the point person with your instructor. Although the entire group is responsible for ensuring the group's project is consistent with the instructor's assignment, the team leader is responsible for setting up meetings and for follow-up e-mails between the group and the instructor. The leader will also be responsible for arranging meeting locations and practice sessions. He or she will also ensure that the group has the resources it needs, such as a computer, visual aids, etc. Although there are many other tasks that the group leader may undertake, these are the most common.

ESTABLISH THE GOAL

Once the group has decided on a leader, it can move toward establishing its goal. As with individual presentations, the goal for any group presentation must be very clear. Just what is it you want your audience to do, think or feel as a result of your presentation? Remember to establish this goal in light of time constraints and other environmental constraints. Will you really be able to accomplish your goals given the budget constraints, etc.? Once your group has decided on its goal, it becomes important that you think about who your audience is and how you can best achieve the goal.

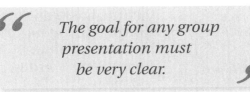

The goal for any group presentation must be very clear.

In regards to the project in this course, you should think very carefully about your goal. Just what type of problem do you want to solve or what kind of problem can you realistically solve with about four weeks of preparation. This is a small amount of time to put together a presentation. You need to think about what you can realistically accomplish given your time and resource constraints. You will not be able to solve the university's parking problem, day-care issue, or transportation issue in this limited amount of time and with the budget constraints you have been given.

Your goal should be to tackle a problem that the university could actually implement. Several of the group presentations in this course have resulted in projects that Purdue has actually funded. One such project sought to strengthen international and domestic student relationships through university-sponsored social activities. The group received funding to form the Purdue Cultural Awareness Committee to coordinate and organize the activities. The goal of these social and educational activities was to increase cultural awareness and to promote student interaction through social gatherings.

Conduct Research

Once the group has a clearly established goal, it can begin to discuss research. As you saw in the opening narrative of this chapter, accounts are won and lost every day because of the research that supports a presentation. Net Worth's failure to work as a group also resulted in faulty research. Unlike Magna Corporation, who went out and surveyed individuals in the target market about what technological needs they had, Net Worth just guessed. In the end, the executives from American Eagle said that their lack of research and, therefore, knowledge of the market, hurt them considerably. In any type of presentation you make, you cannot underestimate the importance of solid research.

The nature of the group presentation in this course rests on good, solid research. Therefore, research is an issue for the entire group. Everybody should take an active role in the research process. Although you don't want to waste time replicating each other's work, you do want to make sure that you thoroughly research each aspect of the presentation. By having two or more individuals researching the same area, you lessen the chance of missing some vital piece of evidence.

Once the general research has been completed, you can ask certain individuals to go back and strengthen specific sections. For example, the Purdue Cultural Awareness Committee decided once their research was collected that they needed to interview the associate dean responsible for diversity at Purdue; obviously, only one individual would need to go out and conduct this interview.

ASSIGN TASKS

At this point the group needs to think about who has certain strengths on the team. In this course you have an advantage. You have seen each other present several times over the course of the semester, so you have a very good idea who on your team is strong in what area. Perhaps one of your team members is very strong in delivery skills; give them the most visible parts of the presentation to deliver. You will want to open and close the presentation with the strongest speaker in the group, so make sure that the group identifies that individual early. Maybe someone else is really good at organizational structure; have them coordinate and finalize the group outline. If someone is technically oriented, have them prepare the PowerPoint template and incorporate the visuals. Everybody in the group has strengths; use them to your advantage.

> *You will want to open and close the presentation with the strongest speaker.*

What you want to avoid, however, is a group presentation that looks like a series of individual presentations presented one after another rather than a group presentation. The presentation should draw on the group and its collective strengths. A team can deliver a much more powerful presentation than an individual. So take advantage of this aspect of working on a team.

In order to achieve a more cohesive presentation, you will want to be careful how you divide the workload. Don't divide the project in the following manner: one person conducts the research, one person constructs the PowerPoint, one person writes the introduction, one person the conclusion, and, finally, someone puts it all together. This will result in disaster. First of all, the introduction and conclusion should be written last, once the body is finalized.

Here is an example of how a group might proceed in assigning tasks. For the first group meeting, each group member should be responsible for coming up with at least two ideas for the group project. The group

Meet early and often with your group to ensure that you stay on task.

should then meet face-to-face and discuss the pros and cons of each group member's proposals. Finally, at this meeting, the group should choose an idea for the project. At this point research becomes an important aspect. Everyone should be involved in conducting preliminary research. Have at least two group members cover each area of research to make sure that the group doesn't miss important details. Once the research has been conducted and you can answer important questions, then you can fine tune. You can determine what holes you have in your arguments and evidence and then decide how to fill those in. Filling in holes is usually a less daunting task. As mentioned before, it won't take the entire group to go out and interview key figures. At this point, that part of the research can be divided up among members.

Next, the group should begin writing the body of the presentation. At least two team members should develop each main point. Then go back and put the body together. The entire group should examine the body and provide input for improvement. Next, two individuals should develop the introduction and at least two individuals should develop the conclusion. The entire group should critique these elements before they are finalized.

The last step in the presentation is developing the visual components. Once the group has decided on the design of the visuals and overall plan, one person on your team can develop the visual aids. However, the entire group should review the final product, looking for typographical errors.

DEVELOP THE PRESENTATION TEMPLATE

As this chapter has stressed, a group should look like a group when it presents. One element that will help you achieve this goal is a PowerPoint template. You can have one person design all the slides for the presentation or each individual can design their own. Regardless of how the presentation is put together, you will want it to appear as if one person designed the entire thing. Make sure that the group has designed a template that everyone can follow so that the presentation takes on a more uniform appearance. You will also want to make sure that font type and size are the same from slide to slide as well. If you prepare a template with enough detail, this step should already be done for you. Also, pay attention to the vocabulary used on each slide. Make sure each team member is using consistent language and abbreviations.

> " *A group should look like a group when it presents.* "

You can use one of the templates Microsoft supplies with its product or you can create your own. Creating your own template is relatively simple and makes the PowerPoint look custom and, therefore, professional. However, if you don't have the skills to customize the templates, don't try it. You will probably be better off with one of the Microsoft templates.

DESIGN PRESENTATION FORMAT

Introductions

As with any other type of presentation, the group presentation will also have an introduction. Within the introduction, you must accomplish all of the tasks emphasized throughout this text: gain attention, establish credibility and relevance, introduce topic (thesis), preview main points, etc. However, you will have an additional component when presenting as a group: you will also have to introduce each group member and their role in the presentation and/or organization. The audience will want to know who each member is and what their role is. So simply saying, "This is Mary from marketing and she will discuss marketing," isn't good enough. Be specific about the point of Mary's segment. In order to achieve this goal, ask each speaker to write one sentence that encapsulates the most important idea in their section of the presentation. Use this material to help structure the introductions of each group member.

Speaker Transitions

Transitions are an important element in any presentation. They become increasingly important in group presentations because they are the element that bridges one speaker to another. Good transitions can help unify the presentation while poor ones can make it seem like one individual presentation after another. According to Peter Giuliano, Chairman, Executive Communications Group, "Each presenter should wrap up his or her own segment, then establish a link to the next presenter" (Giuliano, 2005).

Here is an example: "You have seen from my examples and testimony that there is a lack of cohesiveness among students in our department. I will now turn the podium over to Ken, who will discuss how we may be able to bridge some of these differences between students by employing some unique strategies."

In this example, the speaker has summed up the main point of his or her portion of the presentation and has previewed the main point of the following speaker. It is simply a directional transition with the addition of the name of the next speaker.

Question and Answer Session

The question and answer session is a vital part of the presentation. Make sure the group has a plan for how this section will be handled.

The question and answer session of your presentation is just as important as the actual presentation itself.

There is nothing worse than ending with a Q&A session that has been disorganized. The section on Q&A sessions in this chapter provides greater detail on this issue.

Practice the Presentation

No matter how much individuals practice their individual sections, you cannot overestimate the importance of the group practice session. At the bare minimum, a group should run through their presentation at least once at full dress rehearsal level. This means a run-through from start to finish with no stops. This way you can tell how the group is doing on time, identify rough spots and determine if there are any oversights or replication in terms of material. All visual aids should be employed during the dress rehearsal and should be scrutinized one more time for typographical errors. It is also essential to ensure that all of your technology is working seamlessly. If possible, practice the presentation in the room where it will actually take place.

Don't leave your practice session to the last minute. The group needs to leave enough time to make adjustments if necessary. Remember, practice makes perfect. Although these group practice sessions may be difficult to coordinate, they will pay off!

The Actual Presentation

During the actual presentation, it is essential that all group members stay involved (Newborne, 2002). After all, if group members aren't interested in their presentation, why should the audience be interested? And believe it or not, the audience will be watching all members of the group, not just the person speaking, so it is essential that you show interest. Be very aware of your nonverbals; it is very easy to send negative messages to the audience with a sigh or a yawn.

In addition to appearing interested, you must also pay attention to the audience. Observing audience reaction can help in two ways. First, it can help you adapt to the needs of the audience during the presentation. For example, if during a team member's portion, you notice that he/she is losing the audience's attention, then modify your part of the presentation to compensate. Refer back to Chapter 2 for guidelines on how to adapt to the audience during the presentation. Second, it also helps to watch their reaction to various parts of the presentation. How are various messages being received by the audience (Giuliano, 2005)? For example, when your group presents information on cost, how does the audience react? Do they seem shocked or pleasantly surprised? This information can be very valuable to the group or organization later.

Unless it is absolutely necessary, resist leaning over and whispering to a team member. This shifts the attention and can call professionalism into question. And as Giuliano, from Executive Communication Group, warns, "The worst thing any team member can do, of course, is to show disagreement with what another presenter is saying" (The Total Communicator, 2004).

In order to appear as a group, it is also important that the group dress in a consistent manner. This does not mean that anyone in the group should have to purchase new clothing, but it is important to be cohesive. Imagine an entire group shows up to make their presentation wearing business casual except one member, who wears a suit and tie. It becomes obvious to the audience that the group does not have good communication. Discuss wardrobe as one of the final steps in preparing for the presentation.

THE QUESTION AND ANSWER SESSION

The question and answer session is as important as the presentation itself. It is the last thing the audience hears (recency effect) so it leaves a strong impression. Although most speakers consider the question and answer session an afterthought, it should be at the forefront of your preparation. Many decisions are made and perceptions formed during the Q&A. Accounts are won and lost over this often neglected component. A speaker or group who is unable to answer questions effectively can undermine the impact of a well-prepared presentation. On the other hand, a speaker or group who answers questions well can strengthen the impact of the presentation and enhance credibility.

> *The question and answer session is as important as the presentation itself.*

It is important to a successful presentation that you prepare thoroughly for the Q&A and that you put as much thought and energy into this component as any other. View the question and answer section as another avenue to reach your audience. You will be able to clarify positions or data, and explain details that you may have forgotten to include during the formal part of the presentation. Some guidelines for achieving a successful question and answer session are discussed in the following section.

GUIDELINES FOR AN EFFECTIVE Q&A

PREPARE FOR THE Q&A

Many times speakers ask, "How can someone actually plan for a Q&A? After all, anything could happen, right?" Actually, it may seem overwhelming at first, but you can do many things to prepare for the Q&A. It is much more predictable than you might first imagine. By anticipating questions and developing a plan, you will have more control over the Q&A than you first thought.

Anticipate Questions

Try to put yourself in the place of the audience. Really try to understand their position and perspective. From this vantage point, what questions do you think they could have about the material you presented? For example, sometimes a presentation is so limited by a time constraint that you may have to leave out important details. In this case, it would be easy to anticipate possible questions your audience might have. Obviously, they would ask follow-up questions requesting more detail. Another example is the hostile audience. With this type of audience, it will also be easy to predict where you and the audience differ in terms of attitudes, beliefs and behaviors. Once again, it would be easy to predict their objections and potential questions. Anticipate as many questions as you can and plan in advance how you will deal with these questions and concerns should they arise.

In the two scenarios discussed above, it is relatively easy to predict what an audience might ask; other times, it isn't as apparent. We are often so engrossed in our own material that it becomes difficult to imagine what an audience might find difficult or need further elaboration on. Get feedback from others to help you with this aspect of your presentation. If you can't think of questions a possible audience may have, ask friends and family to sit in on a practice session. Then solicit their questions. It is always a good idea to get as much practice on each aspect of the presentation as you can. Therefore, a trial runthrough with an audience can achieve three goals: it can provide you with an additional practice session for the presentation itself, it can generate possible audience questions, and it can give you the experience of participating in a question and answer session before the real thing.

Have a Plan

If you are in a group situation, developing a plan for how you will handle the Q&A is essential. Will one person take all questions and divert them to the appropriate member of the team, or will all questions be directed at the team leader and answered by the team leader? Which ever way you decide to run the Q&A is fine. There is no prescribed plan that is best in all situations. However, it is essential that you have a plan. It looks completely unprofessional for several team members to jump in to answer the same question or to contradict one another. Make sure the session is as organized as possible.

ANSWERING QUESTIONS

Now that you know how to get prepared for the questions, you will need some strategies for delivering the answers to the questions. Follow the guidelines outlined next and your Q&A should be effective.

Keep Answers Concise and Direct

Answer each question as directly and as concisely as possible. Audiences appreciate a clear and direct response. If the answer is as simple as a yes or no, simply say so and move on to the next question. If you spend too much time on any one question, you may run short on time during the Q&A and some audience members may not have the opportunity to ask their questions.

Repeat Each Question

After each question is asked, repeat or rephrase the question for the entire audience. Oftentimes, it is difficult for other audience members to hear questions. There is nothing more frustrating than listening to a speaker answer a question that you didn't hear. Rephrasing or repeating a question also gives you some additional time to formulate your answer and allows you to make sure that you understood the question.

Listen to the Entire Question

Listen to each audience member's entire question. Don't start formulating your response mentally while they are still speaking. You may miss some important details of the question. Wait to answer until you know exactly what they asked. Make sure you fully understand the question. If you don't, ask for clarification (Giuliano, 2005).

What If I Don't Know the Answer?

If you don't know the answer to a question, be honest. It is better to admit that you do not know than to talk around the issue, use fallacious reasoning or answer as if you are certain, when you are not. Imagine the credibility issues for you as a speaker if you answer a question incorrectly and someone in the audience knows the answer. This can be devastating.

Here are a few strategies that can help in these situations. First, you can always ask an audience member if they know the answer to the question. Let's imagine that you are delivering a presentation on "The Benefits of Alzheimer's Support Groups." The audience is made up of family members of Alzheimer's patients and local aging administrators and social workers who work with families who are experiencing this disease. Maybe someone asks you the question, "How many families in our county are currently using support groups?" Given that you are not from their particular county, you may not know the answer to this question. It would be perfectly acceptable to say, "I am not familiar with the numbers in this county. Does anyone in the audience have that information?" If not, say, "I will try to locate that information and get back to you." It is important to remember, however, that if you promise to get back to an audience member that you do. Your credibility can be called into question if you make empty promises.

> " *If you don't know the answer to a question, be honest.* "

What If No One Asks a Question?

This is a possibility. Audience members suffer from communication apprehension just like speakers do. They often have questions; they just don't want to be the first to ask them. If after you open the floor for questions, there are none, simply say, "A question I am often asked is . . ." and go ahead and answer the question. This will usually loosen an audience up and the questions will come streaming in.

If your audience still fails to ask a few questions, ask them what they think of the issue at hand. This strategy may get them talking. You can also inform the audience that you will be available for questions after the presentation if anyone wants to engage in a one-on-one dialogue.

With Whom Should I Make Eye Contact?

Make eye contact with the individual during the time they ask a question but speak to the entire audience when giving the reply. Also, avoid moving closer to the individual who asked the question as you give your response. These two strategies will keep the entire audience involved while you answer the question and, therefore, keep them interested.

Dealing with the Difficult Audience Member

Most audience members are polite, ask their question and are happy to go on their way. Sometimes, however, you will be confronted with the audience member who is intent on monopolizing the entire session, engaging you in a debate or some other inappropriate behavior.

The most important thing to remember here is to never lose your cool. Handle these situations as delicately as possible. However, it is important to remember that you are in control. Don't be afraid to assert yourself and redirect negative behavior and energy.

It is a mistake to engage this audience member in a one-on-one dialogue. Allow audience members one question and one follow-up question. It is up to you to maintain control of the session. If, after answering their second question, it becomes clear that they are going to ask another one, simply look out to the entire audience and ask if someone else has a question. "Does anyone else have a question?"

Another option is to simply tell the audience member that you find this discussion interesting and perhaps you could talk after the presentation is over. Explain that you want to ensure that everyone in the audience has had a chance to have their questions answered and simply move to the next question.

Often, an audience member will respond with a loaded question. These are questions that are worded so that any response will appear negative. For example, "What are you doing with all the money you are making from our tuition hikes?" Stephen D. Boyd, Ph.D., a noted communication consultant, says, "Don't answer a loaded question; defuse it before you answer" (Boyd, 2004). He uses the following example as an illustration. Suppose an audience member asks the following question, "What are you doing with all the money you are making from increased prices?" Simply reply, "I understand your frustration with the recent rate increase. I believe what you are asking is, 'Why such a sudden increase in rates?'" Then go on to answer that question. By answering a loaded question, you will just set yourself up for conflict.

Similarly, if someone asks a question that you answered in your presentation, refrain from embarrassing them. Simply repeat the material as quickly as you can to answer their question.

Stay Confident

Many times individuals find the Q&A threatening. Whereas you have control over the formal aspect of the presentation, you have less control over questions the audience may ask. It is true that oftentimes audience members may ask difficult questions and try to challenge you or your ideas; however, if you have thought about the Q&A and planned in advance, you can handle these issues effectively and with confidence.

Don't dread the question and answer session. Remember, this is a great opportunity for you to sell yourself, your ideas, your product or even your company. Stand up straight. Look audience members directly in the eye and exude the confidence that you have demonstrated throughout your presentation.

PROVIDE CLOSURE

Just as your presentation comes to a clear ending, so also should your Q&A session. You want to maintain control as much as possible. If you run out of time for additional questions, tell the audience that you are out of time and close the session. If it seems that all questions have been answered, simply respond by saying, "If there are no more questions, I would like to thank you for your time and participation." Regardless of whether you run short or long, always thank the audience for their participation and thoughtful questions. Then provide a very short one or two sentence wrap-up statement that sums up your thoughts or the conclusion of your presentation. You want to have the final word. Take the opportunity to leave the audience on a positive note (Boyd, 2004).

> " *You want to have the final word.* "

CONCLUSION

This chapter is a guide to keep you from encountering the problems experienced by Net Worth that were described in the opening paragraphs. As Net Worth experienced, group presentations can present some unique challenges. As long as the group prepares thoroughly by choosing a leader, establishing a clear goal, conducting good research, and utilizing each member's strengths, the group presentation can be effective. In order to achieve success, it is important that the group function as a team rather than a collection of individuals. Using design templates, effective introductions, adequate transitions, and group practice sessions are the means through which groups can achieve the necessary uniformity to be successful.

Question and answer sessions are extremely important to the presentation. Often overlooked, they are a great opportunity for you to clarify your position and strengthen your connection to your audience. In order to be successful, you need to plan ahead for the Q&A, and then maintain control of the session. By managing questions effectively and having the last word, a question and answer session can enhance the credibility of the speaker.

EXERCISES

1. How would you handle the following situations that arose during a Q&A session?

   a. You have just made a persuasive presentation in support of a proposed campuswide ban on smoking. During the Q&A, Danny, who is from a tobacco farming family, gets belligerent while questioning you. What would you do?

   b. You have just made an informative presentation on Purdue's growing research in nanotechnology. During the Q&A, an audience member questions you about an aspect of nanotechnology you are not familiar with. How do you respond?

   c. Your group has just made a presentation to your COM114 class. During the Q&A, one of your group members fields a question. You realize that he or she has not adequately answered the audience member's question. What should you do?

   d. Your group has just made a presentation to your COM114 class. During the Q&A, one group member appears to be fielding all questions. What can you do?

e. You have just made a presentation on new changes in rules for college basketball. An audience member asks a question you do not understand. What should you do?

2. West Lafayette City Council meetings are televised live on Insight's Channel 13. The Common Council meets the first Monday of the month at 7:30 p.m. at City Hall. Watch one of these televised meetings. What type of Q&A do presenters to the council face? How did the presenters' handling of the Q&A appear to affect council members?

REFERENCES

Boyd, S. D. (2004). The presentation after the presentation. *Techniques*, 79(3), 42–43.

Giuliano, P. (2005, Winter). Ask the expert: Team or group presentations. *The Total Communicator*, 3(1). Retrieved May 10, 2005, from http://totalcommunicator. com/vol3_1/expert2.html.

Newborne, E. (2002). Tag–Team Pitches: Group presentations are a different ball game: Here's how to play. *Sales and Marketing Management*, 3, 154.

When it's time to present as a team (2004). *The Total Communicator*, 2(1). Retrieved May 10, 2005, from http:// totalcommunicator.com/vol2_1/ team_article.html.

Chapter 14

PRESENTING ONLINE

After reading this chapter, you should be able to:

- Explain the differences between asynchronous and synchronous presentations.

- Explain how media richness can impact online presentations.

- Describe how issues of interactivity affect online presentations.

- Build a simple asynchronous online presentation.

- Publish a simple asynchronous presentation to a Web page.

*I*mmediately after graduating, Celeste took a sales position with a small firm that was trying to expand its marketing presence around the country as a way of increasing its customer base. Typically, the company would organize local meetings in different venues to make sales presentations. Celeste was very comfortable delivering these presentations. She was comfortable using PowerPoint and computers to deliver presentations to live audiences. Recently, Celeste has been asked to develop presentations for online delivery to distributed audiences, something the company has never done before. Celeste, while excited about the possibility of delivering online presentations, does not know where to start. What are her options? What initial steps might she take to begin offering remote audiences access to her information? Her company has a Web site, but the Web site does not offer the same rich information that she normally presents in her live presentations.

More than likely, you will find yourself in a situation similar to Celeste. Making presentations that are distributed through the Web is increasingly common. Although you probably have many questions and concerns about online presentations, one of the most common is, "Are they effective?" Much of what is known about online presentations comes from the research being conducted in the area of distance education. This research has indicated that online lectures and presentations can be as effective as traditional learning environments (Tallent-Runnels, Thomas, Lan, Cooper, et al., 2006; Moore & Thompson, 1990) if you choose the right technology for the message you want to deliver. When Celeste was first considering her options, she thought it might be simple to videotape her presentation and then have it digitized for the Web. What she quickly discovered was that once her presentation was digitized for placement on the Web, she was disappointed with the results. Her video was very small, it was hard to recognize her, and the sound was difficult to hear. Also, her PowerPoint presentation that she worked so hard on was small, blurry, and an unreadable part of the background. Celeste was using the wrong tool for the job.

This chapter is designed to introduce you to some of the differences between face-to-face presentations and online presentations. It will also provide some strategies for addressing some of these differences, thereby avoiding some of the mistakes made by Celeste. Additionally, the chapter presents several tutorials for taking the information in your "traditional" presentations and distributing that material online in ways that are effective and take advantage of the benefits of the online environment.

THE IMPORTANCE OF ONLINE PRESENTATIONS

Increasingly, we work, communicate, and interact with people who live in other cities, states, and even countries. Students who understand the role that digital technologies play in facilitating and transforming interaction with distributed audiences have substantial advantages over those who do not. Corporations have already realized this importance. In essence, delivering presentations online facilitates cost savings, labor efficiency, and coordination, and because of this, they are becoming pervasive forms of communication.

Cost Savings

The economic advantages of presenting online are relatively easy to understand. Distributed organizations, and organizations trying to reach ***distributed audiences,*** find much of their expenses consumed by travel. By distributed, it is meant that the organization and/or its clients are geographically dispersed. A company may have offices in many locations, or, even more common, its clients are distributed around the state, nation, or world. Airfares, hotel accommodations, and scheduling of facilities is expensive for both the companies and their clients. The possibility of eliminating or drastically limiting those expenses can save companies substantial amounts of money over time for both internal and external communication. Instead of spending money on these factors, companies are increasingly investing in online technologies that maximize profitability in the long term (Lindstrom, 2002).

Time Savings

In addition to costs associated with travel, traditional presentations are also seen as a less efficient use of employee time. Lost productivity due to traditional presentations that involve travel is also a factor driving investments in online alternatives. Additionally, one online presentation can reach many more people over a span of time than a series of traditional presentations in small venues. Reducing unnecessary redundancy of effort through the presentation of material online can maximize profit.

Coordination

Coordination between presenter and audience is another factor driving online presentations. Depending on your circumstances, it is often very difficult to find common times for meetings and presentations. Additionally, people are often involved in meetings and presentations that are not directly relevant to their work. By presenting online, companies have the ability to target participants who need the information, and participants have the ability to participate in presentations that they know will be beneficial.

Because of the benefits that corporations realize from online presentations, they will continue to grow in popularity. As an employee, you will be expected to understand how to present in traditional mediums, but you will also be expected to have the skills to create a variety of Web-based presentations.

DIFFERENCES BETWEEN ONLINE AND TRADITIONAL PRESENTATIONS

All presentations, whether online or traditional, should share certain things in common. As stressed throughout this course and text, all presentations should be goal-driven, audience-focused, and responsive to feedback. However, the ways in which these things are accomplished can look very different depending on the type of online presentation you are creating. Different types of online presentations have different characteristics that will force you to carefully evaluate your goals in terms of what you are trying to accomplish, evaluate the needs and abilities of your audience, and determine how you will respond to audience feedback.

Additionally, all online presentations are not the same. There is a vast array of possibilities for creating presentations for online delivery. These can range from simple tasks such as uploading a PowerPoint presentation to the Web, to streaming audio and video, to fully interactive Web conferences. Each of these types of online presentations has different characteristics, as well as advantages and disadvantages. Some of these differences include synchronicity, richness of the media and levels of interactivity.

SYNCHRONOUS VERSUS ASYNCHRONOUS COMMUNICATION

When we say that things are *synchronous*, or "in synch," we simply mean they are occurring at the same time. Face-to-face interaction is synchronous, as is Internet chat. When you deliver your presentation to your classroom audience, it is synchronous. Your audience receives your message as you present it. *Asynchronous* communication, on the other hand, does not occur simultaneously. The message you present is not received by your audience as you deliver it, but at some later time. E-mail is an example of asynchronous communication. Online presentations are often asynchronous, though they can be synchronous as well. The issue of synchronicity can have a huge effect on your presentation and will have strong implications for the decisions you make when planning your presentation. The important thing to remember is that each can be very effective. You just have to choose the right method for your message.

When we look at the Web, asynchronous presentations are the most common type of presentation out there. These presentations can take the form of Web pages, streaming audio or video, and multimedia presentations that combine text, graphic, audio, video, animations, etc. We often call asynchronous presentations ***on demand presentations*** because audiences can access this type of presentation at any time.

Synchronous, or *live* presentations, occur when the audience accesses the presentation while you are delivering it. Traditionally, this happens during phone presentations where people dial into a phone conference to hear a presentation, through video conferencing technology where audio and video is delivered to remote points through phone or satellite technology, or through contemporary Web conferencing systems where audio, video, and other data are presented live on the screen while the audience views the presentation. In most cases, synchronous presentations have more in common with traditional presentations than asynchronous presentations do.

Often, live and on demand presentations can work in concert with each other. It is not uncommon for speakers to deliver a live presentation that is simultaneously recorded and distributed for on demand access at a later time. Similarly, a presenter may distribute a presentation as "on demand" but schedule a live question and answer session to be presented through e-mail once the audience has viewed the presentation.

> **TIPS FOR ASYNCHRONOUS PRESENTATIONS**
>
> ◉ On demand content, because of its permanence, should be carefully rehearsed or scripted
> ◉ Online content should be checked for accessibility to ensure people with vision or hearing impairments can access the information
> ◉ Slide information can have more text and other information than traditional slides since the audience can often pause and review material carefully

The nature of your presentation content will often determine which type of presentation you will want to use. If you have timely information that will be quickly outdated, synchronous presentations may be more effective than asynchronous presentations. One of the complaints about the Web is that much of the content is never maintained. It quickly becomes outdated, and, hence, irrelevant or inaccurate. However, if your material will not be obsolete very quickly, then asynchronous presentations may be more effective.

Other considerations should be kept in mind when planning for an asynchronous presentation. First, the on demand and, therefore, permanent nature of the media require more formality on the part of the speaker. This means that you should use a manuscript style when delivering this type of presentation. Part of the benefit of an extemporaneous presentation is flexibility, which allows a speaker the ability to adapt to the needs of the audience. Since adaptability will not be immediately possible, the added formality of a manuscript presentation has more benefits in this context. As mentioned in Chapter 11 of this text, manuscript speeches are difficult to deliver well. Therefore, this type of presentation will need to be carefully rehearsed to achieve the impact you desire.

Secondly, online content should also be checked for accessibility to ensure that people with vision or hearing impairments can access the information. With large distributed audiences, the various needs of audience members can be great. One of the benefits of an on demand presentation is its ability to reach a wide audience. You do not want to artificially limit this audience by failing to adapt to potential impairments. For example, some individuals use screen-reading software to vocally narrate textual material. If you have a lot of images, you need to be sure alternative labels describe the image.

> **TIPS FOR SYNCHRONOUS PRESENTATIONS**
>
> ◉ Practice using the Web conferencing system prior to the presentation to ensure you are comfortable
> ◉ Have a moderator help you monitor audience questions and deal with technical issues so you can focus on the presentation
> ◉ Make sure the audience has a chance to configure their computers correctly and test their connections prior to the start of the meeting
> ◉ Have a backup plan ready in case there are technical difficulties

Finally, presentational aids can be more detailed in an asynchronous presentation. Audiences will have the ability to read your PowerPoint slides at their leisure, so they can contain more detail than they might in more traditional presentations. Charts and figures may also have more detail because they can be more closely scrutinized by audience members.

Synchronous presentations present their own set of challenges. Most of these are related to the technology itself. First, practice to get comfortable with the Web conferencing system you will be using to deliver your material. Plan several run-throughs until you feel completely comfortable with the system. Second, have a moderator to assist you with audience questions and/or technical difficulties. Having this additional support will allow you to focus all of your energy on your message. Third, arrive early and make sure all aspects of the technology are working smoothly. Even though they may have worked the afternoon before, it is essential that you ensure all components will be ready to go when you are. As with any technology, there is always the potential for technology failure. So, have a backup plan. What will you do if one of the components of your presentation simply will not work? If your technology does fail, don't get flustered. Use this opportunity to demonstrate how polished and competent you are in the situation. Quickly revert to plan B and present the presentation with confidence. This will go a long way in building your credibility as a speaker. For instance, if you are using a Web conferencing system, you might schedule a backup phone conference line just in case there are network problems.

MEDIA RICHNESS

Traditional presentations are often characterized by a variety of communication channels. In other words, they are *media rich* in that speakers are presenting slides, conducting demonstrations, showing other media such as video, interacting with audiences, and engaging in other nonverbal interaction. One of the concerns is that particular mediums leave out relevant information that is important. However, with increases in computer power and network availability, it is substantially easier to provide rich presentations that incorporate multiple mediums to help communicate different aspects of a presentation. The key issue for presenters who have to present online is that they need to understand which components of their presentation are the most important, and understand the technologies they need to use to present those components. Not all presentations require high levels of multimedia.

Media richness exists on a continuum from very lean to very rich. *Lean presentations* use only one or two media forms to communicate, while *rich media* presentations use multiple forms of media. For instance, most Web sites consist of text and graphics. This combination, though relatively lean, is often effective and is the most common type of content on the Web. Also, many online presentations are streaming audio and/or video. This type of presentation provides a very different feel from a traditional Web page presentation of content. Richer presentations might incorporate all of these, with parts of the content presented through text and graphics, and parts through audio and video that is also made available through the Web site.

As a rule, increasing the media richness of a presentation is better for most audiences. In education and training research, it has been recognized that audiences have different learning styles (Kolb, 1984). Some individuals learn better by hearing, some by seeing, some by reading, and some through interaction. This is true for both traditional and online presentations. Presenters who understand that different audience members have different needs and process information in different ways increase the potential for impacting a particular audience. Integrated presentations that incorporate textual, graphical, auditory, and video information have an increased likelihood of reaching audiences in different ways.

One important caveat is that not all presentations are well-suited for delivery in an online context. Regardless of how richly they are presented, certain sorts of announcements or situations that are highly emotional are simply not effective when presented online. Because of the emotionality involved with particular situations or topics, there is a high reliance on nonverbal aspects of the message. Both the sender and the receiver need to be face-to-face so that each can observe the nonverbal communication that transpires. No matter how carefully crafted, your narrated PowerPoint will not do a good job communicating the need for necessary layoffs. In this case, it is better to find a way to present the message in person or the presentation will appear insensitive.

INTERACTIVITY

One assumption that is often made is that online presentations suffer from limited amounts of speaker/audience *interactivity*. In this course, one of the key requirements for most speakers is to be extemporaneous. Speakers are expected to adapt to audience needs during their delivery, answer questions, and engage the audience in a variety of ways. How can online presenters hope to accomplish this? Doesn't the technology itself get in the way of interaction? The short answer is, "yes." Online presentations typically provide less traditional ways of responding immediately and effectively to diverse and changing audience needs. However, a better question for communicators to think about is, "How do I leverage appropriate technologies to provide for audience interaction and adaptation?"

Online presenters have responded to this question in different ways, and their answers to this question have largely depended on the type of online presentation they are making. The big difference to consider is whether or not you are presenting synchronously or asynchronously.

In on demand presentations, several options are typically used. Speakers often use technologies such as online discussion forums, e-mail, feedback forms, and other Web technologies as a way of answering audience questions and responding to feedback. While these may seem limited on the surface, they do have their own advantages. First, when feedback to online presentations is provided electronically, there is now an archive of audience questions and responses to those questions. Second, this type of feedback can be used by the presenter to actually adjust portions of the presentation to clarify any problems. So the presentation is being adapted for future audiences based on feedback from past audiences. While the adjusting to feedback isn't necessarily how we typically think about it, it still can occur. Finally, by having this type of asynchronous dialogue between a presenter and an audience, we can begin to see how online presentations persist as a part of a larger conversation between presenter and audience that is not possible in a traditional environment.

In live or synchronous presentations, the situation is different. Like traditional presentations, there are ways to receive feedback immediately, as well as ways to respond immediately. Audiences can ask questions through audio and video, as well as interact in chat rooms during the presentation. This presents an advantage in and of itself. In most Web conferencing environments, a chat room is often available for audience members, as well as the presenter, to use. One of the advantages of this is that audience members can interact with each other, as well as the presenter, during the presentation. In traditional live presentations, this is typically difficult to do.

The key factor is to recognize that speakers need to think of ways to facilitate interaction and recognize that supposed limitations are not always limitations. New technologies provide both new challenges for maintaining interactivity but also create new possibilities for interaction that are not possible in traditional environments.

> **PUBLISHING CONTENT TO YOUR PURDUE WEB ACCOUNT**
>
> At Purdue, it is easy to publish presentations or other content to the Web. Here are the basic steps:
> - Create your content
> - In the ITaP labs, copy the content to the "www" folder on your H: drive.
> - The content is now viewable on the Web at: http://web.ics.purdue.edu/~yourid/file.html
> - Be sure and replace "yourid" with your Purdue Career Account ID and "file.html" with the actual name of your file
> - More information on how to do this is available on ITaP's Web site at: http://www.itap.purdue.edu/tlt/careeraccount/

PRESENTER AND AUDIENCE TECHNOLOGY LIMITATIONS

An additional limitation that needs to be specifically addressed is that new technologies and new techniques for communicating require both a sufficient technology infrastructure to support the presentation and the technical skill to take advantage of that infrastructure. For instance, if you want to build a Web presentation, do you have a Web site to host it? If you want to record audio and video, is there recording and digitizing equipment or computers available? If you want to participate in an online presentation or event, do you have appropriate Web browsers, or plugins, or network connections that allow you to participate? These are the types of things meant by infrastructure. Online presentations require appropriate online environments.

Many times an infrastructure exists, but presenters and their audiences do not have the skills to develop content or view the presentations. These skills are a part of the basic competencies that need to be learned by presenters, or there must be support staff available that can help presenters and audiences use or develop the material. The next section provides some ideas and techniques for developing basic skills.

INTRODUCTORY METHODS FOR BUILDING ASYNCHRONOUS ONLINE PRESENTATIONS

The most popular technology accompanying contemporary presentations is the use of presentation software, like Microsoft PowerPoint, to show slides of text, images, and other multimedia during a live presentation. Most students are familiar with this type of software and learn to use it early in their academic careers if they do not already know how to use it. However, this technology can also be used to create electronic or online presentations.

Being able to create electronic or online presentations is a valuable skill to have for a variety of reasons:

◇ To provide people who could not attend the opportunity to see your presentation.

◇ To provide people with the ability to review information in your presentation at a later date.

◇ To provide an alternative way to present to audiences when it is not possible to provide a live presentation.

On the surface, this may seem like a simple task. It is not uncommon for people to e-mail, burn to CD, or publish to the Web,

> **SPEAKING TIPS FOR THE ONLINE PRESENTATION**
>
> ◉ Practice with the technology. The first time you use the technology should not be during your presentation. Practice with a remote audience ahead of time.
>
> ◉ Wear muted or solid tones. Avoid red and bright white. Red can bleed and white can interfere with the contrast of the video image.
>
> ◉ When referencing visual aids, remember that you cannot draw audience members' attention to specific points in your slides by using a laser pointer, for example. So, pointing should be built into the presentation by using animated arrows and circles, etc. (The Total Communicator, 2004).

standard PowerPoint (.ppt) files for others to view. However, this is problematic for a couple of reasons. First, it assumes viewers of the presentation have a copy of PowerPoint, or a PowerPoint viewer, installed on their computers. This is often not the case. Second, standard PowerPoint presentations are often very large and are difficult to distribute electronically because of this size issue. Because of this, you need to become familiar with alternative ways of working with PowerPoint to provide more effective presentations for Web and electronic delivery that will make it easier for your audiences to access your presentation.

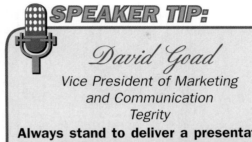

SPEAKER TIP:

David Goad
Vice President of Marketing
and Communication
Tegrity

Always stand to deliver a presentation. You will always have more energy and project better in your online presentations when you are standing, even if there is no audience in the room.

This section will provide you with a basic understanding of how to use PowerPoint to create versions of your presentation that will help meet these different scenarios, overcome the deficiencies of sharing standard PowerPoint files, and provide guidelines on how to modify your presentations to make them more effective for online delivery. Specifically, three techniques will be covered:

◇ Converting PowerPoint slides to HTML.
◇ Creating HTML-based, narrated PowerPoint presentations for online delivery.
◇ Creating a streaming video presentation of your narrated PowerPoint presentation.

Once you have learned how to create your presentations in a form appropriate for Web distribution, this section will overview the process of publishing these types of presentations to the Web so others can view them.

CREATING AN HTML VERSION OF YOUR POWERPOINT PRESENTATION

The simplest way to effectively distribute PowerPoint presentations for online delivery is to convert them to HTML. This process is not difficult, but to maximize your audience's ability to view your presentation, there are several issues you need to be aware of during this process. The primary problem spot presenters need to avoid is the selection of PowerPoint's default options. While these options work fine for some users, the default options typically only work well for audiences who are using Microsoft operating systems and Web browsers. Other users will not be able to view the presentation effectively, or possibly, at all.

Steps in Creating a Web Presentation

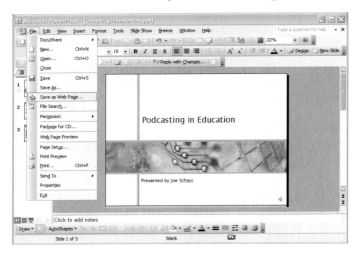

Once you have prepared your presentation you are ready to create a Web version of it. To begin this process:

Select "Save as Web Page..." under the "File" menu.

The default settings on this page need to be changed. By default, PowerPoint wants to save your presentation as an .mht or .mhtml file. This is a Microsoft specific format that is not recommended. Instead:

Select "Web Page (*.htm; *.html)" under "Save as Type."

Give your file a file name. Tip: Do not use spaces or special characters in your file name.

Click the "Publish" button.

You have several options on this page, and even more if you push the "Web Options" button. At a minimum, you should:

Select "All browsers listed above (creates larger files)" to ensure compatibility.

If you use speaker notes in the preparation of your presentation and want them to be visible, check the "Display speaker notes" option.

Check the "Open published Web page in browser box."

Click "Publish."

At this point, your presentation should open in a Web browser to show you what it will look like to your viewers.

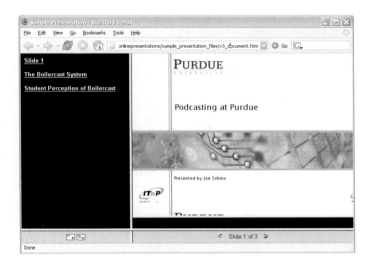

The final step is to publish your presentation to a Web site so that others can view it. You could also e-mail the presentation or burn it to a CD for distribution.

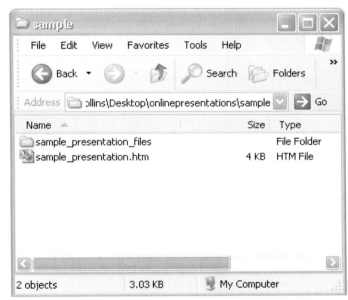

The important point is that the Web version of your presentation is contained in several files. The main file is an .htm file that is the same name as your presentation. There is also a corresponding folder full of additional files that are a part of your Web presentation. When you publish the presentation, you must publish both the main file and the folder of additional files.

CREATING A NARRATED POWERPOINT PRESENTATION

The preceding section described the basic process for creating a Web version of your PowerPoint slides. It is not very difficult, but it also has some limitations itself. If you think about it, a PowerPoint is usually only supplemental to your normal presentations. It is usually either a sketchy outline of your main points and/or some additional supplemental material such as images, charts, or other information. In many cases, this information does not completely represent your overall presentation, the bulk of which is usually spoken. Therefore, it usually cannot stand alone.

PowerPoint, however, allows for the creation of "Narrations," which are recordings of your spoken words that are synchronized with the slides in your presentation. The overall presentation now contains your full spoken text, as well as your slides. This, as a rule, will make your online presentation much more meaningful and complete.

For this step, you will need a microphone on your computer to capture the sound. It is recommended that you use a headset microphone if at all possible. These can be purchased inexpensively for less than $20, though you can pay much more than that if you want special features or very high quality sound. However, inexpensive headsets are fine to start with.

Steps in Creating a Narrated Web Presentation

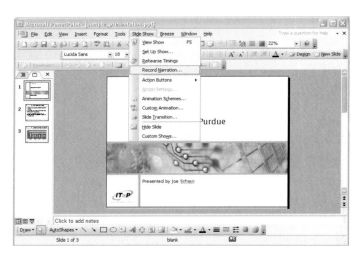

Once your slides are prepared and you are ready to record your audio, you should first:

Select "Record Narration . . ." under the "Slide Show" menu.

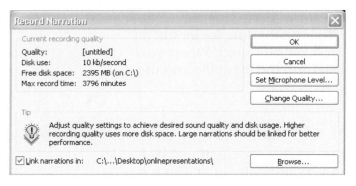

This will bring up a set of options on how to adjust the audio:

Check "Link narrations in: . . ." and browse to the folder you have saved your presentation in. This step links your narration with your slides.

Push the "Set Microphone Level . . ." button.

This slide will ensure your microphone is recognized by the computer and allow you to set the microphone sensitivity.

Adjust the slider bar so that your voice is in the green and yellow bands, but not the red bands.

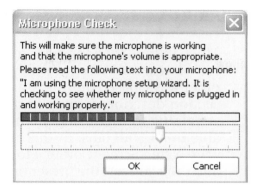

After setting your level, click on the "Change Quality . . ." button. This will help you decide how high or low the quality of your audio should be. This may require some experimentation and will also be impacted by how you distribute it.

Under "Name:" Select the profile that best meets your needs, such as "Radio Quality," or "CD Quality."

Note: The higher the quality, the larger the audio files. Radio quality should work fine if you are publishing the presentation to the Web.

After making these changes and saying "OK," your presentation goes into slideshow mode. All you do at this point is deliver your presentation while advancing your slides normally. At the end of your presentation, you:

Press the "Esc" button on your keyboard
and
Press the "Save" button to save narrations and slide timings.

At this point, your presentation has additional data. You should be able to see a speaker icon in the bottom right hand side of each slide in the presentation. When you are in slideshow mode, the audio will play and advance the slides according to your timings.

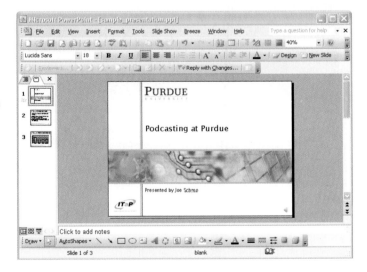

To make this a Web friendly presentation, repeat the "Save as Web Page" instructions described in the previous section.

An Alternate Method for Creating Narrated PowerPoint Presentations as a Streaming Movie

The previous sections explored how to create a PowerPoint presentation as a set of Web pages for online distribution. However, there are other ways, based on your situation, that might be more effective. This section describes how to narrate and convert your presentation to a streaming format using a tool that Purdue has licensed that is available in all ITaP labs. In this section, we will use screen capture software called ScreenCorder 4 to record your delivery of your PowerPoint and then convert the presentation to a Windows Media file that can be uploaded to the Web, or distributed in other ways.

This technique has certain advantages. First, you can use this software to create narrated presentations of any software you are using on your computer. For instance, you might want to give a presentation on how to use a piece of software. In this case, you would use ScreenCorder 4 to record your audio while using the computer to demonstrate the tasks you are describing. In this case, our example will focus on PowerPoint, but recognize it can be used in other circumstances.

Steps in Recording Your PowerPoint as a Streaming Video

After you have prepared your PowerPoint presentation, have it ready to go by launching PowerPoint and opening your presentation. Then:

Launch ScreenCorder 4.

The next step involves selecting options that
will determine how your video and audio
recording is created. These are things you will
want to experiment with to get the best results,
but the steps are relatively straightforward.

Select "New" from the "File" menu.

Under the "Video" tab, identify what part of the
screen you want to record. PowerPoint will run
in full screen mode while you are recording,
press "Full Screen."

Select how many "Frames per second" you want
to record. For this kind of presentation, a low
number will work fine and keep your video's file
size lower. Two frames per second works well.

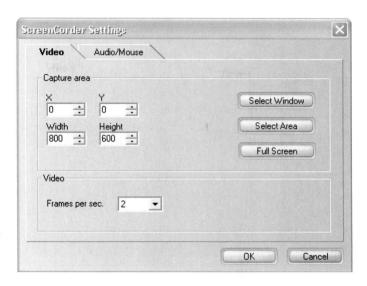

Select the "Audio/Mouse" tab.

Check "Record Audio."

Select your audio options. Mono sound is
appropriate for voice recordings, and a low to
moderate sampling rate, such at 22kHz, should
work fine. You may want to experiment with
these.

Under "Mouse" most of the settings are optional
for PowerPoint. In fact, you might unselect all
of the options.

Once you have selected your settings, you are ready to record your presentation.

Press the red "Record" button at the bottom.

ScreenCorder will then minimize itself and your recording has started. At this point, you simply launch your PowerPoint presentation in slideshow mode and begin delivering your presentation as normal. Your audio will be recorded, along with your slides.

Upon completion, press the "Esc" key on your keyboard. This will stop your PowerPoint presentation, and also end your recording session.

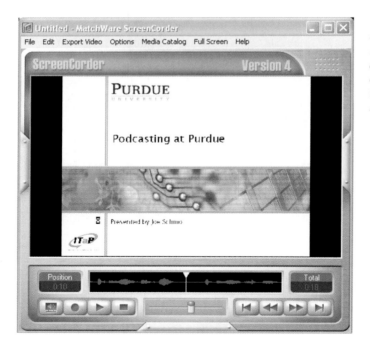

When you have finished recording, ScreenCorder will display your recording in its window. The video is visible in the main area, and the audio waveform is visible below. You can view the whole presentation to ensure it recorded what you intended and that you can hear the sound clearly.

The next step is to make minor adjustments. It is possible that your video has extra, unwanted footage at the beginning or end. You can use ScreenCorder to fix this.

Move the video to where you want to begin the presentation and select "Cut Away Beginning" from the "Edit" menu.

Move the video to where you want to end the presentation and select "Cut Away End."

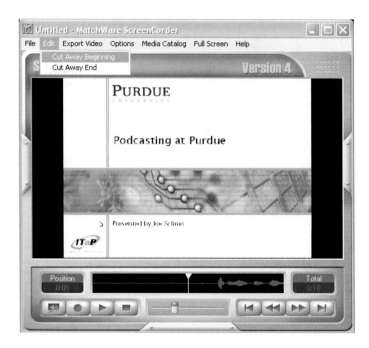

The last set of steps is where you will define how you want ScreenCorder to output your final video so it can be distributed online.

Select "Export Video" from the Menu. This will bring up a wizard to walk you through this process. This is also something you can experiment with several times to achieve your desired result.

Select "Export current recording."

Click "Next."

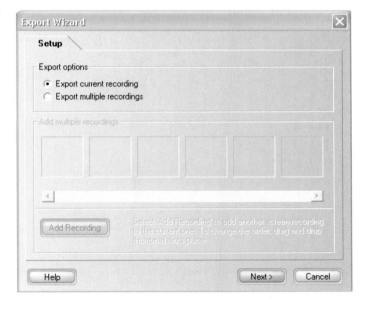

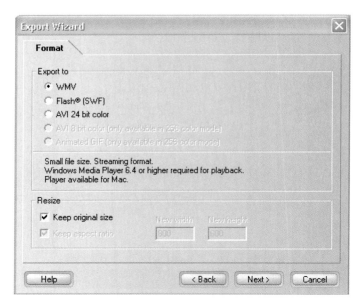

On this screen, you have two main choices: the format of the final video and the size of the final video. We are going to use Windows Media Video (WMV) as our choice, but Flash works well, too. For Web and online distribution, AVI 24 bit color is not a good option because it produces large files.

Select "WMV" under "Export to."

Select "Keep original size" if you recorded your video at the size you need to begin with. If not, select "Keep Aspect Ratio" and select width and height dimensions. 600 X 480 and 320 X 240 are common sizes for Web distribution, but you may need to experiment with these options.

Click "Next."

Compression settings allow you more control over the quality of the audio and video in the final product. You can set these by clicking on "Configure" and picking options. You will also want to experiment with these settings, too.

In this example, we have selected "16Kbits per second, 16000Hz Mono" for audio.

For video, we have selected "128 Kb per sec."

Pick a place on your computer to output the video to, and give your file a name.

Select "Export."

This will complete the export and conversion process.

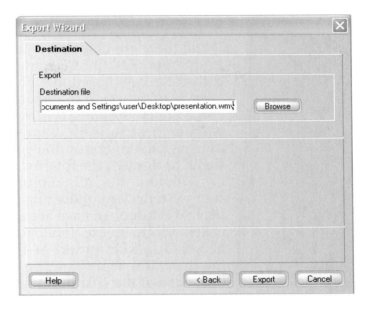

After ScreenCorder converts the video, locate your file and open it. It should open in Windows Media Player. This is what your video will look like upon completion.

The final step is to publish the video to the Web, CD, or other location where your audience can view the presentation.

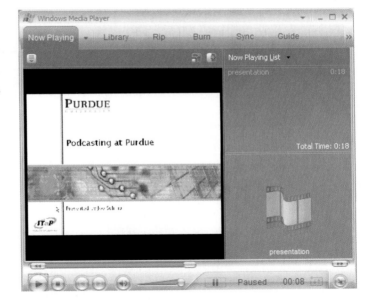

DELIVERING SYNCHRONOUS ONLINE PRESENTATIONS

While there are many ways to produce on demand content, ranging from Web sites to streaming presentations, the tools available for delivering Web-based live presentations are more limited and typically require access to either traditional video conferencing or Web conferencing systems. It is possible to do very lean live presentations without these sorts of systems, but they tend to be less effective, such as using chat rooms or doing simple audio conferencing, either traditional or through the Internet.

With that said, it is common for corporate environments to have such systems for conducting presentations, training events, or meetings. At Purdue, we have licensed a popular Web conferencing system called Adobe Breeze. It allows for very sophisticated interaction that allows for a wide variety of live presentation needs within an online interface. It is representative of several similar systems. It is beyond the scope of the chapter to demonstrate exactly how these work, but here is a screen shot showing types of activities possible within such systems.

Adobe Breeze allows for a variety of online interactions, including:

◇ *Audio/Video*
◇ *Slides*
◇ *Chat Rooms*
◇ *Notes*
◇ *Polls*
◇ *File Sharing*
◇ *Application Sharing*
◇ *Whiteboard*

As you can see from the screenshot, systems like Breeze have a variety of features that can be used concurrently in any given presentation. They provide opportunity for a wide variety of presentations, from highly interactive to the creation of on demand presentations.

CONCLUSION

Online presentations are increasingly popular in today's global marketplace. Understanding the online environment and possessing the skills to make an effective presentation online are real assets for anyone entering the workforce. Although delivering online presentations has much in common with traditional presentations, it also involves developing new skills. Fundamental issues, such as understanding your goal and adapting to your audience, are still present when presenting online. However, the way you meet your goals and adapt to your audience may be different. Asynchronous communication, media richness and interactivity are all important items for you to consider as you develop your online presentation.

KEY TERMS

Asynchronous

Distributed audiences

Interactivity

Lean presentations

Media rich

On demand presentations

Rich media

Synchronous

EXERCISES

1. Practice recording audio with your computer.

2. Upload a Web page you created to the www folder in your Purdue Home Directory and test that it is available on the Web.

3. Export a PowerPoint presentation as a Web page.

REFERENCES

Kolb, D. (1984). Experiential learning: Experience as the source of learning and development. Englewood Cliffs, NJ: Prentice-Hall.

Lencioni, P. M. (2004). Death by meeting. A leadership fable . . . About solving the most painful problem in business. San Francisco: Jossey Bass.

Lindstrom, R. L. (2002). Being visual. *Presenters University*. Retrieved April 19, 2006, from http://presentersuniversity .com/visuals_visuals_being_visual01.php.

Moorer, M. G., & Thompson, M. M. (1990). The effects of distance learning: A summary of literature. ERIC No. ED 330321.

Tallent-Runnels, M. K., Thomas, J. A., Lan, W.Y., Cooper, S., Ahern, T. C., Shaw, S. M., & Liu, X. (2006). Teaching courses online: A review of the research. *Review of Educational Research*, 76, 93–135.

The Total Communicator (2004). Time for your videoconference close-up: What now? Retrieved April 8, 2007 from http://totalcommunicator.com/vol2_3/video.html.

Assignments and Forms

GRADING CRITERIA FOR COM 114 PRESENTATIONS

A GRADE OF C: AVERAGE AND SATISFACTORY WORK

To be judged as average and satisfactory, your speech must:

- Meet all specific requirements for that speech as outlined on the assignment sheet: length, purpose, organization, quality of research, source citation, number of note cards, etc.
- Be delivered on the assigned date.
- Address a topic appropriate to the speaker, audience and occasion.
- Include a body that has
  - Clear and logical organization of main points.
  - Transitions between main points.
  - Accurate, relevant, timely and appropriate evidence and appeals in sufficient quantity.
  - A visual aid (when necessary) that is relevant, appropriate, clearly designed and clearly explained.
- Be delivered using a communication style that emphasizes extemporaneous speaking.
- Be accompanied by a sentence outline and bibliography.

A GRADE OF B: ABOVE AVERAGE WORK

To be judged as above average, your speech must meet the criteria for a C speech, as well as:

- Exhibit skillful use of internal summaries and/or transitions.
- Demonstrate above average use of active verbs, descriptive language, and compelling main points.
- Include content that shows a greater depth of research and thinking than the average student speech.
- Involve the audience in the topic.
- Use a variety of supporting materials in an interesting and original way.
- Be delivered with poise and ease, exhibiting the personal involvement of the speaker.

A GRADE OF A: SUPERIOR WORK

To be judged as superior, your speech must meet the criteria for a B speech, as well as:

- Constitute a genuinely individual contribution by the speaker to the thinking of the audience.
- Demonstrate exceptional understanding of the difficult concepts or processes of winning agreement from listeners initially inclined to disagree with the speaker's ideas or in moving an audience to action.
- Address a topic of significance.
- Be delivered with an interesting, forceful delivery style which catches attention, motivates interest, and uses personalized directness.

The below average speech (D or F) is seriously deficient in the criteria required for the C speech.

Useful Information Presentation

Point Value: 100 points
Length: 3 to 5 minutes
My presentation date: _____

ASSIGNMENT OVERVIEW

In this assignment you are asked to share some information with your classmates that is useful to their everyday lives here on campus or in the community. Your topic will be assigned by your instructor and will describe a service offered on campus or in the community.

This assignment will require a little research. All of the information associated with your topic can be found on a Web page. Use this site as the primary source for information regarding your topic. A class as large as ours can easily overwhelm the campus and community. Therefore, interviews are not appropriate for this assignment. We simply cannot take up the time of individuals who are associated with these organizations. Although one source is usually not adequate, it should do the trick for this assignment.

This assignment emphasizes organization and delivery. It is important that you present the material in an appropriate organizational pattern for an oral presentation. You must have an introduction, body, and conclusion. This will help your audience understand and retain the information you provide. You also will be asked to pay specific attention to your delivery. Simple presentations are an excellent opportunity to become comfortable speaking in front of an audience. They also provide opportunities to practice such delivery techniques as eye contact, hand gestures, tone and volume without having to worry about sharing large volumes of knowledge.

SPECIFIC REQUIREMENTS:

◇ Inform the audience of services on campus or in the community.
◇ Time limit: 3 to 5 minutes. If your speech fails to meet the time criteria, you will be penalized 10 points, so practice your speech.
◇ Base the presentation on one Web source. This Web site should be cited in your presentation and documented on your bibliography.
◇ Develop a thesis statement that meets the criteria discussed in class and in the textbook (full sentence, one distinct idea, etc.).
◇ Pick an appropriate organizational pattern.
◇ Develop an appropriate introduction and conclusion.
◇ Demonstrate skillful use of transitions.
◇ Use an extemporaneous speaking style. This means that you are not to read your speech or to memorize your speech, but are to talk to the audience from notes. You must be concerned with both physical and vocal delivery.
◇ A **typed** full-sentence outline of your presentation is due on <u>Sep. 10th</u>. **Your instructor must approve your outline before you can deliver your presentation. If you do not turn in an outline before your speaking date, you will not be able to deliver your presentation.**
◇ You must also meet any additional requirements as outlined in class by your instructor.

EVALUATION:

Your presentation should meet the requirements of a properly presented informative presentation.

A. Preparation of the full-sentence outline
B. Topic guidelines met
C. Proper speech structure (introduction, body, conclusion)
D. Appropriate organizational pattern
E. Refined delivery

Use the attached presentation checklist to make sure you have completed all of the requirements for this assignment.

OUTLINE CHECKLIST: Useful Information Presentation

Speaker: _____ *Time Limit:* _____
Topic: _____ *Situation/audience:* _____

SPECIFIC PURPOSE:

1. Is it stated as an infinitive phrase? _____ yes _____ no
2. Does it contain only one idea? _____ yes _____ no
3. Does it use clear and concise language? _____ yes _____ no
4. Is the focus clearly defined? _____ yes _____ no

THESIS STATEMENT:

1. Is the focus clearly defined? _____ yes _____ no
2. Are main points previewed? _____ yes _____ no
3. Is it written as a complete sentence? _____ yes _____ no

INTRODUCTION:

Contains all necessary components: attention getter, credibility statement, relevance, thesis? _____ yes _____ no

Attention getter

◇ Is it appropriate for topic? _____ yes _____ no
◇ Is it appropriate for selected audience? _____ yes _____ no
◇ Does it have impact? _____ yes _____ no
◇ Is it appropriate in length? _____ yes _____ no

Credibility statement

◇ Does it sound professional/believable? _____ yes _____ no
◇ Does it point out personal experience/interest? _____ yes _____ no

Relevance statement

◇ Does the statement create an immediate need to listen? _____ yes _____ no
◇ Is it appropriate for the selected audience? _____ yes _____ no

Thesis (see above)

◇ Make sure thesis is same in introduction as written above. _____ yes _____ no

TRANSITION:

1. Is there a directional transition between introduction and body? _____ yes _____ no

ORGANIZATION:

1. Is the appropriate organizational pattern used? _____ yes _____ no
2. Are the main points significant? _____ yes _____ no
3. Are the main points balanced? _____ yes _____ no
4. Do the main points contain one distinct idea? _____ yes _____ no
5. Are they written as complete sentences? _____ yes _____ no
6. Are there directional transitions between main points? _____ yes _____ no
7. Are the subpoints organized correctly? _____ yes _____ no
8. Do the points coordinate? _____ yes _____ no
9. Is there correct subordination? _____ yes _____ no

EVIDENCE:

1. Does each main point have sufficient evidence? _____ yes _____ no
2. Is evidence cited appropriately? _____ yes _____ no
3. Does evidence actually support main points/ _____ yes _____ no

TRANSITION:

1. Was there a directional transition from the body _____ yes _____ no

CONCLUSION:

1. Is thesis restated? _____ yes _____ no
2. Does conclusion contain a clincher? _____ yes _____ no
   ◇ Is it memorable? _____ yes _____ no
   ◇ Is it appropriate for selected audience? _____ yes _____ no
3. Did conclusion (erroneously) introduce new information? _____ yes _____ no

LENGTH/STYLE:

1. Can material be covered in time frame allotted? _____ yes _____ no
2. Was outline typed? _____ yes _____ no

BIBLIOGRAPHY/REFERENCE PAGE:

1. Citations meet the minimum requirement in number? _____ yes _____ no
2. Citations use the appropriate style/format (APA)? _____ yes _____ no

PRESENTATION CHECKLIST:
Useful Information Presentation

Speaker: _____   *Time Limit:* _____
Topic: _____   *Situation/audience:* _____

INTRODUCTION:

	yes	no
1. Captured attention	_____ yes	_____ no
2. Stated thesis	_____ yes	_____ no
3. Related topic to audience	_____ yes	_____ no
4. Established speaker credibility	_____ yes	_____ no
5. Previewed main points	_____ yes	_____ no
6. Provided transition to body	_____ yes	_____ no

BODY:

	yes	no
1. Organized main points clearly and logically	_____ yes	_____ no
2. Included transitions between main points	_____ yes	_____ no
3. Used accurate, relevant and timely supporting materials in sufficient quantity	_____ yes	_____ no
4. Cited sources accurately in speech	_____ yes	_____ no
5. Used an oral language style appropriate to topic	_____ yes	_____ no

CONCLUSION:

	yes	no
1. Provided transition to conclusion	_____ yes	_____ no
2. Restated thesis	_____ yes	_____ no
3. Summarized main points	_____ yes	_____ no
4. Ended with a memorable final thought (clincher)	_____ yes	_____ no

DELIVERY:

	yes	no
1. Used adequate and inclusive eye contact	_____ yes	_____ no
2. Used effective vocal delivery	_____ yes	_____ no
(appropriate rate and volume, clear articulation,	_____ yes	_____ no
varied inflection, and no vocal fillers)	_____ yes	_____ no
3. Used effective physical delivery (posture, gestures, movement)	_____ yes	_____ no
4. Speech was extemporaneous	_____ yes	_____ no

ADDITIONAL MATERIALS REQUIRED:

1. Video or CD for taping presentation   _____ yes   _____ no
2. Folder with note cards and evaluation sheet   _____ yes   _____ no
3. Outline with bibliography   _____ yes   _____ no
4. Copies of reference materials   _____ yes   _____ no

SPEECH EVALUATION FORM: Useful Information Presentation

Speaker: _____   Time Limit: _____
Topic: _____   Situation/audience: _____

INTRODUCTION: (Captured attention, stated thesis, relevance, credibility, transition)

Strengths:

Weaknesses:

_____/_____ Section total

BODY: (Organization, transitions, sources, visual aids, language)

Strengths:

Weaknesses:

_____/_____ Section total

CONCLUSION: (Transition, restated thesis, clincher)

Strengths:

Weaknesses:

_____/_____ Section total

DELIVERY: (Eye contact, vocal variety, physical delivery, extemporaneous, rehearsed)

Strengths:

Weaknesses:

_____/_____ Section total

OTHER: (Audience analysis, timely, creative)

Strengths:

Weaknesses:

_____/_____ Section total

COMMENTS

Major Strengths:

Areas Needing Improvement:

Total Points/Grade:

NEWS PRESENTATION

Point Value: 150
Length: 4 to 6 minutes
My Presentation Date:_____

ASSIGNMENT OVERVIEW

In today's workplace, a common form of presentational speaking is sharing new and interesting information. In this assignment you will be asked to go to the library and find an article from a magazine or periodical that you find interesting and novel. After selecting that article, you must also locate two other printed sources of material that support your original article. From this research you are to assemble a presentation that provides useful or interesting information to your audience. Remember, in order to be useful/interesting, the information you present must be novel, or new, to your audience. Audience analysis is an important aspect of this assignment. Think about specific information that an audience made up of primarily college age students would find interesting and helpful. This is not a speech about political or social issues, but rather a speech that should reveal information that should have some clear relevance for the audience.

It is important that you take the articles and combine them in an appropriate organizational pattern for an oral presentation. Your presentation will not meet the guidelines of this assignment if you simply reproduce material from your six sources.

Outline due Monday Oct. 1st

SPECIFIC REQUIREMENTS

- ◇ Present information that the audience will find useful or interesting.
- ◇ Time Limit: 4–6 minutes. *If your speech does not meet the time criteria, you will be penalized 10 points.*
- ◇ Base the speech on at least three printed sources of research, published within the last year. All of these sources must be cited correctly within your presentation and must be from within the last year. **Web pages do not count as printed research material.** *All material cited on your bibliography must be turned in to your instructor the day of your presentation. Failure to do so results in a loss of 10 points.* *cnn.com*
- ◇ Develop a thesis that meets the criteria discussed in class and in the textbook (full sentence, one distinct idea, etc.) and fits one of the organizational patterns discussed in class.
- ◇ Develop two or three main points. Main points should meet class criteria (balance, mutually exclusive, etc.).
- ◇ Present well-reasoned and well-documented evidence for your main points.
- ◇ Appropriate development of an introduction and conclusion.
- ◇ Demonstrate skillful use of transitions.
- ◇ Refined delivery: Your speaking style should be extemporaneous. This means that you are not to read your speech, or to memorize your speech, but are to talk to the audience and adapt to the audience as you speak. Work for both effective physical and vocal delivery.

◇ A **typed** full-sentence outline of the speech along with a bibliography of your sources is due on _____. **Your instructor must approve your outline before you can deliver your presentation. If you do not turn in an outline before your speaking date, you will not be able to deliver your presentation.**

◇ You must also meet any additional requirements as outlined in class by your instructor.

EVALUATION:

Your speech should meet the requirements of a properly presented informative speech.

A. Preparation of the sentence outline and bibliography
B. Analysis of the topic and audience
C. Organization of speech
D. Research
E. Use of evidence and appeals
F. Refined delivery

Use the attached presentation checklist to make sure you have completed all of the requirements for this assignment.

OUTLINE CHECKLIST: News Presentation

Speaker: _____ *Time Limit:* _____
Topic: _____ *Situation/audience:* _____

SPECIFIC PURPOSE:
1. Is it stated as an infinitive phrase? _____ yes _____ no
2. Does it contain only one idea? _____ yes _____ no
3. Does it use clear and concise language? _____ yes _____ no
4. Is the focus clearly defined? _____ yes _____ no

THESIS STATEMENT:
1. Is the focus clearly defined? _____ yes _____ no
2. Are main points previewed? _____ yes _____ no
3. Is it written as a complete sentence? _____ yes _____ no

INTRODUCTION:
Contains all necessary components: attention getter, credibility statement, relevance, thesis? _____ yes _____ no

Attention getter
◇ Is it appropriate for topic? _____ yes _____ no
◇ Is it appropriate for selected audience? _____ yes _____ no
◇ Does it have impact? _____ yes _____ no
◇ Is it appropriate in length? _____ yes _____ no

Credibility statement
◇ Does it sound professional/believable? _____ yes _____ no
◇ Does it point out personal experience/interest? _____ yes _____ no

Relevance statement
◇ Does the statement create an immediate need to listen? _____ yes _____ no
◇ Is it appropriate for the selected audience? _____ yes _____ no

Thesis (see above)
◇ Make sure thesis is same in introduction as written above. _____ yes _____ no

TRANSITION:
1. Is there a directional transition between introduction and body? _____ yes _____ no

ORGANIZATION:
1. Is the appropriate organizational pattern used? _____ yes _____ no
2. Are the main points significant? _____ yes _____ no
3. Are the main points balanced? _____ yes _____ no
4. Do the main points contain one distinct idea? _____ yes _____ no

5. Are they written as complete sentences? _____ yes _____ no
6. Are there directional transitions between main points? _____ yes _____ no
7. Are the subpoints organized correctly? _____ yes _____ no
8. Do the points coordinate? _____ yes _____ no
9. Is there correct subordination? _____ yes _____ no

EVIDENCE:

1. Does each main point have sufficient evidence? _____ yes _____ no
2. Is evidence appropriate for selected audience? _____ yes _____ no
3. Is evidence timely? _____ yes _____ no
4. Are a variety of types of supporting materials used? _____ yes _____ no
5. Is evidence from credible sources? _____ yes _____ no
6. Is evidence cited appropriately? _____ yes _____ no
7. Does evidence actually support main points/conclusion/arguments? _____ yes _____ no

ARGUMENTS:

1. Do arguments follow sound reasoning? _____ yes _____ no
2. Is fallacious reasoning avoided? _____ yes _____ no
3. Do arguments make appropriate appeals (logos, ethos, pathos)? _____ yes _____ no

VISUAL AIDS:

1. Are visual aids included in outline? _____ yes _____ no
2. Is explanation included on how visual aid enhances/explains information? _____ yes _____ no
3. Are visual aids appropriate? _____ yes _____ no

TRANSITION:

1. Was there a directional transition from the body _____ yes _____ no

CONCLUSION:

1. Is thesis restated? _____ yes _____ no
2. Does conclusion contain a clincher?
   ◇ Is it memorable? _____ yes _____ no
   ◇ Is it appropriate for selected audience? _____ yes _____ no
3. Did conclusion (erroneously) introduce new information? _____ yes _____ no

LENGTH/STYLE:

1. Can material be covered in time frame allotted? _____ yes _____ no
2. Was outline typed? _____ yes _____ no

BIBLIOGRAPHY/REFERENCE PAGE:

1. Citations meet the minimum requirement in number? _____ yes _____ no
2. Citations use the appropriate style/format (APA)? _____ yes _____ no

PRESENTATION CHECKLIST:
News Presentation

Speaker: _____   *Time Limit:* _____

Topic: _____   *Situation/audience:* _____

INTRODUCTION:

1. Captured attention   _____ yes   _____ no
2. Stated thesis   _____ yes   _____ no
3. Related topic to audience   _____ yes   _____ no
4. Established speaker credibility   _____ yes   _____ no
5. Previewed main points   _____ yes   _____ no
6. Provided transition to body   _____ yes   _____ no

BODY:

1. Organized main points clearly and logically   _____ yes   _____ no
2. Included transitions between main points   _____ yes   _____ no
3. Used transitions within main points (internal summaries/   _____ yes   _____ no
   previews, signposts)
4. Used the correct explanatory type with the appropriate components   _____ yes   _____ no
5. Used accurate, relevant and timely supporting materials in   _____ yes   _____ no
   sufficient quantity
6. Cited sources accurately in speech   _____ yes   _____ no
7. Used relevant, professional visual aids that enhanced   _____ yes   _____ no
   audience understanding
8. Explained visual aids clearly   _____ yes   _____ no
9. Used an oral language style appropriate to topic   _____ yes   _____ no
   and audience

CONCLUSION:

1. Provided transition to conclusion   _____ yes   _____ no
2. Restated thesis   _____ yes   _____ no
3. Summarized main points   _____ yes   _____ no
4. Ended with a memorable final thought (clincher)   _____ yes   _____ no

DELIVERY:

1. Used adequate and inclusive eye contact   _____ yes   _____ no
2. Used effective vocal delivery (appropriate rate and volume,   _____ yes   _____ no
   clear articulation, varied inflection, and no vocal fillers)   _____ yes   _____ no
3. Used effective physical delivery (posture, gestures, movement)   _____ yes   _____ no
4. Speech was extemporaneous   _____ yes   _____ no

TOPIC:

1. Topic choice was appropriate for the audience   _____ yes   _____ no
2. Presented new and relevant information   _____ yes   _____ no
3. Other comments: _____ yes   _____ no

ADDITIONAL MATERIALS REQUIRED:

1. Video or CD for taping presentation   _____ yes   _____ no
2. Folder with note cards and evaluation sheet   _____ yes   _____ no
3. Outline with bibliography   _____ yes   _____ no
4. Copies of reference materials   _____ yes   _____ no

SPEECH EVALUATION FORM: News Presentation

Speaker: _____   *Time Limit:* _____
Topic: _____   *Situation/audience:* _____

INTRODUCTION: (Captured attention, stated thesis, relevance, credibility, transition)

Strengths:

Weaknesses:

____/____ *Section total*

BODY: (Organization, transitions, sources, visual aids, language, new information)

Strengths:

Weaknesses:

____/____ *Section total*

CONCLUSION: (Transition, restated thesis, clincher)

Strengths:

Weaknesses:

____/____ *Section total*

DELIVERY: (Eye contact, vocal variety, physical delivery, extemporaneous, rehearsed)

Strengths:

Weaknesses:

____/____ *Section total*

OTHER: (Audience analysis, timely, creative)

Strengths:

Weaknesses:

____/____ *Section total*

377

COMMENTS

Major Strengths:

Areas Needing Improvement:

Total Points/Grade:

Explaining Information Presentation

Point Value: 150
Length: 4 to 6 minutes
My Presentation Date:_____

ASSIGNMENT OVERVIEW

In today's information age we are often faced with presenting difficult or challenging information to an audience who may have little experience with the ideas we are presenting. It becomes particularly important that we can take these ideas and express them in an understandable way to audiences with varying levels of information. In this assignment you will be asked to choose a difficult topic and explain it in detail to your audience through a quasi-scientific, transformative, or elucidating explanation. You will want your audience to be able to grasp and remember the material in your presentation after hearing it only once. In order to do this effectively it is important that you draw analogies between your audiences' experiences and the material you are presenting in your presentation. This assignment requires excellent audience analysis in order to provide information at a level the audience can process and understand. It is your job to analyze your audience effectively so that your presentation is effective.

SPECIFIC REQUIREMENTS

◇ Presentation must use one of the strategies discussed in class: elucidating explanations, quasi-scientific explanations, or transformative explanations. It is important that you include all of the appropriate components of each type of these explanations (e.g., quasi-scientific explanations must include: organizing analogy, visual aid, internal summaries and reviews, and repetition)

◇ Time Limit: 4–6 minutes. If your speech does not meet the time criteria, you will be penalized 10 points.

◇ Base the speech on at least three sources of published research or material. This material must be current. All of these sources must be cited correctly within your presentation. **Web sites do not count as published material.** Check with your instructor for allowable Web material. All sources included on bibliography must be turned in to your instructor the day of your presentation. Failure to do so results in loss of 10 points.

◇ Adequately explain the ideas of the presentation by fully developing main points with concrete supporting material.

◇ Relate unfamiliar ideas to what the audience knows and values.

◇ Develop a thesis that meets the criteria discussed in class and in the textbook (full sentence, one distinct idea, etc.).

◇ Develop two or three main points. Main points should meet class criteria (balance, mutually exclusive, etc.) and fit one of the organizational patterns discussed in class.

◇ Present well-reasoned and well-documented evidence for your main points.

◇ Appropriate development of an introduction and conclusion.

◇ Demonstrate skillful use of transitions.

◇ Refined delivery: Your speaking style should be extemporaneous. This means that you are not to read your speech, or to memorize your speech, but are to talk to the audience and adapt to the audience as you speak. Work for both effective physical and vocal delivery.

◇ A typed sentence outline of the speech along with a bibliography of your three sources. These must be submitted through your WebCT account to your instructor. Due date:_____. **Your outline must be approved by your instructor before you can deliver your presentation. If you fail to have your outline approved by your instructor before your assigned speaking day, you will lose your opportunity to speak and will receive a ZERO on this assignment.**

◇ You must also meet any additional requirements as outlined in class by your instructor.

EVALUATION:

Your speech should meet the requirements of a properly presented explanatory presentation.

A. Preparation of the sentence outline and bibliography
B. Analysis of the topic and audience
C. Organization of speech
D. Research
E. Use of evidence and appeals
F. Refined delivery

Use the attached presentation checklist to make sure you have completed all of the requirements for this assignment.

OUTLINE CHECKLIST: Explaining Information Presentation

Speaker: _____   *Time Limit:* _____
Topic: _____   *Situation/audience:* _____

SPECIFIC PURPOSE:

1. Is it stated as an infinitive phrase? _____ yes _____ no
2. Does it contain only one idea? _____ yes _____ no
3. Does it use clear and concise language? _____ yes _____ no
4. Is the focus clearly defined? _____ yes _____ no

THESIS STATEMENT:

1. Is the focus clearly defined? _____ yes _____ no
2. Are main points previewed? _____ yes _____ no
3. Is it written as a complete sentence? _____ yes _____ no

INTRODUCTION:

Contains all necessary components: attention getter, _____ yes _____ no
credibility statement, relevance, thesis?

Attention getter

- Is it appropriate for topic? _____ yes _____ no
- Is it appropriate for selected audience? _____ yes _____ no
- Does it have impact? _____ yes _____ no
- Is it appropriate in length? _____ yes _____ no

Credibility statement

- Does it sound professional/believable? _____ yes _____ no
- Does it point out personal experience/interest? _____ yes _____ no

Relevance statement

- Does the statement create an immediate need to listen? _____ yes _____ no
- Is it appropriate for the selected audience? _____ yes _____ no

Thesis (see above)

- Make sure thesis is same in introduction as written above. _____ yes _____ no

TRANSITION:

1. Is there a directional transition between introduction and body? _____ yes _____ no

ORGANIZATION:

1. Is the appropriate organizational pattern used? _____ yes _____ no
2. Are the main points significant? _____ yes _____ no
3. Are the main points balanced? _____ yes _____ no
4. Do the main points contain one distinct idea? _____ yes _____ no

5. Are they written as complete sentences?	_____ yes	_____ no
6. Are there directional transitions between main points?	_____ yes	_____ no
7. Are the subpoints organized correctly?	_____ yes	_____ no
8. Do the points coordinate?	_____ yes	_____ no
9. Is there correct subordination?	_____ yes	_____ no

EVIDENCE:

1. Does each main point have sufficient evidence?	_____ yes	_____ no
2. Is evidence appropriate for selected audience?	_____ yes	_____ no
3. Is evidence timely?	_____ yes	_____ no
4. Are a variety of types of supporting materials used?	_____ yes	_____ no
5. Is evidence from credible sources?	_____ yes	_____ no
6. Is evidence cited appropriately?	_____ yes	_____ no
7. Does evidence actually support main points/	_____ yes	_____ no

ARGUMENTS:

1. Do arguments follow sound reasoning?	_____ yes	_____ no
2. Is fallacious reasoning avoided?	_____ yes	_____ no
3. Do arguments make appropriate appeals (logos, ethos, pathos)?	_____ yes	_____ no

VISUAL AIDS:

1. Are visual aids included in outline?	_____ yes	_____ no
2. Is explanation included on how visual aid enhances/explains information?	_____ yes	_____ no
3. Are visual aids appropriate?	_____ yes	_____ no

TRANSITION:

1. Was there a directional transition from the body to the conclusion?	_____ yes	_____ no

CONCLUSION:

1. Is thesis restated?	_____ yes	_____ no
2. Does conclusion contain a clincher?		
◇ Is it memorable?		
◇ Is it appropriate for selected audience?		
3. Did conclusion (erroneously) introduce new information?	_____ yes	_____ no

LENGTH/STYLE:

1. Can material be covered in time frame allotted?	_____ yes	_____ no
2. Was outline typed?	_____ yes	_____ no

BIBLIOGRAPHY/REFERENCE PAGE:

1. Citations meet the minimum requirement in number?	_____ yes	_____ no
2. Citations use the appropriate style/format (APA)?	_____ yes	_____ no

PRESENTATION CHECKLIST:
Explaining Information Presentation

Speaker: _____   *Time Limit:* _____
Topic: _____   *Situation/audience:* _____

INTRODUCTION:

1. Captured attention   _____ yes   _____ no
2. Stated thesis   _____ yes   _____ no
3. Related topic to audience   _____ yes   _____ no
4. Established speaker credibility   _____ yes   _____ no
5. Previewed main points   _____ yes   _____ no
6. Provided transition to body   _____ yes   _____ no

BODY:

1. Organized main points clearly and logically   _____ yes   _____ no
2. Included transitions between main points   _____ yes   _____ no
3. Used transitions within main points (internal _____ yes   _____ no
   summaries/previews, signposts)
4. Used the correct explanatory type with the   _____ yes   _____ no
   appropriate components
5. Used accurate, relevant and timely supporting _____ yes   _____ no
   materials in sufficient quantity
6. Cited sources accurately in speech   _____ yes   _____ no
7. Used relevant, professional visual aids that enhanced _____ yes   _____ no
   audience understanding
8. Explained visual aids clearly   _____ yes   _____ no
9. Used an oral language style appropriate to topic _____ yes   _____ no
   and audience

CONCLUSION:

1. Provided transition to conclusion   _____ yes   _____ no
2. Restated thesis   _____ yes   _____ no
3. Summarized main points   _____ yes   _____ no
4. Ended with a memorable final thought (clincher) _____ yes   _____ no

DELIVERY:

1. Used adequate and inclusive eye contact   _____ yes   _____ no
2. Used effective vocal delivery (appropriate rate and volume, _____ yes   _____ no
   clear articulation, varied inflection, and no vocal fillers) _____ yes   _____ no
3. Used effective physical delivery (posture, gestures, movement) _____ yes _____ no
4. Speech was extemporaneous   _____ yes   _____ no

TOPIC:

1. Topic choice was appropriate for the audience   _____ yes   _____ no
2. Presented new and relevant information   _____ yes   _____ no
3. Other comments: _____ yes   _____ no

ADDITIONAL MATERIALS REQUIRED:

1. Video or CD for taping presentation   _____ yes   _____ no
2. Folder with note cards and evaluation sheet   _____ yes   _____ no
3. Outline with bibliography   _____ yes   _____ no
4. Copies of reference materials   _____ yes   _____ no

SPEECH EVALUATION FORM: Explaining Information

Speaker: _____   *Time Limit:* _____
Topic: _____   *Situation/audience:* _____

INTRODUCTION: (Captured attention, stated thesis, relevance, credibility, transition)

Strengths:

Weaknesses:

_____/_____ *Section total*

BODY: (Organization, transitions, sources, visual aids, language, complex material explanation, appropriate explanatory method)

Strengths:

Weaknesses:

_____/_____ *Section total*

CONCLUSION: (Transition, restated thesis, clincher)

Strengths:

Weaknesses:

_____/_____ *Section total*

DELIVERY: (Eye contact, vocal variety, physical delivery, extemporaneous, rehearsed)

Strengths:

Weaknesses:

_____/_____ *Section total*

OTHER: (Audience analysis, timely, creative)

Strengths:

Weaknesses:

_____/_____ *Section total*

COMMENTS

Major Strengths:

Areas Needing Improvement:

Total Points/Grade:

SPEECH EVALUATION FORM: Explaining Information

Speaker: _____   **Time Limit:** _____
Topic: _____   **Situation/audience:** _____

INTRODUCTION: (Captured attention, stated thesis, relevance, credibility, transition)

Strengths:

Weaknesses:

_____/_____ Section total

BODY: (Organization, transitions, sources, visual aids, language, complex material explanation, appropriate explanatory method)

Strengths:

Weaknesses:

_____/_____ Section total

CONCLUSION: (Transition, restated thesis, clincher)

Strengths:

Weaknesses:

_____/_____ Section total

DELIVERY: (Eye contact, vocal variety, physical delivery, extemporaneous, rehearsed)

Strengths:

Weaknesses:

_____/_____ Section total

OTHER: (Audience analysis, timely, creative)

Strengths:

Weaknesses:

_____/_____ Section total

COMMENTS

Major Strengths:

Areas Needing Improvement:

Total Points/Grade:

PERSUASIVE PRESENTATION

Point Value: 200
Length: 5 to 7 minutes
My Presentation Date:_____

ASSIGNMENT OVERVIEW

outline due 10-30

On this round, you will be asked to deliver a presentation on a question of fact, value or policy. It is important that you use the correct organizational pattern for your speech type. Check the class readings so that you can ensure that you use the appropriate one. The focus of this presentation is on making and evaluating arguments. Specifically, you'll be expected to use examples, statistics, and expert testimony for supporting material, as well as weave these elements together in a way that provides complete and logical documentation and reasoning for the key ideas in your speech. You will need to demonstrate effective reasoning skills by using good solid arguments that are free from fallacies. **You will also need to demonstrate proficiency at designing and utilizing a visual aid.**

Speech topic is always crucial in a persuasive presentation. You have a very short time frame to persuade your audience. Think about persuasion as a process; you simply cannot persuade the class to change their attitudes on controversial topics. It is simply not possible given the situational constraints of this assignment. Therefore, your goals for this presentation should be modest. You should seek to persuade your audience on local issues rather than global issues. Garnering support for the policies regarding printing in computer labs on campus is well suited for this assignment, while a speech about abortion, gun control, or gay marriage would not. **Your topic must be approved by your instructor before you begin work on your presentation.** Failure to receive prior approval may result in unnecessary work on your part.

SPECIFIC REQUIREMENTS

◇ Time Limit: 5–7 minutes. If your speech does not meet the time criteria, you will be penalized ten points.

◇ Base the speech on at least four sources of published research or material. This material must be current. All of these sources must be cited correctly within your presentation. **Web sites do not count as published material.** Check with your instructor for allowable Web material. All sources included on bibliography must be turned in to your instructor the day of your presentation. Failure to do so results in loss of 10 points.

◇ Present well-reasoned and well-documented evidence for the major arguments.

◇ Avoid bias in presenting arguments.

◇ Develop a thesis that meets the criteria discussed in class and in the textbook (full sentence, one distinct idea, etc.).

◇ Develop two or three main points. Main points should meet class criteria (balance, mutually exclusive, etc.) and fit one of the organizational patterns discussed in class.

◇ Appropriate development of an introduction and conclusion.

◇ Demonstrate skillful use of transitions.

◇ Effective use of a visual aid. Ask the following questions: is it necessary and does it enhance audience understanding? Is it professional and free from errors?

◇ Refined delivery: Your speaking style should be extemporaneous. This means that you are not to read your speech, or to memorize your speech, but are to talk to the audience and adapt to the audience as you speak. Work for both effective physical and vocal delivery.

◇ A **typed** sentence outline of the speech along with a bibliography of your sources. These must be submitted through your WebCT account to your instructor. Due date:_____. **Your outline must be approved by your instructor before you can deliver your presentation. If you fail to have your outline approved by your instructor before your assigned speaking day, you will lose your opportunity to speak and will receive a ZERO on this assignment.**

◇ You must also meet any additional requirements outlined by your instructor.

AREAS FOR EVALUATION:

Your speech should meet the requirements of a properly presented persuasive speech.

A. Preparation of the sentence outline and bibliography
B. Analysis of the topic and audience
C. Organization of speech
D. Research
E. Use of evidence and appeals
F. Refined delivery

Use the attached presentation checklist to make sure you have completed all of the requirements for this assignment.

OUTLINE CHECKLIST: Persuasive Presentation

Speaker: _____   *Time Limit:* _____
Topic: _____   *Situation/audience:* _____

SPECIFIC PURPOSE:

1. Is it stated as an infinitive phrase? _____ yes _____ no
2. Does it contain only one idea? _____ yes _____ no
3. Does it use clear and concise language? _____ yes _____ no
4. Is the focus clearly defined? _____ yes _____ no

THESIS STATEMENT:

1. Is the focus clearly defined? _____ yes _____ no
2. Are main points previewed? _____ yes _____ no
3. Is it written as a complete sentence? _____ yes _____ no

INTRODUCTION:

Contains all necessary components: attention getter,
credibility statement, relevance, thesis? _____ yes _____ no

Attention getter

- ◇ Is it appropriate for topic? _____ yes _____ no
- ◇ Is it appropriate for selected audience? _____ yes _____ no
- ◇ Does it have impact? _____ yes _____ no
- ◇ Is it appropriate in length? _____ yes _____ no

Credibility statement

- ◇ Does it sound professional/believable? _____ yes _____ no
- ◇ Does it point out personal experience/interest? _____ yes _____ no

Relevance statement

- ◇ Does the statement create an immediate need to listen? _____ yes _____ no
- ◇ Is it appropriate for the selected audience? _____ yes _____ no

Thesis (see above)

- ◇ Make sure thesis is same in introduction as written above. _____ yes _____ no

TRANSITION:

1. Is there a directional transition between introduction and body? _____ yes _____ no

ORGANIZATION:

1. Is the appropriate organizational pattern used? _____ yes _____ no
2. Are the main points significant? _____ yes _____ no
3. Are the main points balanced? _____ yes _____ no
4. Do the main points contain one distinct idea? _____ yes _____ no

5. Are they written as complete sentences? _____ yes _____ no
6. Are there directional transitions between main points? _____ yes _____ no
7. Are the subpoints organized correctly? _____ yes _____ no
8. Do the points coordinate? _____ yes _____ no
9. Is there correct subordination? _____ yes _____ no

EVIDENCE:

1. Does each main point have sufficient evidence? _____ yes _____ no
2. Is evidence appropriate for selected audience? _____ yes _____ no
3. Is evidence timely? _____ yes _____ no
4. Are a variety of types of supporting materials used? _____ yes _____ no
5. Is evidence from credible sources? _____ yes _____ no
6. Is evidence cited appropriately? _____ yes _____ no
7. Does evidence actually support main points/conclusion/arguments? _____ yes _____ no

ARGUMENTS:

1. Do arguments follow sound reasoning? _____ yes _____ no
2. Is fallacious reasoning avoided? _____ yes _____ no
3. Do arguments make appropriate appeals (logos, ethos, pathos)? _____ yes _____ no

VISUAL AIDS:

1. Are visual aids included in outline? _____ yes _____ no
2. Is explanation included on how visual aid enhances/explains information? _____ yes _____ no
3. Are visual aids appropriate? _____ yes _____ no

TRANSITION:

1. Was there a directional transition from the body to the conclusion? _____ yes _____ no

CONCLUSION:

1. Is thesis restated? _____ yes _____ no
2. Does conclusion contain a clincher? _____ yes _____ no
   ◇ Is it memorable?
   ◇ Is it appropriate for selected audience?
3. Did conclusion (erroneously) introduce new information?

LENGTH/STYLE:

1. Can material be covered in time frame allotted? _____ yes _____ no
2. Was outline typed? _____ yes _____ no

BIBLIOGRAPHY/REFERENCE PAGE:

1. Citations meet the minimum requirement in number? _____ yes _____ no
2. Citations use the appropriate style/format (APA)? _____ yes _____ no

PRESENTATION CHECKLIST
Persuasive Presentation

Speaker: _____ *Time Limit:* _____

Topic: _____ *Situation/audience:* _____

INTRODUCTION:

1. Captured attention   _____ yes   _____ no
2. Stated thesis   _____ yes   _____ no
3. Related topic to audience   _____ yes   _____ no
4. Established speaker credibility   _____ yes   _____ no
5. Previewed main points   _____ yes   _____ no
6. Provided transition to body   _____ yes   _____ no

BODY:

1. Organized main points clearly and logically   _____ yes   _____ no
2. Included transitions between main points   _____ yes   _____ no
3. Used transitions within main points (internal summaries/previews, signposts)   _____ yes   _____ no
4. Arguments are free from fallacies   _____ yes   _____ no
5. Used accurate, relevant and timely supporting materials in sufficient quantity   _____ yes   _____ no
6. Cited sources accurately in speech
7. Used relevant, professional visual aids that enhanced audience understanding   _____ yes   _____ no
8. Explained visual aids clearly   _____ yes   _____ no
9. Used an oral language style appropriate to topic and audience   _____ yes   _____ no

CONCLUSION:

1. Provided transition to conclusion   _____ yes   _____ no
2. Restated thesis   _____ yes   _____ no
3. Summarized main points   _____ yes   _____ no
4. Ended with a memorable final thought (clincher)   _____ yes   _____ no

DELIVERY:

1. Used adequate and inclusive eye contact   _____ yes   _____ no
2. Used effective vocal delivery (appropriate rate and volume, clear articulation, varied inflection, and no vocal fillers)   _____ yes   _____ no
3. Used effective physical delivery (posture, gestures, movement)   _____ yes   _____ no
4. Speech was extemporaneous   _____ yes   _____ no

TOPIC:

1. Topic choice was appropriate for the audience   _____ yes   _____ no
2. Presented new and relevant information   _____ yes   _____ no
3. Other comments: _____ yes   _____ no

ADDITIONAL MATERIALS REQUIRED:

1. Video or CD for taping presentation   _____ yes   _____ no
2. Folder with note cards and evaluation sheet   _____ yes   _____ no
3. Outline with bibliography   _____ yes   _____ no
4. Copies of reference materials   _____ yes   _____ no

EVALUATION FORM: Persuasive Presentation

Speaker: _____   *Time Limit:* _____

Topic: _____   *Situation/audience:* _____

INTRODUCTION: (Captured attention, stated thesis, relevance, credibility, transition)

Strengths:

Weaknesses:

_____/_____ *Section total*

BODY: (Organization, transitions, sources, visual aids, language, well-reasoned arguments, avoided fallacies)

Strengths:

Weaknesses:

_____/_____ *Section total*

CONCLUSION: (Transition, restated thesis, clincher)

Strengths:

Weaknesses:

_____/_____ *Section total*

DELIVERY: (Eye contact, vocal variety, physical delivery, extemporaneous, rehearsed)

Strengths:

Weaknesses:

_____/_____ *Section total*

OTHER: (Audience analysis, timely, creative)

Strengths:

Weaknesses:

_____/_____ *Section total*

COMMENTS

Major Strengths:

Areas Needing Improvement:

Total Points/Grade:

SMALL GROUP PERSUASIVE PRESENTATION

Point Value: 200 Points
Length: 50 Minutes
*My Group's Presentation Day:*_____

For this assignment you will need to take everything you have learned this semester and apply it to this presentation. You will draw on your delivery skills, organizational abilities, reasoning and argumentation skills, critiquing skills, as well as your ability to interact and communicate effectively in small groups. This presentation will require some role-playing.

The situation:

Purdue President Martin Jischke controls the distribution of funds from an incentive grant pool. These grants are used to improve campus or to improve campus-community relations. Previously, President Jischke funded a proposal to create the Purdue Cultural Awareness Committee to help unite various campus ethnic groups and promote diversity, and a proposal to fund the creation of video public service announcements and posters to promote exposure to Purdue's Sexual Harassment Network. These grants award a maximum of $2,500 to each recipient. *5000*

You are part of a group who has a particular campus concern but has lacked the funds necessary to address the problem. Your group sees these incentive grants as an opportunity to bring some of your ideas to the public forefront and actually make a difference here on campus. President Jischke will be entertaining several proposals from other groups. Your group will essentially be competing for this grant against the other groups in your section.

Your task:

Your group will need to identify a campus concern or problem and present a solution to this problem.

Remember, you will be competing for the resources, so your proposal must be compelling and persuasive. You will present your proposal to President Jischke's appointed committee and your instructor. The committee will be comprised of other classmates. While your instructor will be responsible for grading the assignment, the committee will have an input in the final appraisal of the proposal.

SPECIFIC REQUIREMENTS

You and four or five other classmates will form a group and identify a campus/community concern or problem and propose a solution to that problem. Each group should select a distinct problem. Each group should get their problem approved by their instructor to ensure that each group's problem is distinct. Problems will be approved on a first-come, first-served basis.

- ◇ Every person in the group should take a **speaking** part in the presentation and have knowledge of the proposal.
- ◇ Each presentation will follow the problem-solution format discussed in class. Pay particular attention to the need, plan, and practicality issues related to questions of policy.

- The last part of the presentation will consist of a question and answer session with the selection committee (members of the class). The committee should try their best to find problems with the proposal. So, the presenting group must cover every possible angle of the problem and solution. Be sure you are prepared to defend health, social, economic, environmental, etc., concerns.
- The group has the entire class period for the presentation and question and answer session.
- Every class member will also serve on a selection committee. As a member of this committee, you will be required to ask very thoughtful and knowledgeable questions about other groups' proposals and provide a critique of the proposals.

If there is a shirker in your group, you (NOT your instructor) will need to deal with him/her. That is, it will be the responsibility of the group to set up rules pertaining to attending planning meeting(s), who will do what, sanctions for not doing what was expected, etc. The group will sign a group contract, and every member will be held to the behavioral guidelines as outlined by that contract. Get these issues settled as soon after group formation as possible so that on presentation day, when Joe Blow doesn't show up or shows up unprepared, the group will have a known procedure for dealing with Joe!!!!

RECEIVING CREDIT

You may receive a total of 200 points for participating in this assignment. Point breakdown is as follows:

Criteria for Group Presentation (160 points): All group members will receive the same score for this portion of the assignment.

1. **Presentation and Group Effectiveness** (125 points)
   - Creativity and vividness of presentation.
   - How well you engaged the audience. The best way to fulfill this criteria is to use a variety of methods to present your ideas—rather than rely solely on a lecture approach, use videos, have handouts, ANYTHING to break the monotony of a string of individual presentations.
   - Perceived productivity of the group—Did you accomplish your task? How informative and persuasive is the information? Was the presentation well-organized?
   - Perceived cohesiveness of the group—How well did the group members seem to work together? Did everyone take an active part?
   - Elements of Effective Speaking (all those things we have talked about all semester long).
     - Organization
     - Effective use of evidence
     - Refined delivery
     - Audience analysis
     - Appropriate use of visual aids
2. Executive summary of the proposal: This is just the outline of the presentation. (25 points)
3. Feedback from the committee members. (10 points)

Criteria for Individual Evaluation (40 points) Individual scores will be assigned for this portion.

1. Individual presentation skills: Basically, your instructor will be evaluating your delivery on the presentation, how well you answered questions from the committee, and your overall demeanor during your group's presentation. (15 points)

2. Group Evaluation Form: Each member is to complete the attached questionnaire regarding contributions of each group member in an honest and thorough manner. Your instructor evaluation of this questionnaire will be based on the thoroughness of your responses. (5 points)

3. Responses to the group evaluation questionnaire. Did your group say you participated and were a good group member? (10 points)

4. Committee member responsibilities: Were you prepared with <u>thoughtful and thorough</u> questions during one other group's presentation? Did you provide a thorough and honest critique of the other group's proposal and presentation. (10 points)

The instructor reserves the right to lower any student's final grade on this assignment based on group feedback and level of participation in the project.

SMALL GROUP PRESENTATION
Group Evaluation Form

Speaker: _____   *Time Limit:* _____

Topic: _____   *Situation/audience:* _____

INTRODUCTION:

1. _____Captured attention
2. _____Stated thesis
3. _____Related topic to audience
4._____ Established credibility

5. _____Previewed main points
6. _____Provided transition to body
7. Other comments:

BODY:

1. _____Organized main points clearly and logically
2. _____Included transitions between main points
4. _____Used accurate, relevant and timely supporting materials in sufficient quantity
5. _____Cited sources accurately in speech
6. _____Used relevant, professional visual aids that enhanced audience understanding
7. _____Used visual aids appropriately
8. _____Used an oral language style appropriate to topic and audience
9. Other comments:

CONCLUSION:

1. _____Provided transition to conclusion
2. _____Restated thesis
3. _____Summarized main points
4. _____Ended with a memorable final thought (clincher)
5. Other comments:

QUESTION AND ANSWER SECTION:

1. _____Rephrased questions
2. _____Answered questions clearly and completely
3. _____Answered questions succinctly

4. _____Q&A was well organized and professional
5. Other comments:

OVERALL GROUP ASSESSMENT:

1. _____Project demonstrated creativity
2. _____Accomplishment of group persuasive and informative goals
3. _____Presentation demonstrated group cohesiveness
4. _____Transitioning from one speaker to another was smooth
5. Other comments:

EVALUATION OF PROPOSAL

1. _____Proposal clearly identified and defined campus issue/problem
2. _____Proposal presented a clear plan for dealing with issue
3. _____Proposal presented a practical solution
4. Other comments:

COMMENTS:

Major Strengths:

Areas Needing Improvement:

Overall Evaluation:

Total Points/Grade:

Presentation Score   _____

Executive Summary   _____

Committee Evaluation   _____

Total Group Score   _____

Photo Credits

Chapter 1
p. 2 © Nico Kai/Getty Images
p. 10 © Andrew Fox/CORBIS
p. 12 © Jeff Cadye/Getty Images

Chapter 2
p. 30 © Andrew Errington/Getty Images
p. 44 © Randy Faris/CORBIS
p. 48 © Digital Vision RF/Getty Images

Chapter 3
p. 56 © Dag Sundberg/Getty Images
p. 63 © Ben Rice/Getty Images
p. 71 © Ron Chapple/Getty Images

Chapter 4
p. 80 © Stockbyte RF/Getty Images
p. 89 © Britt Erlanson/Getty Images
p. 91 © Royalty-Free/CORBIS

Chapter 5
p. 104 © Digital Vision RF/Getty Images
p. 112 © Stephen Marks/Getty Images
p. 117 © Fisher/Thatcher/Getty Images

Chapter 6
p. 122 © Naile Goelbasi/Getty Images
p. 129 © Taxi/Getty Images
p. 142 © PhotoDisc RF/Getty Images

Chapter 7
p. 150 © Altrendo Images/Getty Images
p. 159 © Digital Vision/Getty Images
p. 163 © Digital Vision/Getty Images

Chapter 8
p. 180 © Stockbyte/Getty Images
p. 184 © Hans Nelman/Getty Images
p. 194 © Alex Freund/Getty Images

Chapter 9
p. 202 © Chris Ryan/Getty Images
p. 205 © Jonathan Nourok/Getty Images
p. 209 © Martin Barraud/Getty Images

Chapter 10
p. 240 © PhotoDisc/Getty Images
p. 245 © Colin Hawkins/Getty Images
p. 252 © James Leynse/CORBIS
p. 256 © Louise Gubb/CORBIS SABA

Chapter 11
p. 262 © Stockbyte RF/Getty Images
p. 275 © Jose Luis Pelaez, Inc./CORBIS
p. 277 © Royalty-Free/CORBIS

Chapter 12
p. 286 © Digital Vision/Getty Images
p. 288 © Walter Bibikow/Getty Images
p. 289 © Luca Trovato/Getty Images
p. 297 © Bettmann/CORBIS
p. 298 © Royalty-Free/CORBIS
p. 299 © Jeff Albertson/CORBIS

Chapter 13
p. 310 © Tom & Dee Ann McCarthy/CORBIS
p. 315 © Royalty-Free/CORBIS
p. 318 © Rob Lewine/CORBIS

Chapter 14
p. 328 © PhotoDisc RF/Getty Images

Index

A

Active agreement, 224
Agreement
  active, 224
  passive, 224
American Psychological
    Association (APA). *See* APA
    style
"America's Most Wanted", 4
Analogical reasoning, 249
Analogy, 249
  invalid, 249
Answering questions, 321–23
Anxiety
  over topic selection, 62
  See also Communication
    apprehension
APA style (American
    Psychological Association),
    146–47, 160
Apathy, 43
Appeals, 242–58
  ethos, 243–45
  fear, 254
  guilt, 254
  logos, 245–55
  pathos, 255–58
  See also individual headings;
    Persuasive presentations
Appearance, 278–79
Argument ad hominem (against
    the person), 251
Arguments
  order of, 223
Aristotle, 242
Asynchronous presentations,
    338–49

See also Online
    presentations
  steps in creating, 340–49
  streaming video, 344–49
  vs. synchronous, 332–35
  tips for, 333
Attention, 226–27
Attention gaining devices,
    83–92, 94–95, 97, 98.
    See also Introductions
Attitudes, 208–9
  behaviors and, 39–40
  defined, 38
  vs. values, 39
Audience
  attention getters and, 91–92
  complimenting, 87
  difficult members of, 322–23
  identifying with, 88
  participation of, 89–90
  presentation aids and, 306
  technology and online
    presenters, 337–38
Audience analysis, 31–55
  age of audience, 34–35
  audience attitudes, 38–43
  audience knowledge, 45–46
  audience motivation, 43
  direct methods of collecting
    information about
    audiences, 51–52
  favorable audiences, 40–41
  geographical location, 35–36
  group affiliation, 36
  hostile audiences, 41–42
  identification and, 33
  importance of, 32–33

indirect methods of collecting
    information about
    audiences, 52–53
  neutral audiences, 43
  occasion, 47–48
  order of speakers, 49
  persuasive presentations
    and, 205–6
  physical setting, 47
  presentational speaking and,
    9–10
  See also Demographic
    audience analysis;
    Environmental audience
    analysis; Psychological
    audience analysis
  sex and gender, 35
  socioeconomic factors,
    36–38
  technology, 50–51
  time of day, 48–49
  time/length of presentation,
    49–50
  topic selection and, 59
Audio-visual aids, 88–89,
    299–300

B

Backup plans, 305
Balance
  main points and, 111–12
  outlines and, 154
Bandwagon, 252–53
Bar charts, 293–94
Behaviors, 209–10
  attitudes and, 39–40
Beliefs, 208

415